Barack Obama
and the
Rhetoric of Hope

MARK S. FERRARA

McFarland & Company, Inc., Publishers
Jefferson, North Carolina, and London

LIBRARY OF CONGRESS CATALOGUING-IN-PUBLICATION DATA

Ferrara, Mark S.
    Barack Obama and the Rhetoric of Hope / Mark S. Ferrara.
      p.   cm.
    Includes bibliographical references and index.

    ISBN 978-0-7864-6793-8
      softcover : acid free paper ∞

    1. Obama, Barack — Oratory.   2. Obama, Barack — Language.
3. Obama, Barack — Philosophy.   4. United States — Politics
and government — 2009- — Philosophy.   5. Communication in
politics — United States — History — 21st century.   6. Discourse
analysis — Political aspects — United States.   7. Rhetoric —
Political aspects — United States.   I. Title.
E908.3.F47 2013
973.932092 — dc23   2013020007

BRITISH LIBRARY CATALOGUING DATA ARE AVAILABLE

On the cover: Barack Obama speaking in Houston on the
eve of the Texas primaries (photograph by Tim Bekaert);
democratic campaign button (Hemera/Thinkstock)

Manufactured in the United States of America

McFarland & Company, Inc., Publishers
  Box 611, Jefferson, North Carolina 28640
  www.mcfarlandpub.com

Barack Obama
and the
Rhetoric of Hope

In loving memory
of my father, Paul B. Ferrara,
who departed the Red Dust world
during the writing of this book

Table of Contents

Acknowledgments

I am indebted to many people who helped this study of American presidential rhetoric find its final form. Foremost among them must be my mentor and friend of more than twenty-five years, Walter R. Coppedge, emeritus professor of English at Virginia Commonwealth University. I continue to learn to write from him and aspire to do so someday with his concision and elegance. My wife, Liangmei Bao, was instrumental in preparing this work. In addition to the tedious task of checking quotations for accuracy, she read through the text as it approached completion, making important suggestions along the way. My good friend Wesley Graves improved the readability of the manuscript. R. A. Brown and Ronald Gray, both colleagues whom I met while teaching at Kyungnam University in South Korea in the late 1990s, perused the text.

I am grateful for the support of many people at the State University of New York College at Oneonta. This book benefited from a workshop by a reading group composed of junior faculty and organized by Suzanne Black. Suzanne also provided incredibly useful suggestions for revision to Chapters Seven, Eight, and Ten weeks before submission. Bianca Tredennick, Jonathan Sadow, and Roger Hecht, the other members of this reading group, contributed insights that improved many chapters. Several other colleagues at SUNY Oneonta also deserve acknowledgment and sincere thanks. Eileen Morgan-Zayachek, currently our department chair, helped to arrange a course-release for writing during the fall 2011 semester. Richard Lee and Daniel Payne reviewed the prospectus and provided continual encouragement to explore subjects outside of my areas of specialization (a natural consequence of writing a genealogy of ideas like this one). My friend and colleague Patrick Meanor reviewed early parts of the manuscript as well. The College at Oneonta's Faculty Diversity Research Grant Program provided important funding for research, and the faculty and staff at Milne Library deserve recognition for their gracious assistance at the circulation desk, in the inter-library loan office, and in acquisitions.

Sincere thanks also are due to Cliff Edwards of Virginia Commonwealth University who urged me, in the very early stages, to pursue this study of Barack Obama's rhetoric of hope. Cathie Brettschneider likewise encouraged me to continue with my analysis of the 2008 campaign rhetoric (even before it became apparent that in doing so I was also mapping Obama's 2012 rhetoric). My dear mother, Nicole Ann Jones, has in this case, as always, believed in her child's ability to accomplish almost anything (whether teaching in Shanghai, writing a book or dissertation, or learning electric guitar). And speaking of guitar, how could I have completed this endeavor without the refuge provided by my musician friends in this small city in upstate New York: Jennie Williams, Brian Dolber, Matt Voorhees, Roger Hecht, Daniel Payne, and many others, including Joe Von Stengel, J. Jeremy Wisnewski, Gregory Smith, Marc Shaw, Parker Troist, Paul French, Joe Lafave, and Marcia Bowne. Special thanks also to Arno Brichon, Bryan Walpert, Paul G. Ferrara, Christy Jaromack, Dina Smith, Charlie Nelson, Tim Knepper, Dan Alexander, Ruth Carr, Adam Spingler, Charlie Ragozzine, Art Derouin, Alice Cudlipp, and Ed Eades.

Preface

This book locates the historical and literary antecedents of the president's utopian political rhetoric in the idealistic traditions of the Western world. By rhetoric of hope, I mean deliberately constructed political discourse that envisions social betterment brought about by the force of shared values and culminating in a promise of a "more perfect union" in the future.

The introduction briefly traces the origins of American idealism, beginning with early colonial settlers who sought religious freedom in the New World, through the American romantic movement, and into the late nineteenth-century flirtation with intentional communities. An in-depth analysis of the central features of the rhetoric of hope begins in Chapter One with the utopian tropes of Judeo-Christianity. Chapter Two follows allusions to European Enlightenment thought found in seminal American documents, while Chapter Three outlines Obama's debt to African American slave narratives, the pulpit style of the black church, and the civil rights movement. The role that three American presidencies had in shaping central themes of the rhetoric of hope (those of Thomas Jefferson, Abraham Lincoln, and Franklin Roosevelt) are explored in Chapter Four, while the force of music, literature, and popular culture on Obama's campaign rhetoric comprise the focus of Chapter Five.

Next, in chapters Six and Seven, we move from historical and literary contextualization to the important role of moral values in the rhetoric of hope, for they undergird the prophetic persona that Obama employed effectively to rally the country toward "Change We Can Believe In." Chapter Eight enlarges the focus of this study beyond American borders by exploring the pronounced universalism of the rhetoric of hope, particularly in regard to multicultural globalization. The remaining two chapters cover

Obama's final political race for office. Chapter Nine analyzes the formation of the new campaign rhetoric through 2011, while Chapter Ten treats the period from January 2012 to Election Day in November.

The myth of the American Dream, which Barack Obama endlessly mines in his rhetoric of hope, is founded upon a fundamental belief in the innate goodness of nature and man. Perhaps it could not have been otherwise in a country with seemingly unlimited natural resources, a place where a person was supposedly judged not on his origins, but on what he accomplished through diligence and hard work. Indeed, millions of immigrants uprooted themselves from every corner of the globe to come to this "land of opportunity," and it was they who constructed a myth of American exceptionalism (and passed it along by retelling idealized stories about themselves). This study, meant to be suggestive rather than exhaustive, was inspired by all of those who came to American shores and dreamed together, perhaps naïvely, of a better future.

Introduction: Idealism and the American Mind

This project began with a simple personal observation. During the course of the 2008 Democratic Party nomination for the presidency, I noticed that the rhetoric of one candidate was charged with an optimistic idealism that seemed to evoke many of the motifs of utopian literature (on which I wrote my dissertation). When Barack Obama returned to Des Moines, Iowa, in early 2007, my wife and I attended the campaign event. At a dingy local high school gym, stuffy and seething with more than 2,000 Iowans priding themselves on their political savvy, Obama delivered a lackluster speech. Yet, like many other listeners (as I would find out in the course of researching this book), I could not escape a feeling that I had just heard from the next president of the United States. The narrative of the rise of this man, and the extraordinary air of almost fatalistic inevitability that surrounds his political and personal life, has already been the subject of several excellent books by professional journalists.

My interest, by contrast, is in Barack Obama's rhetoric of hope. At the heart of his political rhetoric are values, many of them quintessentially American, including work, discipline, temperance, self-reliance, duty, fairness, and compassion towards those less fortunate in our communities. It is a rhetoric of social mobility based on merit, a belief in the principles of freedom and the pursuit of happiness laid out in the Constitution. As a result, it seeks the middle ground between ideology and realism, and at its heart lies a social compact based on freedom of worship, release from want, and deliverance from fear. In this sense, the rhetoric of hope finds in American history the clear signs of social amelioration.

Barack Obama's rhetoric of hope therefore has utopian propensities.

To be utopian means to look out at the world — at its continued poverty, war, and oppression — and to imagine a better place. It means enduring discontentment with the status quo and holding fast to a stubborn impatience for a new day. Forward-looking thinkers, from Plato and Augustine to More and Bellamy, imagined societies in which the ills of their day had been ameliorated and humanity had come closer to fulfilling its potential. Even the Judeo-Christian notion of a Promised Land, which itself inspired generations to cast off the manacles of oppression and create new societies, points clearly toward a redemptive future. In fact, one can trace the arc of the influence of this utopian idealism from the ancient Greek world, through the rise of Judeo-Christianity, and into the writings of Enlightenment thinkers like Charles-Louis de Montesquieu and John Locke — who in turn fired the American quest for liberty in the eighteenth century and infused the founding documents of the United States with a burning idealism. These idealistic traditions that the United States inherited would be transformed in time into what we recognize today as the myth of the American Dream.

From a study of Obama's two books, *Dreams from My Father* (1995) and *The Audacity of Hope* (2006), as well as numerous speeches and interviews from both campaigns, I have attempted to trace Obama's rhetoric of hope to its historical and literary antecedents in enduring utopian traditions in the Western world. I seek, not simply to identify those origins, but to understand how the success of the deliberate rhetorical construction of Obama as a quasi-prophetic figure relies on the familiarity of repackaged tropes from American mythologies. So it is that many of the antecedents of the rhetoric of hope are predictable: Judeo-Christianity; liberation theology; American founding documents such as the Constitution and Bill of Rights; the genius of Lincoln and FDR's New Deal; the civil rights movement; and transformational figures like Martin Luther King, Jr., and Gandhi. Other sources of the rhetoric of hope are perhaps more unexpected: Paul Tillich, Reinhold Niebuhr, the anti-colonial liberation movements in Africa, Martin Buber, Hegelian notions of historical progress, as well as a host of universal religious values (possibly the result of Obama's anthropologist mother, who kept a Bible, Koran, Bhagavad-Gita, Dao de Jing, and books on world mythology around the house).

Since this is a rhetorical study, one that focuses on forensic analysis of usage, I am grateful to be spared the burden of aligning the word with reality — a task best left to the political pundits. My interest is specifically in the evocation of a better future toward which we progress gradually, one that offers a sort of collective salvation (a decidedly utopian ideal, if one means by the term a belief in social amelioration and not necessarily perfection). When Thomas More coined the term "utopia" (Greek for "no place"), he made an intentional homophonic pun on "eutopia" ("good place"), giving it a double meaning. Contemporary usage of the term "utopian" has come to connote an impractical scheme of social regeneration, something "ideal" or "chimerical." One aim of this project is to reclaim that term from its derogatory meaning in current political discourse by tracing it to those idealistic traditions in the Western world that Obama draws upon freely.

Indeed, hope itself is a utopian ideal. In his three-volume study *The Principle of Hope* (1959), Ernst Bloch mixes the religiosity of utopia with materialist Marxism. He argues that anticipatory consciousness may be found in every field of human endeavor from fairy tale to film, architecture to technology.[1] In *Paths in Utopia* (1949), Martin Buber explores the utopian wish for what should be in the context of that same longing for a perfect time and place in Hebrew prophetic eschatology. Buber finds traces of this desire for that "right order" in science and utopian socialism as well. His messianic view is tied to a belief in the redemption of the world through a leap out of the realm of necessity into that of freedom.[2]

The influential sociologist Karl Mannheim asserts that a state of mind is utopian when it is incongruous with the immediate situation. It means harboring a discontentment with the status quo, but acting on that impulse puts oneself at odds with the actual order of things. Moreover, when the utopian impulse passes into action and succeeds, it tends to shatter the order of things (the status quo) prevailing at the time. In this sense, historical progress results directly from the dialectical tension between the two poles of the ideal and actual, which defines utopia. Moreover, because the utopian impulse initiates the transformation of current social conditions, it must reject all criticism that it is unrealizable under present circumstances.[3]

Utopian ideas, then, are those fulfilled not in the present but in the succeeding social order. For example, in the context of nineteenth-century America, the dream of African Americans for freedom and true equality under the law was a utopian hope that would not be realized until the next century. Mannheim also recognizes that the "representatives of a given order will label as utopian all conceptions of existence which from their point of view can in principle never be realized." Practically, this means that the "very attempt to determine the meaning of 'utopia' shows to what extent every definition in historical thinking depends necessarily on one's perspective."[4] In the early twenty-first century, with gains in civil rights clearly discernible from the course of American history, to be utopian now might mean positing the need for a new global order that celebrates multiculturalism and in which all sit at the table of nations as equals. Utopias, therefore, should be distinguished from ideologies because if they succeed, they change the world. What seems impossible, chimerical, unattainable in the present order is realized in succeeding ones—such is the force of the utopian impulse.

Following this line of thought, those who are utopian are not hopeless dreamers but actually diviners of a future order. Historical progress is dialectical; it moves toward a goalpost that is moving ever forward. Change is the creed of those who seek a future where the arc of progress becomes self-evident. The course of human history, Barack Obama reminds us, is toward "a better today." In the rhetoric of hope, he calls the American electorate and the citizens of the world toward a better future. Together, "we as a people will get there." The union "can be perfected." He envisions a global multicultural utopia that generally corresponds to an idealized version of American democracy, only stripped of its cultural baggage and extended to the people around the world. Here, at the farthest reaches of his utopian thought, we can understand why Obama's rhetoric of hope inspired people in America, and around the world, in 2008 with its vaulting idealism. Before beginning a detailed analysis of each component of Barack Obama's rhetoric of hope, the following overview of utopianism in American political and literary discourse will provide a brief historical framework (one that will be expanded in Chapter Six).

Many early European settlers in North America came to those shores seeking to realize their own vision of heaven on earth (Philadelphia, the City of Brotherly Love, for example, was planned as a "holy experiment" in living harmoniously). For utopian writers of the sixteenth century, America became a place of promise. Founding fathers of this fledgling nation, like Thomas Jefferson, imbued it with a sense of unrealized potential. Jefferson saw freedom of the body and mind as the cornerstone of American possibility, and he felt that the state control of the freedom to choose constituted "tyranny over the mind of man." Jefferson wrote famously: "We hold these truths to be self-evident, that all men are created equal, that they are endowed by their Creator with certain unalienable Rights, that among these are Life, Liberty and the pursuit of Happiness."[5]

The modern formulation of the American Dream can be traced back to the romantic movement (ca. 1830–1865) in the United States. Much more than simply the attainment of material comforts, it is a founding national myth, an ideology in which the future and the frontier always beckon, a progressive and ameliorative vision that includes certain beliefs by which the American people (rightly or wrongly) define themselves: freedom, equality, optimism, creativity, and perhaps most importantly, the possibility of self-transformation regardless of past or present conditions. Out of these principles, the idealistic American hero emerges. He models action over indolence, like the American frontiersman who, independent from society, strikes out on his own to establish a new life. James Fenimore Cooper's Natty Bumppo is "fearless and miraculously resourceful, he survives the rigors of nature and the villainy of man by superior strength and skill."[6] Walt Whitman also praises this American propensity:

> All the past we leave behind,
> We debouch upon a newer and mightier world, varied world,
> Fresh and strong the world we seize, world of labor and march,
> Pioneers! O pioneers![7]

Because the natural outgrowth of romantic idealism is optimism, if Americans have any debt to the past, it is only something to learn from or from which to escape, not something by which to be bound. Ralph Waldo Emerson declares that "Genius looks forward: the eyes of man are set in his forehead, not in his hindhead: Genius creates ... [while] inaction is cowardice."[8] Americans venerate those who rise from a lowly station through diligence and perseverance to positions of affluence.

The literary persona of Benjamin Franklin provides one of the best-known examples of American social mobility as the result of the confluence of hard work and opportunity. In the opening pages of his *Autobiography* (begun in 1771), Franklin observes with pride: "From the poverty and obscurity in which I was born and in which I passed my earliest years, I have raised myself to a state of affluence and some degree of celebrity in the world."[9] He even offers the reading public his formula for success so that they, too, might remake themselves. As John Seelye has pointed out, "the Horatio Alger story is a ritualized fiction based on the Franklin formula, a fabulization of the American dream of success."[10]

Typical American heroes embody beliefs in both self and social transformation. By substituting the religious conception of a God from afar for a more immediate and tangible God, the self-actualized, self-transforming American person (or hero) is Man-become-God, to use the philosopher and writer Merezhkovsky's phrase.[11] Other literary and historical figures we might cull from the tradition of letters as embodiments of American idealism include Abraham Lincoln, Frederick Douglass, who escaped bondage by arduously overcoming unimaginable obstacles in his flight to freedom, and Henry David Thoreau, who chose to "live deliberately, to front only the essential facts of life and see if I could not learn what it had to teach."[12]

During the nineteenth century, the United States witnessed an increase in intentional communities, such as Oneida in New York and Amana in Iowa, informed by a diversity of communal principles. There were others inspired by the French utopian socialist Charles Fourier. The first full American literary utopia, *Equality or, A History of Lithconia* (1802), appeared in the Philadelphia weekly *The Temple of Reason* and featured a society where land was held in common, money was abolished, and women had full rights. In Edward Bellamy's *Looking Backward* (1888), crime, war, class struggle, competition, and other social ills are eliminated, and the state guarantees the nurture, education, and comfortable maintenance of every citizen from cradle to grave. Bellamy, drawing heavily from the late nineteenth-century nationalist movement in the United States, portrays the beneficial effects of the centralization of communication, production, and distribution.

In addition to this emphasis on communal living and equitable distribution of resources, itself a critique of the perceived shortcomings of industrialization (such as the exploitation of labor and increasing environmental destruction), American utopianists in the twentieth century explored the religious, psychological, scientific, and even sexual dimensions of social reform in their depictions of fictional societies. For instance, in Walter Henry's *Equitania, or the Land of Equity* (1914), four parties consisting of Buddhists, Christians, Jews, and Muslims all land simultaneously on an island. In light of the circumstances, they all agree that religion is a personal matter that should be separated from the joint government they form. Since they deem abiding happiness the aim of existence, selfishness, which is wholly incompatible with it, must be eliminated and moral virtue cultivated so that one's desires might be satisfied without hurting others.

In this religious utopia, morality is the sum of all individual duties owed to the community and the natural world.

In *Walden Two* (1948), B. F. Skinner, the famed psychologist, describes a behaviorally engineered utopia that actually inspired a number of communal societies, including Twin Oaks in Virginia and East Wind in Missouri. The fictional Walden Two community contains one thousand people living together with the stated goals of happiness and an active drive toward the future. To achieve them, behavioral engineering is employed to effect a change in human nature through the use of positive reinforcement. Members endeavor to lower consumption and thereby raise the living standard for everyone, and by working together and practicing a code of behavior based on the principles of liberty, equality, and brotherhood, they strive to increase leisure time by distributing social responsibility. So, while each of the fictional societies noted above are unique and challenge the status quo in different ways, they share a common grounding in idealistic and forward-looking American mythologies.

As this brief overview is meant to suggest, the United States inherited utopian propensities from the classical world, Judeo-Christianity, and the European Enlightenment, and shaped them into a unique form of optimistic idealism. The effectiveness of Barack Obama's rhetoric of hope has a lot to do with the fact that it taps into central features of the American narrative, particularly those that are forward-looking and progressive. Admittedly, the historical moment of crisis lent his rhetoric of hope more force and gave it broader appeal in 2008. As the Chinese proverb has it, "chaotic times make heroes (*shi shi zao ying xiong*)." The United States was entangled in two foreign wars, and then only a few months before the election the worst American financial crisis since the Great Depression struck, leading to a global economic recession. With improbable optimism, a relatively unknown junior senator named Barack Obama deftly conflated his own life story with the myth of the American dream, and, through a carefully crafted prophetic narrative persona, urged a war-weary electorate toward a better future. Using that persona, he calls the world to embrace a similar vision of dignity, freedom, and opportunity grounded in universal human values. In the pages that follow, we will trace the narrative threads that together make up the rhetoric of hope, beginning with the Judeo-Christian prophetic tradition.

CHAPTER ONE

Judeo-Christianity
and the Rational Utopia

In *Dreams from My Father* (1995), Barack Obama writes that community organizing held "a promise of redemption." By promise, he does not mean simply individual salvation but "collective redemption." His memoir brims over with similar youthful and idealistic formulations, yet they would in the fullness of time mature into the rhetoric of hope that propelled him to victory in the 2008 presidential campaign. When Barack Obama first decided to become a community organizer, he reports that his college classmates asked him what a community organizer did. He remained unable to answer them directly due to his limited experience with organizing at Occidental College and Columbia University, so he spoke more generally to the importance of political and social transformation: "I'd pronounce on the need for change. Change in the White House, where Reagan and his minions were carrying on their dirty deeds. Change in the congress, compliant and corrupt. Change in the mood of the country, manic and self-absorbed. Change won't come from the top, I would say. Change will come from a mobilized grass roots."[1] Although Obama would eventually see the need for a top-down and policy-driven transformation of poverty-stricken communities (hence his decision to run for elected office), the motto "Change We Can Believe In" later featured on placards and on every podium from which he spoke during the 2008 presidential campaign.

Organizing communities in Chicago also led Barack Obama to a discovery of the paradox of "individual advancement and collective decline."[2] For although he knew certain individuals benefited from his efforts to empower South Chicago communities, he witnessed those comparatively

21

small gains against a backdrop of overall economic decline. His attempt to decipher this paradox of the individual versus group welfare, in many ways, charts the path of his intellectual development and marks a maturing in his notion of collective redemption. In today's America, some readers might find assertions of the importance of the common good as proof of Obama's socialist agenda (he does admit to attending "socialist conferences" and "African cultural fairs" at Occidental College).[3] However, Obama's vision of social progress articulated in the rhetoric of hope is grounded firmly in Judeo-Christianity, not Marxism.

Barack Obama writes convincingly of his decision to dedicate himself to Christianity. The moral values in the social gospel appealed to him and informed his community organizing. He was particularly drawn to the power of the "African American religious tradition to spur social change," for it "understood in an intimate way the biblical call to feed the hungry and clothe the naked and challenge powers and principalities." In the history of those struggles, Obama was "able to see faith as more than just a comfort to the weary or a hedge against death; rather, it was an active, palpable agent in the world." His decision to embrace that religious tradition "came about as a choice and not an epiphany." He recalls that conversion experience: "kneeling beneath that cross on the South Side of Chicago, I felt God's spirit beckoning me. I submitted myself to His will, and dedicated myself to discovering His truth."[4]

Not surprisingly, Obama drew inspiration for his rhetorical vision of a better America from biblical narratives of emancipation, from belief in the New Jerusalem, and even from the myth of the apocalypse. Likewise, images of collectivist rebellion against the evils of racial discrimination during the civil rights movement became transformed into "a form of prayer" that channeled his energy, bolstered his spirits, and pointed toward a better future.[5] Here, in recent history, Obama finds a concrete example of an old social order founded in inequality and injustice being replaced by a new one based on the ideal of universal human rights. Like this radical break with the existing order, and the creation of a better place, Obamian rhetoric envisions a future society based on adherence to collective ethical codes. His is a progressive view of history.

The rhetoric of Christian eschatology that Obama appropriates in his political discourse starts out "from a definite reality in history" (the status quo), and "announces the future of that reality, its power over the future" (the ideal).[6] Consequently, the anticipatory nature of rational utopias, like Obama's rhetoric of hope, exploits the dialectical tension between the ideal and the existing order implicit in the forward glance. In *The Audacity of Hope*, Barack Obama clearly points to this gap "between our professed ideals as a nation and the reality we witness every day." The political status quo includes the "escalating ferocity of Washington's political battles," the "unremitting cultural wars," and the erosion of American global competitiveness. By contrast, for Obama the ideal order consists of a government that "truly represents" everyday Americans. In an ideal future, individual freedom is reconciled with the demands of the community and results in the creation of a truly multiracial nation. "America's genius" is to "absorb newcomers, to forge a national identity out of the disparate lot that arrived on our shores."[7]

In his 2008 campaign rhetoric, Barack Obama suggests that while true utopian perfection may elude us, we should nevertheless look forward to a better future. "I would not be running for president if I didn't believe with all my heart," Obama states, that although this "union may never be perfect ... generation after generation has shown that it can always be perfected." A keen understanding of successful struggles against inequity should "give us something to build on" because they "tell us that more progress can be made."[8] As one academic commentator observes, this dialectical tension between status quo and the ideal world (the distance between things as they are and things as they should be) fundamentally defines utopia.[9]

Utopian discourses like the rhetoric of hope thus often point toward what Augustine calls the realm of the "Not Yet"—a place where "future things do not yet exist, they are not yet, and if they are not yet, it is not possible for them to be seen. However these future things can be foretold by means of present things that already exist and are seen."[10] In the same way, the aforementioned history of the civil rights movement became for Obama an augury of future things. In his vocabulary, "perfect" is an instrumental verb emphasizing movement toward the ideal. This utopian wish for what "should be" is also the same longing in Hebrew prophetic eschatology for a perfect time and place.[11] Because time is conceived linearly in the biblical tradition, it therefore has an end. For Ernst Bloch, this eschatological belief in the "Last Thing" remains a perennial subject of "those religions which also set a time-limit to time." Above all, we find it in the "Judaeo-Christian philosophy of religion."[12]

Indeed, Christianity is also "full to the brim with future hope of a messianic kind for the world." In Christian eschatology, expectations for end time include "the return of Christ in universal glory, the judgment of the world and the consummation of the kingdom, the general resurrection of the dead, and the new creation of all things."[13] Biblical prophets such as Isaiah filled their narratives of exile, captivity, and suffering with allusions filled with yearning for Zion (Jerusalem or the biblical land of Israel) and with tropes of the restoration of City of God. For Isaiah, the Babylonian exile, the exodus of the Israelites from Egypt and the destruction of the Temple in Jerusalem all foretold of a future in which the city would be rebuilt to provide a home for God's scattered people:

> Rejoice ye with Jerusalem, and be glad with her, all ye that love her:
>   rejoice for joy with her, all ye that mourn for her:
> That ye may suck, and be satisfied with the breasts of her consolations;
>   that ye may milk out, and be delighted with the abundance of her glory.
> For thus saith the LORD, Behold, I will extend peace to her like a river,
>   and the glory of the Gentiles like a flowing stream: then shall ye suck, ye
>   shall be borne upon her sides, and be dandled upon her knees.
> As one whom his mother comforteth, so will I comfort you; and ye shall
>   be comforted in Jerusalem [Isaiah 66.10–13].

In this passage, the Lord promises peace and comfort to the faithful in exile. The hope for a return to Jerusalem becomes emblematic of God's covenant with his chosen people, from among whom shall come the Messiah, or redeemer of the world. This intensive view into the future is characteristic of the prophets for whom the exodus leads to a city destined for rebuilding,[14] and it is part of the eschatological expectations of that tradition.

Historically, the fabled city of Jerusalem, after the celebrated but relatively short empires of David and Solomon, was reduced to a little kingdom called Judah. Later it was a vassal city of Assyria and Babylonia and then finally "a provincial city of the Persian, Greek, and Roman empires."[15] Yet, despite this modest history, Jerusalem was shown for the Jews of the Diaspora as the emblem of a promised future when the kingdom would be reestablished. As one scholar explains, Exodus leads to a city destined for rebuilding and guaranteed by Yahweh (Isa. 44:26; 45:13; 49:14f.; 54:1ff.; 11ff.; etc.) and to a future home for God's people — and even the Gentiles (Isa. 49:22ff.; 45:14).[16]

The prophets of the New Jerusalem foretold of the restoration of this City of God, because "the Zion tradition was indissolubly bound up with the idea of the reign of Yehweh." Like Isaiah 66, Psalm 137 evokes the loss of Jerusalem and exhorts its readers to never forget its destruction:

> By the rivers of Babylon, there we sat down, yea, we wept when we
>   remembered Zion.
> We hanged our harps upon the willows in the midst thereof.
> For there they that carried us away captive required of us a song; and
>   they that wasted us required of us mirth, saying, Sing us one of the
>   songs of Zion.
> How shall we sing the Lord's song in a strange land?
> If I forget thee, O Jerusalem, let my right hand forget her cunning.
> If I do not remember thee, let my tongue cleave to the roof of my mouth;
>   if I prefer not
> Jerusalem to my chief joy [137:1–6].

Here, the state of exile holds within itself the promise of return, so long as the holy city, the symbol of God's covenant, is not forgotten.

These transitions from one historical era to another are also an "important element of the apocalyptic tradition." (The apocalypse, as most people know, is not the end of the world but rather the final revelation.) Since apocalypse "projects its ... patterns on to history," the promise of end time implies a revolutionary overthrowing of the existing order.[17] Here in the book of Revelation looms the restored city of Jerusalem (itself a symbol of prophetic longing) and the awesome vision of the Last Judgment in Isaiah:

> And I saw the holy city, new Jerusalem, coming down out of heaven from God, prepared as the bride adorned for her husband; and I heard a great voice from the throne saying, "Behold, the dwelling of God is with men. He will dwell with them, and they shall be his people, and God himself will be with them; he will wipe away every tear from their eyes, and death shall be no more, neither shall there be no mourning no crying nor pain any more, for the former things have passed away" [21:3].

This apocalyptic imagery conjures a future judgment day when those who kept the covenant will be separated from the sinners:

> For, behold, the LORD will come with fire, and with his chariots like a
>   whirlwind, to render his anger with fury, and his rebuke with flames
>   of fire.
> For by fire and by his sword will the LORD plead with all flesh: and the
>   slain of the LORD shall be many.
> They that sanctify themselves, and purify themselves in the gardens
>   behind one tree in the midst, eating swine's flesh, and the

> abomination, and the mouse, shall be consumed together, saith the
> LORD.
> For I know their works and their thoughts: it shall come, that I will
> gather all nations and tongues; and they shall come, and see my glory
> [Isaiah 66:15–17].

In the passages above, the fact that the Lord knows the works and directs the thoughts of his people suggests the importance of collective ethical behavior in establishing a new social order. Here again, we meet with a central feature of the rational utopia: the progressive striving toward a utopian goal by following prescribed actions. Many literary depictions of utopian communities featured ethical codes derived from Christianity, including notable works by Thomas More (1478–1535), Tommaso Campanella (1568–1639), Francis Bacon (1561–1626), and Edward Bellamy (1850–1898). Obama's rhetoric of hope draws freely upon this utopian tradition informed by Judeo-Christian ethics.

The influence of prophetic discourse on Obama's rhetoric of hope is not unique in American politics. The Bible has exercised an enormous presence in American public discourse from the earliest colonial settlements to the present day. This power derives from the deliberate use of symbols, rhetoric, moral guidance, and a biblical understanding of history.[18] As one scholar of early American history asserts, "the frequent biblical allusions in the rhetoric of the Revolution confirm our historical understanding of the importance of the Bible as a prominent model of discourse in the lives of the colonists." Moreover, biblical discourse continues to provide rhetorical models into the twenty-first century because "it is a highly visible discourse of radical reform that strikes an amenable balance between the contradictory elements of freedom and duty."[19]

At the heart of American rhetorical constructions of duty lies a central concern with collective ethical action that helps to bring about a new social order based on a doctrine of perfectibility. Roosevelt's New Deal, Kennedy's "New Frontier," Johnson's "Great Society," and Clinton's "New Covenant" themes[20] all tap into the prophetic promise of a radically new social order, one that represents at once a break with the past and the continuity of it (insofar as the historical pattern of the collapse of an old social order and the establishment of a better one delineates progress). In this sense, "change does not occur at any moment but as the culmination of historical evolution."[21] Obama often evokes this gradualism in that prophetic tradition in his rhetoric of hope when he speaks of the promise of the future.

Returning to the motif of change with which this chapter began, in his 2008 speech on race Obama asserts that Jeremiah Wright's "profound mistake" was not recognizing "what we know — what we have seen ... that America can change." For Obama, Wright's error lay in not his self-righteous condemnation of the abuses of slavery, segregation, and their ongoing legacy of disenfranchisement, but in simply failing to see the obvious: that what "we have already achieved gives us hope — the audacity of hope — for what we can and must achieve tomorrow." The "path to a more perfect union" will be gradual and driven by shared ethical and religious values. "In the end," Obama observes, "what is called for is nothing more, and nothing less than what all the world's great religions demand — that we do unto others as we would have them do unto us. Let us be our brother's keeper, Scripture tells us. Let us be our sister's keeper."[22]

In accepting the Democratic nomination for the presidency after a bruising fight against Hillary Clinton, Obama referenced John F. Kennedy's call for individual responsibility coupled with mutual responsibility as "the essence of America's promise." It is this American spirit, Obama observes, that "pushes us forward even when the path is uncertain; that binds us together in spite of our differences, that makes us fix our eyes not on what is seen, but what is unseen, that better place around the bend." He concludes with a plea to "keep that promise — that American promise — and in the words of scripture hold firmly, without wavering, to the hope that we confess."[23] It is here, in this yearning for a better place, that the anticipatory function of hope is actualized. Obama's ideal of gradual progress made over time speaks to a conception of utopia as a historical unfolding. It also corresponds to the Old Testament prophetic tradition whose messianic vision and ethical demands for the realization of the Kingdom of Heaven constitute a central motif in Judeo-Christianity.

Barack Obama emphasizes the collective ethical action required to create a better place in his 2009 inaugural address. Invoking "the words of Scripture," he tells us that the time has come "to set aside childish things," for we continue together a journey on which countless "men and women struggled and sacrificed and worked until their hands were raw so that we might have a better life." This onerous duty, Obama acknowledges, "is the price and the promise of citizenship." Because of its prominent place in the world, and the power of the enduring values upon which it was founded, "America must play its role in ushering in a new era of peace."[24]

Finding himself suddenly in charge of a polarized country facing economic crisis and at war on two fronts, his 2009 Inaugural Address creates a rhetorical vision of a "future world." With "eyes fixed on the horizon and God's grace upon us," says Obama, and in a better future, it will be known that "we carried forth that great gift of freedom and delivered it safely to future generations."[25] Obama asserts that "hard work and honesty, courage and fair play, tolerance and curiosity, loyalty and patriotism" have been "the quiet force of progress throughout our history." His emphasis on the common good means asking the individual to set aside what might be in his or her own self-interest for the sake of others.

Like a Judeo-Christian prophet, Obamian rhetoric enjoins Americans to respond with a "spirit of service" and "a willingness to find meaning" in something greater than ourselves.[26] We will recall that for Obama, social organizing, and later holding political office, held "the promise of redemption,"[27] and that this redemption was not so much individualistic as it was collective and founded on the Golden Rule. It is an ethic rooted in an empathy that Obama claims is "at the heart of my moral code."[28] Together, the hope for a new order and the collective ethical striving for its realization in historical time will bring about that more perfect order.

Moreover, Obama's rhetoric of hope makes clear the distinction between the need for values and the necessity of ultimately freeing them from ideology: "Values are faithfully applied to the facts before us, while ideology overrides whatever facts call theory into question." Obama's message of unification frees values from ideology because "the lines between sinner and saved were ... fluid; the sins of those who came to church were not so different from the sins of those who didn't." Perhaps here we find something of an agapeistic ethic in Obama's rhetoric of hope that moves the individual out of the self toward the universal love that Jesus and Paul outline. In Acts, we find a similar emphasis on the moral action to bring about the resurrection and Last Judgment and with it the promise of a just social order (25:14). What makes tropes like these so forceful in the rhetoric of hope is that they are borrowed directly from Judeo-Christianity, and therefore easily recognizable to a significant portion of the American electorate.

For instance, David Remnick notes that Obama's use of the "trope of Moses and Joshua as a parable of struggle and liberation" makes explicit the "comparison between the Jewish slaves in Pharaoh's Egypt and the black American slaves on Southern plantations."[29] In my view, Obama's depiction of history as a culmination of transition and transformation results in his rhetorical formulation a multicultural utopia (the subject of Chapter Eight). "In a sense," Obama admits, "I have no choice but to believe in this vision of America."[30] Like "Gramps and the Old Man," Obama concedes, "I am something of a dreamer."[31]

Yet, his dreamy idealism was not merely youthful naïveté; it had roots in a religious tradition that Obama consciously chose to embrace as an adult: "In our household the Bible, the Koran, and the Bhagavad Gita sat on the shelf alongside books of Greek and Norse and African mythology. On Easter or Christmas Day my mother might drag me to church, just as she dragged me to the Buddhist temple, the Chinese New Year celebration, the Shinto shrine, and ancient Hawaiian burial sites. But I was made to understand that such religious samplings required no sustained commitment on my part — no introspective exertion or self-flagellation."[32]

During his first service at Trinity United Church of Christ, Obama recounts watching as people began to shout, clap, and sing. In writing about the experience, Obama evokes the prophets directly and acknowledges their influence on the rhetoric of his own story: "And in that single note — hope! — I heard something else; at the foot of that cross, inside the thousands of churches in the city, I imagined the stories of ordinary black people merging with the stories of David and Goliath, Moses and Pharaoh, the Christian's in the lion's den, Ezekiel's field of dry bones. Those stories — of survival, freedom, and hope — became our story, my story."[33] Noting his rhetorical debt to the genre of the Sunday sermon, Remnick observes that Obama "adapted the emblematic biblical story of bondage and emancipation to describe a circumstance that was, at once, personal ('my story'), tribal, national, and universal."[34]

In his Selma Voting Rights March Commemoration speech on March 4, 2007, Obama explicitly evokes biblical tropes of promise, hope, and redemption already familiar to his audience:

> If you want to change the world, the change has to happen with you first and that is something that the greatest and most honorable of generations has taught us, but the final thing that I think the Moses generation teaches us is to remind ourselves that we do what we do because God is with us. You know, when Moses was first called to lead people out of the Promised Land, he said I don't think I can do it, Lord. I don't speak like Reverend Lowery. I don't feel brave and courageous and the Lord said I will be with you. Throw down that rod. Pick it back up. I'll show you what to do. The same thing happened with the Joshua generation.

Joshua said, you know, I'm scared. I'm not sure that I am up to the challenge, the Lord said to him, every place that the sole of your foot will tread upon, I have given you. Be strong and have courage, for I am with you wherever you go. Be strong and have courage. It's a prayer for a journey.

Obama closes his address by asking his audience to struggle together to bring about the full promise of the United States. Employing frequent biblical allusions, he asks his listeners again to be "strong and have courage and let us cross over that Promised Land together."[35]

Obama's better place is a meritocracy based on the principle of social mobility. As he explains, the status quo problems of racism, poverty, and unemployment "are rooted in societal indifference and individual callousness—the desire among those at the top of the social ladder to maintain their wealth and status whatever the cost, as well as the despair and self-destructiveness among those at the bottom of the social ladder." (In his 2012 campaign rhetoric, Obama will align himself with populist movements like Occupy that likewise find fault with the self-interest of the elite in American society.) Referencing the theologian Martin Buber again, Obama suggests that we must take religion seriously and "recognize that the call to sacrifice on behalf of the next generation, the need to think in terms of 'thou' and not 'I,' resonates in religious congregations across the country."[36]

Implicit in the projection of a better place forward in time is a criticism of the status quo, and it is this dialectical tension between the ideal and the actual that defines utopia and gives Obama's rhetoric of hope its utopian dimensions. His critique of the existing order, which he masterfully contrasts with images of a "more perfect union," includes health care "that is too costly" and schools that "fail too many," as well as the fact that our energy use strengthens our adversaries and threatens our planet.[37] Speaking to workers in Flint, Michigan, just six weeks before the 2008 election, Obama criticizes the lack of proper investment "in innovation" or in rebuilding "our crumbling roads and bridges." During that campaign, the promise of a better place was constantly held up in contrast to the existing order. "We have a choice," Obama asserts in Flint, to "continue the Bush status quo—as Senator McCain wants to do—and we will become a country in which a few reap the benefits of the global economy, while a growing number work harder for less and depend upon an overburdened public sector."

Obamian rhetoric offers another alternative, one that points toward social amelioration. "We can choose to rise together," but, he warns like the prophets of yore, "it won't be easy." To concretize the better place, everyone needs to strive for the collective good, to "work at it by studying harder, training more rigorously, working smarter, and thinking anew." Appealing to nationalism, Obama asserts that we can "do that, because this is America — a country that has been defined by a determination to believe in, and work for, things unseen."[38] In contrast to the status quo, Obama envisions a future that "ends poverty in America," provides "universal healthcare," harnesses "alternative fuels" to create more efficient vehicles, and defends equal access to "justice and opportunity."[39]

Declaring his candidacy for the presidency on a blustery day in February 2007 in Springfield, Illinois, Obama evokes the motif of a journey to describe "one people ... building a more perfect union"[40] rhetorically patterned after Moses, leading his people out of bondage to a Promised Land. Likewise, in his victory night speech on November 4, 2008, Obama asserts: "That is the true genius of America — that America can change. Our union can be perfected. And what we have already achieved gives us hope for what we can and must achieve tomorrow."[41] Because of the efforts of "men and women of every race, from every walk of life," Obama reminds us, "today we have the chance to face the challenge of this millennium together, as one people."[42]

Clearly, he sees in history that the arc of progress favors the ideal (the promise of betterment) rather than the actual (the status quo). This kind of historical movement forms the basis of his ideal of progress. Obama explains that for "my grandfather, who marched in Patton's army, and my grandmother, who [worked] on a bomber assembly line while he was at war, it was the liberation of Europe and the rebuilding of America that offered unrivaled opportunity and mobility for the middle class. Decades later, men and women from all walks of life marched and struggled and sacrificed for civil rights, women's rights, and worker's rights. Free people from across the world tore down a wall to end a cold war, while the revolutions in communications and technology that followed have reduced global barriers to prosperity and cooperation."[43]

In his commentary "Let Reconstruction Begin," Thomas Friedman acknowledges the historical significance of Obama's election, specifically the fact that it represents progress towards an ideal land and so should spur us onward toward the realm of the "Not Yet." He writes:

> What I am more certain of, though, is this: of all the changes that will be ushered in by an Obama presidency, breaking with our racial past will turn out to be

the least of them. There is just so much work to be done, so many radical departures to be set in motion. The Civil War is over. Let Reconstruction begin.

By making present the continuing consequences of the Civil War, Friedman also realizes that history points to a better future. So significant was the election of Barack Hussein Obama to the presidency of the United States in 2008 that Friedman almost prophetically sings of the emancipation of future generations of Americans: "Let every child and every citizen and every new immigrant know that from this day forward everything really is possible in America."[44] Such an exuberant response may now seem naïve, but such was the force of Obama's rhetoric when it was coupled with the compelling personal narrative of its multiracial messenger.

By bringing to light several features of the rhetoric of hope that correspond to the paradigm of the rational utopia, itself grounded in Judeo-Christianity, we have discovered a central concern with moral action that brings nearer the promised realization of an ideal social order. In the millennial society that Obama envisions, a heightened emphasis on the ideal results in the promise of an altruistic and communal morality ultimately informed by an eschatological underpinning. In a prophetic voice, on election night 2008, Obama prepared his listeners for the difficulties of the journey: "The road ahead will be long. Our climb will be steep. We may not get there in one year or even one term, but America — I have never been more hopeful than I am tonight that we will get there. I promise you — we as a people will get there."[45]

Reading the rhetoric of hope through the lens of the Judeo-Christian prophetic tradition shows how a dialectical approach makes possible a new understanding of the importance of religion to Obama's construction of hope. For Obama, this dialectical tension between the ideal and the existing orders makes historical progress possible through the promise of continual improvement. The following chapters are dedicated to Obama's utopian vision and the nature of those shared values that are the vehicle for reaching it. In Chapter Three, we will return to an examination of the influence of Judeo-Christianity on Obama's campaign rhetoric in the context of a discussion of American slave narratives, the black church, and the civil rights movement. For the moment, let us turn our attention to another set of distinct antecedents to the rhetoric of hope, specifically those arising from American founding documents, some of which (like the Constitution) Obama would teach at the University of Chicago.

CHAPTER TWO

American Founding Documents

The Founding Fathers of the United States imbued the Declaration of Independence, the Constitution, and the Bill of Rights with an ample measure of idealism but tempered it with hard-nosed pragmatism. Out of these opposing forces, they forged a new form of government that was a unique expression of the American mind. Supremely concise and elegant, clear and logical, these documents have become classics in American studies and have helped to shape the constitutions of Canada, South Africa, Australia, France, Italy, and Germany (among others). Together, they provided the moral justification for revolution, proclaimed the indestructibility of the union, created a system of checks and balances— all the while protecting individual rights. The delegates to the Constitutional Convention of 1787 understood that to get bogged down in the minute particulars of eighteenth-century American political life would mean failure, so they created a clockwork-like mechanism of self-government for the people that, once set into action, would, like a finely tuned Swiss watch, run efficiently and effectively. As a result of favoring the general over the particular, the Constitution often requires interpretation, spawning continual debate about judicial restraint versus activism, for instance. Yet, despite its brevity and deliberate vagueness, the Constitution has proven agile in adapting to historical progress. The framers of the Constitution understood that they were providing "a model of self-government for all humanity,"[1] hence its universalist dimensions.

In his intellectual biography of the president, James Kloppenberg notes that Obama was "trained in two of America's leading colleges, Occidental and Columbia. He earned his law degree at one of its leading law schools, Harvard, then taught law for more than a decade at another top-flight institution, the University of Chicago Law School."[2] Barack Obama's ideas about American culture emerge from close study of the "Constitution, antebellum American democracy, Lincoln and the Civil War, and the reform movements of the Progressive, New Deal, and civil rights eras." While teaching constitutional law at University of Chicago, Obama came to reject conservative evocations of original intent, observing instead that "the decision to leave the document open to amendment testified to the framers' realization that the nation's Constitution would have to change, albeit slowly, with American culture in order to survive."[3]

The United States Constitution is best understood as a never-ending interpretive process, and American democracy is an ongoing deliberation with its progress continually witnessed in history. The Constitution gives us a way of resolving problems, which edges us closer to that ever-elusive "more perfect union." Kloppenberg notes that Obama believes the Constitution gave form to a deliberative democracy that forces us to "engage in a process" of testing ideals against external reality and continually building shifting alliances of consent.[4] Although I quote him above to establish Obama's fluency with the founding documents, Kloppenberg argues that out of a matrix of political and intellectual persuasions Obama ultimately turns to philosophical pragmatism. No doubt, there is a pragmatic streak in the president's intellectual disposition, but out on the campaign trail his rhetoric is steeped in a heady mix of both idealism and pragmatism. It is charged with the language and sentiment of the founding documents, and by mixing it with themes from Judeo-Christianity, Obama constructs a complex prophetic persona, which he then uses to graft his own personal narrative onto American history.

Rather than begin by illustrating one-to-one correspondences between the language of the founding documents and the rhetoric of hope, we start instead with a series of observations on the spread of idealism in the eighteenth century, before turning to an overview of the central features of the Declaration of Independence and Constitution that distinguish American democracy from other forms of government. Along the way, we will trace the sources of the utopian idealism that permeate these founding documents, in order to illustrate the grounding of the rhetoric of hope in traditions of idealism that the United States inherited from the Greeks, the Romans, and the Scots, to name but a few. Those deferred correspondences between Obamian rhetoric and the language of the founding documents conclude this chapter.

During the European Renaissance, classical humanism reemerged, religious dogmatism was challenged, and empirical knowledge confirmed by the senses was championed over religious faith. Perhaps no Renaissance thinker anticipated the subsequent Age of Reason more than Francis Bacon. Responding in part to More's *Utopia* (1516) and Campanella's *City of the Sun* (1623), Bacon penned a literary utopia entitled *New Atlantis* (1624) in which the dictates of reason are followed in order to bring about social betterment. Reason, as Bacon refigures the use of it, allows the scientist-priests of Bensalem to "discern (as far as appertainth to the generations of men) between divine miracles, works of nature, works of art, and impostures and illusions of all sorts."[5] If mankind understood rationally all the laws of the universe, Bacon asserts, we could create "a new and better world — A New Atlantis."

Because he yokes science together with government, at the heart of Bacon's literary utopia is Salomon's House, a research complex on the island. In order to improve their understanding of the physical world, its citizens rely on an "aggregation of observatories, laboratories, libraries, zoological and botanical gardens manned by scientists, economists, technicians, physicians, psychologists, and philosophers, chosen (as in Plato's *Republic*) by equal tests after equal educational opportunity."[6] Again following the *Republic*, progress in the *New Atlantis* is made by joining "humanity and policy together" through the improvement of perception.[7] The result is a fictional society in which the state respects the rights of the individual and which proclaims hope that an age of science will usher in social amelioration. Barack Obama taps this utopian tradition that begins with Plato and blossoms during the Renaissance.

Some of the soaring idealism in works by More, Campanella, Bacon, and others found its way into the nation's founding documents, and as a result informs a worldview still recognizable in the modern formulation of the American Dream. As Bacon presciently foresaw more than a hundred years earlier, the expansion of commerce and industry compelled the development of science in later centuries. The need arose for tools of observation and recording (like the microscope and calculus). Moreover, the principles of reason and ratiocination increasingly challenged, and even substituted for, religion in the eighteenth century. In time, the American and French revolutions would overturn feudal and colonial models of governance based on an idea that mankind was endowed with natural rights, a supposition that also provided the justification for self-rule.

Due to many factors, prominent among them the religious language of the colonial charters and the Revolution of 1688 (which overthrew King James II of England and created a Bill of Rights), the American Founding Fathers understood civil government as social contract or covenant. As a consequence, when it came time to declare independence from the Crown, "they had to demonstrate that 'life, liberty, and the pursuit of happiness' were according to Nature and the will of God, whereas tyranny and cruelty and the taking of property without consent were not."[8] Nature for the American Founding Fathers became the new God (the supreme workman of the universe) who revealed laws to the rational mind, which in turn furnished "a reliable and immutable standard for testing ideas, the conduct, and the institutions of men."[9]

In addition, the explosion of printing in the eighteenth century meant the dissemination of ideas at a pace hitherto unseen, and it fed the rise of a culture of reading and public debate. Many of the American colonists who signed the Declaration of Independence, and subsequently created the Constitution, benefited immensely from this availability of books. Winter Solberg, in his study of the Constitutional Convention, catalogs many ideas in currency during the eighteenth century and their influence on those proceedings (in part based on the records kept by James Madison). What follows is a brief overview, for in them are early figurations of the American mythologies that we are tracing through the eighteenth century and into the campaign rhetoric of President Obama.

Classical antiquity clearly had a tradition of constitutionalism, and both Plato and Aristotle "envisioned a state embodying perfect justice." The word "republic" used by Plato to describe his ideal commonwealth came to signify an "image of perfection" that spurred delegates at the Constitutional Convention "to seek its earthly realization."[10] This republic was made up of just men governed by *nous*, or reason. In its exemplary leader, reason rules over bodily appetites to achieve physical and mental harmony. Right behavior therefore arises naturally (rather than as the result of moral precepts followed blindly). Once inner harmony and justice are established in this philosopher king, they naturally extend outward, making the state harmonious as well. Because it promised to provide the greatest happiness for all, this principle of justice became the sum of all virtues. While Plato emphasized universal justice derived from nature and reason, Aristotle's belief in natural justice (as reformulated by James Harrington) "became a basic principle of American constitutional theory."[11]

Important also to the framers of the United States Constitution were Roman influences by way of the Stoics, who built on Aristotle and espoused a belief that true knowledge could only be obtained by reason and be verified by collective judgment. Cicero was also popular among the American colonists. He thought that nature endowed human beings with wisdom so that they might penetrate the universal rules that governed the natural world. In the Renaissance, as we saw above, the discovery of natural laws that governed the cosmos were assumed to have correlates in the study of human society.[12] The Glorious Revolution in 1688 provided the framers of the Constitution with a model of power roughly divided between the executive and legislative branches, and many of the provisions of the Bill of Rights "passed over almost unchanged through the American state instruments in the Federal Constitution."[13]

The ideas of the seventeenth-century utopian thinker James Harrington also permeated the Constitutional Convention. His novel *Oceana* (1656) was so influential in America that it became a guide for constitution-making after 1776 principally by way of John Adams.[14] Harrington's fictional commonwealth is a kingdom of laws, not men, and one that reconciled public and private interests. He makes land the source of power and wealth, an idea that appealed to the American colonists due to their agrarian economy. In the interest of social justice, by law no one in Oceana was to possess property worth more than two thousand pounds. While Harrington retained an aristocracy, it was one based on merit and virtue. Citizens voted to choose between candidates and offices were term limited. In addition to this agrarian common law, *Oceana* featured a bicameral legislature (a small conservative senate and a popular house).[15] His utopian novel was, in short, a thinly disguised metaphor for what Harrington had hoped England would become under Oliver Cromwell.

In addition, the ideas of two other philosophers exerted considerable influence over the Constitutional Convention (and subsequently Obamian rhetoric): Locke and Montesquieu. According to Walter Mead, no philosopher "was more often or more favorably quoted by the delegates than John Locke."[16] Among his ideas that held sway in the convention were a notion of individual rights tied to natural law and a belief that a people always possessed the ability to overthrow a government that abuses its power.[17] Locke stressed "preservation of property as a very essential feature both of self-preservation and happiness," and he thus laid the foundation of American enterprise.[18] The central role of government became the preservation of property, and it was by reason that mankind came into a "social contract" that required the surrender of their individual rights to the community as a whole (and not a king with divine right).[19] For Becker, it was through Locke in the eighteenth century that "a valid morality would be a 'natural morality,' a valid religion would be a 'natural religion,' a valid law of politics would be a 'natural law' popularly accepted as self-evident."[20]

While the influence of Locke's emphasis on property was immense, Montesquieu was the most cited in Philadelphia in terms of establishing the three branches of government with separate powers. Montesquieu also recognized what he called a "spirit of the nation" to describe the unique character of a people. In the case of the United States, the deliberators were reminded that due to the size of their country, what he called a "confederate republic" of smaller states establishing a larger one might serve their purposes.[21] Mead notes that the Founding Fathers, particularly James Madison, frequently quoted this French advocate of republicanism. Indeed, Montesquieu's insistence on representative government found fertile ground in Philadelphia,[22] as did his idea that administrative powers be separated by the judicial, legislative, and executive.

Nor were these the only ideas prevalent in the eighteenth century that found their way into the nation's founding documents. The representative government of the Roman Republic impressed the framers of the Constitution for "its popular — not its aristocratic — elements."[23] While the American colonists knew Rousseau, and his conception of a social contract held some appeal to them, his ideas were generally rejected at the Constitutional Convention. No doubt William Blackstone's survey of English law was also influential, as were Calvinistic beliefs in mankind's sinful nature, divine law, and covenant.[24] The Scottish School of Common Sense that James McCosh brought to Princeton University as its president also enjoyed popularity in eighteenth-century American intellectual circles. This philosophy held that views contrary to common sense should be rejected and helped to temper the soaring idealism unleashed by the possibility of the freedoms of self-determination. Common sense could be measured by the degree of agreement held by those with whom one conversed daily, and it was a principle which made one capable of distinguishing truth from falsity in matters that are self-evident. While any of these ideas circulating through the eighteenth century America deserve book-length treatment, let us return to the task at hand: to trace the streams of idealistic political thought in the nation's founding documents that Obama recontextualizes and redeploys in his rhetoric of hope.

Once a professor of constitutional law, Barack Obama frequently references the founding documents in his rhetoric of hope and the ideas in currency in the American colonies that informed them. Citing verbatim the section of the Preamble to the Declaration of Independence (concerning the inalienable rights to life, liberty, and the pursuit of happiness), Obama writes in *Audacity*:

> Those simple words are our starting point as Americans; they describe not only the foundation of our government but the substance of our common creed. Not every American may be able to recite them; few, if asked, could trace the genesis of the Declaration of Independence to its roots in eighteenth-century liberal and republican thought. But the essential idea behind the Declaration — that we are born into this world free, all of us; that each of us arrives with a bundle of rights that can't be taken away by any person or any state without just cause; that through our own agency we can, and must, make of our lives what we will — is one that every American understands. It orients us, sets our course, each and every day.[25]

For Obama, the Declaration of Independence is not simply a political document, but rather it is a moral one where the spirit of the nation may be said to reside. Obama notes the still radical nature of that declaration of individual freedom and points out that some parts of the world still reject its call (he cites the Kenyan government, for instance, as one that jails citizens for expressing opposition to its policies).

In the rhetoric of hope, Obama observes that the Constitution rejects absolute authority in favor of a "deliberative democracy" in which all citizens engage in a conversation. In Obama's view, the Constitution spurns notions of absolute truth. "In sum," Obama concludes, "the Constitution envisions a road map by which we marry passion to reason, the ideal of the individual freedom to the demands of community."[26] When he taught constitutional law, Professor Obama wanted his students to appreciate how accessible the Declaration of Independence, Constitution, and the Bill of Rights remain after two centuries— and just how much our attitudes, for instance about inalienable rights, were shaped by them.

The Declaration of Independence is a marvel of concision, clarity, logic, and organization. Contrary to the fate of many documents that go through committee, the Declaration of Independence is widely considered to have benefited from changes made to it. Thomas Jefferson, well known for the quality of his writing by his contemporaries, was chosen to draft the document, and rhetorically he adopted a tone of high seriousness with restrained passion boiling underneath. Its central reason for being was to proclaim to the world the rationale for the United States to declare its independence from England. As such, it gives the rhetorical appearance of unity among the colonies, when in fact there was a great deal of discord that would be played out in Philadelphia in 1787. We will see this trope of unity expropriated by Barack Obama as early as his 2004 Democratic National Convention keynote speech, which is widely credited with making him a national political player purveying a message of unity as a result of assertions like "there is not a liberal America and a conservative America — there is the United States of America."

The central tenets of the Declaration of Independence, and those that help to distinguish it historically from previous such documents, include: reason as a foundation of just government (echoing utopian thought from Plato to Bacon), the affirmation of the right of a people to overthrow its own government (inherited from Locke), the acknowledgment of the natural rights of mankind (from Montesquieu, Locke, and perhaps tangentially Rousseau), and finally a moral and legal justification for their rebellion against the divine right of kings (the 1688 Bill of Rights). Carl Becker notes that in the Declaration's opening, Jefferson combines simplicity of statement with "an urban solemnity of manner in such a way as to give that felicitous, haunting cadence" that adorns his best writing[27]:

> When in the course of human events it becomes necessary for one people to dissolve the political bands which have connected them with another and to assume among the powers of the earth, the separate and equal station to which the Laws of Nature and of Nature's God entitle them, a decent respect to the opinions of mankind requires that they should declare the causes which impel them to the separation.

After this justification for independence grounded in natural law, Jefferson outlines a political philosophy that affirms the right of the people to establish their own government. This argument, because it can apply to oppressed people anywhere, has lent the document a universalism that Obama evoked in his quest for the presidency. Jefferson roots his Declaration of Independence in broad theoretical terms before moving on to the historical particulars of the perceived abuses of these natural rights by the Crown:

We hold these truths to be self-evident, that all men are created equal, that they are endowed by their Creator with certain unalienable Rights, that among these are Life, Liberty and the pursuit of Happiness. That to secure these rights, Governments are instituted among Men, deriving their just powers from the consent of the governed; That whenever any Form of Government becomes destructive of these ends, it is the Right of the People to alter or to abolish it, and to institute new Government, laying its foundation on such principles and organizing its powers in such form, as to them shall seem most likely to effect their Safety and Happiness.

Here, Jefferson gives a central role to governments in securing those inalienable rights. Obama, as we shall see shortly, likewise views government as critical to safeguarding individual rights from the forces of commerce and power deriving from property and wealth. "Such has been the patient sufferance of these Colonies," Jefferson writes, that necessity requires them to "alter their former Systems of Government." Thus the framers of the Declaration of Independence "formulated a philosophy of government which made revolution right under certain conditions." The colonies were breaking with England "solely on account of the deliberate and malevolent purpose of their king to establish over them an 'absolute tyranny.'"[28]

The framers of the Constitution and Bill of Rights were charged with rewriting the nation's first constitution (the Articles of Confederation and Perpetual Union) in 1787 due to an economic crisis that highlighted the need for a stronger national government, one that could raise its own revenue rather than relying on voluntary donations by the states. Like the Declaration of Independence, the Constitution (with the Bill of Rights) is remarkable for its concision. The original nineteen resolutions of the Constitution were only twelve hundred words in length yet exceedingly precise where there was agreement.[29] The general principles of the Constitution can be summarized neatly as a result of this brevity. Firstly, it affirms the indestructibility of the union in perpetuity and promises its continued betterment. The Preamble to the United States Constitution sets forth the guiding principles and fundamental purposes of its composition:

We the people of the United States, in order to form a more perfect union, establish justice, insure domestic tranquility, provide for the common defense, promote the general welfare, and secure the blessings of liberty to ourselves and our posterity, do ordain and establish this Constitution for the United States of America.

Obama evokes this promise of a more perfect union frequently in the rhetoric of hope in a variety of contexts (not simply when employing religious tropes of the Promised Land).

The United States Constitution separates the powers of the United States government into executive, legislative and judicial branches, then it establishes a series of checks and balances to ensure one branch cannot lord over the others. For example, although the powers of the presidency were significantly increased from those under the Articles of the Confederation, Congress was given the government purse strings. The Constitution also regulates the nation-state relationship (states cannot issue their own currency, for instance), as well as the state-to-state relationship (states are prohibited from erecting their own trade barriers to favor local commerce), and it provided elections and term limits (a nod to Harrington's *Oceana*). The United States Bill of Rights also afforded extensive protections to the individual citizen from government intrusion, including the freedom of speech and the press, the right to bear arms, and no unreasonable searches and seizures.

Thus, in these founding documents, the framers of the nation blended the old and new into a unique form of law and government. As Solberg explains, although "extremely practical in their approach, they nevertheless constantly invoked both European history and European theorists," and I would argue its utopian traditions as well, to "illuminate their way." Ultimately, however, these founding documents are "primarily a product of American growth — a skillful synthesis of mainly indigenous elements" drawn from "the Articles of the Confederation and other native sources."[30] It was these indigenous features, the spirit of the nation, as Montesquieu put it, that Alexis de Tocqueville noted in his renowned volume *Democracy in America* (1840). Traveling in the United States less than fifty years after the adoption of its Constitution, Tocqueville observed among its citizens a strong ambition to improve their condition, a remarkable individualism, and a singular perpetual striving to acquire more power and material gain. He marveled at Americans' lack of any loftier ambitions and their boundless self-esteem, yet so new was the government that they created that Tocqueville declared the "new word to express this new thing does not yet exist."[31] Here we find another source of the myth of American exceptionalism that Barack Obama evokes in the rhetoric of hope.

In Obamian rhetoric, the United States provides a unique model for global progress due to its ability to balance the tension between the individual and the group, for it "allowed us to form a multicultural nation the likes of which exists nowhere else on earth."[32] James Petre argues that Obama has a progressive interpretation of American exceptionalism rooted in a history and born "of continual struggle for inclusion" that extends into the future through a call for hope. Obama differs from nearly all other presidents and political figures who frequently reference the term "American exceptionalism" by reminding audiences that American actions must match its idealistic words.[33] The rhetoric of hope is built upon historical interpretations that locate the true genius of America in its capacity for reform, for change.

Working together to improve the nation requires hope and a sense of common purpose. "Hope," Obama explains in his Iowa Caucus Night address, "is what led a band of colonists to rise up against an empire.... Hope ... hope ... is what led me here today — with a father from Kenya; a mother from Kansas; and a story that could only happen in the United States of America."[34] Introducing Barack Obama in early 2008 to an audience of two thousand worshippers on a blustery Sunday morning, the Reverend Raphael Warnock explained: "We invited this brother because he's committed, he's brilliant. He has spiritual foundation. And he is the embodiment of the American dream. Regardless of whether you are a Democrat, a Republican, or an Independent, when you think about the long history of America, Barack Obama makes us proud."[35] As we shall see in Chapter Seven of this book, Obama invites these correspondences between his story and the story of America.

In the rhetoric of hope, Obama makes deliberate and repeated allusions to the figures and language of the founding documents. Obama explains to his readers that Enlightenment thinkers like Hobbes and Locke suggested governments created by free men should preserve liberty and prevent tyranny. Clearly well versed in the historical antecedents of American democracy, Obama notes how the founding documents created a republican form of representational government that was in part a response to Athenian experiments in direct democracy. The Constitution and the Bill of Rights are a "novel contribution to the world," Obama writes, for in addition to protecting individual rights, separating national government yet balancing interests and checking factions, these documents provided a map by which Hamilton's "jarring of parties" could take place.[36]

In these documents, the Founding Fathers, Obama suggests, tell us how to think, not what to think. Pointing to a defining feature of the eighteenth century preserved in them, Obama argues that the Constitution requires constant interpretation based on reason. He rejects strict constructionist views of the Constitution as fixed or unwavering. This is a living document that must be read in the context of an ever-changing world.[37] The framework of the United States Constitution therefore provides Obama with a way to argue about the future on the campaign trail. This futurity becomes a noteworthy characteristic of the rhetoric of hope, one that invites the listener, and the reader, to look forward in anticipation of that more perfect union.

For Obama, evidence that the union can be perfected may be found in the Thirteenth, Fourteenth, and Fifteenth Amendments to the Constitution that outlawed slavery, for they demonstrate clear historical progress in race relations. In a speech delivered on the night of the North Carolina and Indiana primaries in 2008, Obama remarks, "I believe in our ability to perfect this union because it's the only reason I'm standing here today. And I know the promise of America because I have lived it." Here again, we note the conflation of Obama's life story with the quintessentially American promise of continual betterment. He invokes the shadowy image of his absent father from Africa, and juxtaposes it with that of his white grandfather, and then combines the two with allusions to the nation's founding documents: "It is the light of opportunity that led my father across an ocean./It is the founding ideals that the flag draped over my grandfather's coffin stands for — it is life, liberty, and the pursuit of happiness."[38]

As Kloppenberg observes, "Barack Obama's intellectual and political persuasions emerged from a particular matrix formed not only from his personal experience but also from the dynamics of American history." Obama's professor at Occidental College, Roger Boesche, introduced the future president to the line of argument that the United States was designed from the beginning to be a democracy "in which the people would deliberate together to discover the meaning of justice and advance the common good."[39] In the rhetoric of hope, Obama harkens back to an early Republican formulation of freedom shared by Adams, Jefferson, and Madison, namely that self-determination has "always been a question of disciplining impulses according to ethical principles and considering the demands of the common good."[40] The importance of moral values in the rhetoric of hope will be the subject of a later chapter. For the moment, it is enough to understand that Obama's use of the notion of the common good has deep roots in American history. Let us now move on to another intersection of history and idealism in Obamian discourse derived from the African American experience.

CHAPTER THREE

Slave Narratives, the Black Church and Civil Rights

Thus far, we have considered the rhetorical debt that Barack Obama's campaign rhetoric owes to Judeo-Christianity (with its prophetic tradition and tropes of the New Jerusalem) and to the idealistic traditions in currency during the eighteenth century that permeated the founding documents of the United States. We now take up another thread in the tapestry of the rhetoric of hope, one that begins with the narratives of American slaves— a group to whom the proposition that "all men are created equal" did not apply. Out of their continual suffering, documented in those narratives, emerged an African American religious tradition that applied Judeo-Christian tropes of hope and salvation to their own condition of bondage. The theology of liberation that followed provided the religious justification for the American civil rights movement under the leadership of Dr. Martin Luther King, Jr. The nation's founding documents supplied the ideals (already encoded into law) that vindicated their demand for equality and access to opportunity. Tragically, it would be more than one hundred years after the Civil War before the victims of the Founding Fathers' failure to resolve the divisive issue of slavery would win the barest measure of the American Dream.

The three-fifths compromise reached by the Constitutional Convention in 1787 preserved the Union, at that time under serious threat of collapse due to a weak federal government created by the Articles of the Confederation, but at the cost of the continuance of the institution of slavery (and a mere postponing of the day of reckoning). That compromise meant that black slaves would count as three-fifths of a person in determining the legislative representation of southern states in the House of

Representatives. Through this agreement, the more sparsely populated southern states, which feared marginalized representation in any new government, were appeased, and the present Constitution was ratified. However, the fact that the nation's founding documents failed to extend protections of "life, liberty, and the pursuit of happiness" to blacks and other minorities did not go unnoticed by abolitionists, who dedicated their pens to making this incongruity between word and deed apparent to all, especially to slaveholding Christians.

Among both free blacks and slaves, recognition of such hypocrisy resulted in a rejection of the white church, whose interpretation of Christianity was used to justify both the enslavement of others and the continuance of colonialism. This realization also led to the formation of a distinctly African American form of Christianity that borrowed from both American and biblical narratives of bondage and emancipation to fashion a theology of hope. As Lawrence Jones observes, African American Christianity "looked forward to the New Jerusalem — the city of God," and it also "possessed an implicit hope, rooted in the Declaration of Independence and in the Constitution, that one day the ideals enshrined in these historic documents would be actualized and there would arise an earthly city, a beloved community, in which they would be citizens with all the rights, prerogatives, and responsibilities with which white men were invested."[1] This chapter briefly charts that quest for social equality beginning with accounts of slavery written by those who experienced its horrors firsthand. It follows the formation of the black church and shows how that religious institution provided the theological foundation for the American civil rights movement. By way of closing, we consider Barack Obama's appropriation of these African American traditions in his rhetoric of hope.

Slave narratives enjoyed tremendous popularity between 1836 and 1865. They were compelling accounts that stirred emotion and found positive reception among members of emancipation movements as well as the greater reading public. Their authors were slaves who "had to represent themselves as 'speaking subjects' before they could begin to destroy their status as objects, as commodities in Western Culture."[2] Perhaps for this reason, their narratives often begin with an assertion of selfhood like this one: "I, JOHN JEA, the subject of this narrative, was born in the town of Old Callabar, in Africa, in 1773.... At two years and a half old, I and my father, mother, brothers, and sisters, were stolen, and conveyed to North

America, and sold for slaves; we were then sent to New York, the man who purchased us was very cruel, and used us in a manner, almost too shocking to relate."[3] Likewise, another contemporary account opens: "I JOHN MARRANT, born June 15th, 1755 in New York, in North America, with these gracious dealings of the Lord with me to be published, in hopes they may be useful to others, encourage the fearful, to confirm the wavering, and to refresh the hearts of true believers."[4]

In their narratives, these Americans vividly recounted the violence inflicted on them and chronicled the brutal nature of the institution by which they were continually oppressed. For instance, Moses Roper describes how he was tortured using a cotton screw for trying to escape from Mr. Goosh, his master: "This is a machine used for packing and pressing cotton. By it he hung me up by the hands," says Roper. Using this contraption for a purpose it was not designed, Goosh raises Moses ten feet off the ground and spins him in the air from his tied hands (by having a horse drive the cotton screw). Several months later, when Moses escapes and is recaptured yet again, Mr. Goosh put the fingers of his left hand in a vise and squeezed all of his nails off, then he did the same to both feet while beating his toes.[5] This physical suffering, unimaginable to most, was accompanied by mental agony as well.

Harriet Jacobs, who wrote her narrative of captivity secretly at night, described the psychological effects of slavery on women, many of whom were stalked like prey and repeatedly sexually abused by their white masters. They were property in every sense of the word. Jacobs recounts her experience with one such lascivious slave owner: "My master met me at every turn, reminding me that I belonged to him, and swearing by heaven and earth that he would compel me to submit to him. If I went out for a breath of fresh air, after a day of unwearied toil, his footsteps dogged me." Fellow slaves who witnessed this relentless sexual pursuit pitied Harriet, for "they knew too well the guilty practices under that roof; and they were aware that to speak of them was an offense that never went unpunished."[6] One might be struck by Jacobs' oblique accounts of her master's sexual transgressions, but due to social taboos in the eighteenth and nineteenth centuries, concrete descriptions of sexual abuse are rare in slave narratives. Instead, figures of substitution are employed to hint at that abuse.

In addition to chronicling their abuse and the conditions of their enslavement, the narratives of American slaves share several other features that contributed in time to the formation of a distinctly African American religious tradition, one that Barack Obama thoroughly mines in his rhetoric of hope. Slave narratives mix storytelling, racial awareness, social critique, and self-reflection (as do traditional sermons in the black church that emerge out of the experience of slavery). They also tend to be episodic, demonstrate a strong resistance to oppression, and aim to counter the rhetorical defenses of slave owners by revealing their deplorable behavior.[7] Because the mode of their emplotment claims to be factual thereby purporting to provide a non-memorialized (and not fictionalized) description of events, slave narratives often have a didactic function vis-à-vis the institution of slavery.

In their published form, American slave narratives most often include an engraved portrait or photograph, the testimonials of others, poetic epigrams, illustrations, and a wide range of documents in an appendix to reinforce the authenticity of the account.[8] These paratextual materials not only served to confirm the identity of the writer, but they also authenticate their accounts of slavery to audiences of non-slave-holders or others who might not have direct knowledge of that institution and its practices. American slave narratives also employ the conventions of realism, tropes of elevation (both individual and collective), leitmotifs of moral and psychic regeneration, and feature a dialectic tension between the promise of freedom and the reality of bondage. A brief analysis of the *Narrative Life of Frederick Douglass* (1845) exemplifies the use of many of these defining features of the slave narrative. We see in them the rhetorical origins of the black church and the civil rights movement, the subjects of the latter part of this chapter, as well as the establishment of a uniquely African American artistic tradition (itself the focus of Chapter Five).

In 1845, Frederick Douglass published one of the most influential accounts of American slavery written in the characteristically realistic mode of such narratives. Consider the matter-of-fact tone Douglass employs in providing detailed exposition to the reader:

> I have had two masters. My first master's name was Anthony. I do not remember his first name. He was not considered a rich slaveholder. He owned two or three farms, and about thirty slaves. His farms and slaves were under the care of an overseer. The overseer's name was Plummer. Mr. Plummer was a miserable drunkard, a profane swearer, and a savage monster. He always went armed with a cowskin and a heavy cudgel. I have known him to cut and slash the women's heads so horribly, that even master would be enraged at his cruelty, and would threaten to whip him if he did not mind himself. Master, however, was not a humane slaveholder. It required extraordinary barbarity on the part of an

overseer to affect him. He was a cruel man, hardened by a long life of slave-holding. He would at times seem to take great pleasure in whipping a slave. I have often been awakened at the dawn of day by the most heart-rending shrieks of an own aunt of mine, whom he used to tie up to a joist, and whip upon her naked back till she was literally covered with blood. No words, no tears, no prayers, from his gory victim, seemed to move his iron heart from its bloody purpose.[9]

In addition to using short declarative sentences that reinforce the rhetorical supposition of accurate reporting, Douglass reveals the deplorable behavior of his master and overseer. Douglass' detached tone and use of specific details (of names and places, for instance) adds force to his account and highlights the ultimate intention of these narratives: to instruct the reader concerning the brutal reality faced every day by himself and his fellow slaves. As this quotation illustrates, the realistic mode of (re)telling employed by writers such as Douglass was highly compelling, and it is easy to see why these narratives contributed so significantly to American emancipation movements.

In addition to employing these traditional features of the slave narrative, Douglass uses tropes of elevation and leitmotifs of moral and psychic regeneration to create a dialectical tension between the reality of bondage and the promise of freedom. This is the same utopian dialectic between the ideal and the actual traced in previous chapters. Concerning his arrival in the free state of New York, Douglass writes: "It was a moment of the highest excitement I have ever experienced. I suppose I felt as one may imagine the unarmed mariner to feel when he is recused by a friendly man-of-war from the pursuit of a pirate."[10] As in many slave narratives, Douglass's movement from a condition of bondage to freedom is recounted using the metaphor of a journey. "It is well known," reports the former slave William Wells Brown, "that a great number of fugitives make their escape to Canada, by way of Cleveland; and while on the Lake, I always made arrangements to carry them on the boat to Buffalo or Detroit, and thus effect their escape to the 'promised land.'"[11] This remark betrays the extent to which slaves evoked biblical figures of liberation as they journeyed toward emancipation.

References to religious conversion also abound in slave narratives, as do tropes of the talking book through which slaves recount hearing the Bible read aloud for the first time. That many white adherents failed to live up to the tradition's moral teachings was not lost on these slaves who embraced Christianity. Moses Roper, after being forcibly separated from his mother to whom he had escaped on one occasion, wrote of the religious hypocrisy that he saw all around him:

> I was told afterwards that some of those men who took me were professing Christians, but to me they did not seem to live up to what they professed. They did not seem, by their practices, at least, to recognize that God as their God, who hath said, "Thou shalt not deliver unto his master, the servant which is escaped from his master unto thee; he shall dwell with thee, even among you, in that place which he shall choose, in one of the gates, where it liketh him best; thou shalt not oppress him."[12]

Declarations of white religious hypocrisy in slave narratives like this one have led C. Eric Lincoln to conclude that the creation of separate black churches in the nineteenth century was "in part a response to the failure of white churchmen to treat their brothers with equity, respect, care, concern, and love."[13] Indeed, most blacks in eighteenth- and nineteenth-century America were treated with anything but respect by their Christian neighbors and masters, and their exclusion from white ministries meant turning to their own communities for spiritual succor.

The black church has been called the "invisible institution"[14] due to its stealthy emergence. The formation of the black church in secret slave gatherings prior to Emancipation shaped a rhetoric of endurance and transcendence in the face of hardship, and at its core was hope for liberation from bondage. It is to the rise of that social, religious, and political institution we move next in our quest for antecedents to Barack Obama's rhetoric of hope. The recollection of the historical struggle of American slaves for the equality promised in the Constitution, a struggle that reached an apex during the civil rights movement, became for Barack Obama "a form of prayer." So strong an impact did that historical fight for equality have on Obama that even in the words of the Declaration of Independence he heard "the spirit of Douglass and Delany, as well as Jefferson and Lincoln; the struggle of Martin and Malcolm."[15]

Historically, the black church was formed from slave religion, itself a complex mixture of traditional polytheistic African religious beliefs brought with them into bondage. It was infused with European and American elements (particularly Judeo-Christianity) over several centuries, and it developed into a spirituality that directly addressed the need for survival among its practitioners. In his acclaimed book *Black Religion and Black Radicalism*, Gayraud Wilmore observes that a distinctive African American

Christianity sprang from this amalgam of traditions, and thereby a new religion of the oppressed took root in the black community. Its theology would emphasize the "rejection of the spiritual and political despotism of the white man" and chart the course for an epic journey to freedom laid out in the slave narratives that preceded it.

This African American form of Christianity relied on interpretations of Old Testament stories (particularly Exodus), prophetic pronouncements, and New Testament apocalypse, all of which were read so as to make manifest the "compelling signals of God's concern for their freedom."[16] The otherworldly mysticism that accompanied these eschatological beliefs inspired some, like Nat Turner, to advocate the violent overthrow of the slave system. By contrast, "for most whites, Christianity was largely viewed as an instrument of social control" seen as effective in producing slaves who were more obedient.[17] These differing interpretations of Christian doctrine contributed to the rise of a distinct religious culture that developed in slave communities in the north and south and employed the rhetoric of communal obligation. In the early nineteenth century, Methodist and Baptist mass conversion of slaves during the Second Great Awakening resulted in the founding of the first authentic black churches that preached and practiced a social gospel of community welfare. In them, Jesus becomes a liberator of the poor and oppressed (and therefore very much a political actor and rebel against unjust authority). Perhaps in emulation of that vision of Jesus, the preacher in the black church is often an educator, a political leader, a liberator, a healer, an advocate for the oppressed, and, crucially, he possesses a solid command of language (the medium through which we saw slaves affirm their identities).

Preaching in the black church is accompanied by singing, shouting, and dancing. The black spirituals (which would develop into the popular musical genres of blues, gospel, and jazz) undoubtedly grew out of the musical call and response between the preacher and the congregation. Like the sermon, "prayer was also delivered in a kind of sing-song declamation which evoked musical response from the worshipers."[18] Black politicians, including Barack Obama, still employ the cadences, repetitions, and rhythmic delivery of the preacher. Indeed, as the only stable institution to survive slavery, the black church became the womb of black culture[19] and informed artistic and political movements from the Harlem Renaissance to Civil Rights.

Although each is unique, the seven major denominations that make up the black church in America share several identifiable features. Among them are a concern with bondage and redemption, a belief in nondiscrimination, an understanding that God calls one to freedom, the use of music and the shout to display emotions, dialogue with a preacher, and a personal conversion experience of being "born again."[20] This emphasis on individual conversion is balanced against a collectivist concern with the welfare of the group. As a result, one of the major functions of black churches in American politics has been mobilizing and community organizing.[21] In fact, the traditions of the black church are so deeply embedded in black culture that they cannot easily be separated from the politics of the African American community.

As Obama explains, his baptism into the black church "came about as a choice and not an epiphany."[22] Barack Obama's embrace of black Christianity, and his rhetorical debt to that tradition and its tenets, springs from a rational and deliberate process on his part. His rhetoric of hope draws heavily from the black church, an institution that grew out of the oppression of slavery chronicled in slave narratives. In an October 2006 article for *Time* entitled "My Spiritual Journey," Barack Obama discusses his secular yet spiritual upbringing, as well as how his studies in political philosophy and community organizing in Chicago led him to embrace African American Christianity. Through his own community organizing in Chicago, Obama came to believe in shared sacrifice as part of what he calls "a promise of redemption."[23] He explains: "Christians with whom I worked recognized themselves in me; they saw that I knew their Book and shared their values and sang their songs. But they sensed that a part of me remained removed, detached, an observer among them." Obama sometimes felt that he, like his mother, might never find a community or shared tradition in which to ground his "most deeply held beliefs." It was the unique historical attributes of the black church, and the tradition of bondage from which it emerged, that helped Obama to, in his own words, "shed some of my skepticism and embrace the Christian faith."

Coming as it does in 2006, this *Time* article, like *Dreams from My Father*, is an early figuration of the rhetoric of hope. Reading it today, four years after Obama's election to the presidency in 2008, one is struck by Obama's nuanced understanding of both American political and religious discourse, and by his ease in speaking of either Lincoln or Jesus. Noting the truism that "Americans are a religious people," Obama urges progressives not to cede the use of religious language to the Republicans (who had used it effectively to defeat Al Gore in 2000 and John Kerry in 2004):

> More fundamentally, the discomfort of some progressives with any hint of religiosity has often inhibited us from effectively addressing issues in moral terms. Some of the problem is rhetorical: Scrub language of all religious content and we forfeit the imagery and terminology through which millions of Americans understand both their personal morality and social justice. Imagine Lincoln's Second Inaugural Address without reference to "the judgments of the Lord," or King's "I Have a Dream" speech without reference to "all of God's children." Their summoning of a higher truth helped inspire what had seemed impossible and move the nation to embrace a common destiny.

Obama acknowledges that the failure of progressives "to tap into the moral underpinnings of the nation" was not simply rhetorical, but one that risked discounting the role that values and culture play in redressing social ills. The rhetoric of hope is unique in American political discourse because its progressive interpretation of American exceptionalism means that rhetoric must match action.[24]

His intellectual biographer James Kloppenberg notes, "Obama's religious conversion had enabled him to put together several forms of realism." He slowly came to understand that Christian love "required a commitment to justice that is deep enough—fierce enough— to enable one to withstand resistance without abandoning hope."[25] Not surprisingly, when it came time to campaign for the presidency, Barack Obama filled his political rhetoric with American history, religious idealism drawn from the black church, and universal secular values. So clearly established were those influences on Obama's writing that Jon Favreau, Obama's new speechwriter, soon "knew the books to read (anything about Lincoln)," and he "knew whom to quote (Martin Luther King Jr. and Scripture)."[26]

Obama had written most of his own speeches up until the demands of the campaign trail made that impossible, and even with speech writers like Favreau, Obama often worked and reworked revisions of important speeches by hand in order to make prominent elements derived from the African American experience. As Richard Wolffe observes in his second book on the president, Obama "idolized" the civil rights movement and Dr. King, and "he deployed the language and techniques of the movement, the idealism and impatience, to help propel his presidential campaign."[27] In his own writing, Martin Luther King exemplifies the rhetorical linkages between the slave narrative, the black church, and the civil rights movement, for he espoused a black gospel of social justice.

Dr. King's pulpit style was above all didactic, and his sermons often blended biblical allegory and juxtaposition with moralism. King's political discourse features rhetorical figures and tropes commonly employed by black preachers. Like his father and grandfather who were pastors, King used the "intonation and pitch, dynamics and rhythm, movement and timing" of his voice to build toward an emotional climax.[28] In his "I Have a Dream" speech, King begins softly by evoking Lincoln using Lincolnian language:

> Five score years ago, a great American, in whose symbolic shadow we stand today, signed the Emancipation Proclamation. This momentous decree came as a great beacon light of hope to millions of Negro slaves who had been seared in the flames of withering injustice. It came as a joyous daybreak to end the long night of their captivity.

Using similes of light and daybreak to denote the hope of black slaves for an end to oppression after the signing of the Emancipation Proclamation in 1863, King in the next part of his speech points out the ongoing betrayal of that promise:

> But one hundred years later, the Negro still is not free. One hundred years later, the life of the Negro is still sadly crippled by the manacles of segregation and the chains of discrimination. One hundred years later, the Negro lives on a lonely island of poverty in the midst of a vast ocean of material prosperity. One hundred years later, the Negro is still languished in the corners of American society and finds himself an exile in his own land. And so we've come here today to dramatize a shameful condition.

In this section, the imagery has shifted from light motifs to those of bondage and disenfranchisement (manacles, chains, island, and vast ocean). Note also the rhythmic use of the repeated phrase, "one hundred years later," reminiscent of traditional black preaching.

King also peppers his speech with direct allusions to the Bible and American founding documents. "I have a dream," says King, "that one day this nation will rise up and live out the true meaning of its creed: 'We hold these truths to be self-evident, that all men are created equal.'" Citing Amos 5:24, King declares: "No, no, we are not satisfied, and we will not be satisfied until 'justice rolls down like waters, and righteousness like a mighty stream.'" The refrains "I have a dream" and "let freedom ring" are repeated to a bell-like crescendo. King closes with an image of hope.

In it, all American people "join hands and sing in the words of the old Negro spiritual: *Free at last! Free at last! Thank God Almighty, we are free at last!*"

As can be gleaned from the foregoing pages, a significant part of Barack Obama's rhetoric of hope derives from a long African American tradition of idealism that begins with slave narratives, grows in complexity in the black church, and comes to fruition in the civil rights movement. After a failed experiment with equality during Reconstruction, black Americans suffered under Jim Crow laws that increasingly mandated racial segregation from the post–Reconstruction period through the 1940s. In order to evade the Fifteenth Amendment protecting the right to vote, "southern states required voter applicants to pay poll taxes, pass literacy tests, satisfy residency requirements" and more just to cast a ballot.[29] Even Franklin Delano Roosevelt's New Deal failed to help blacks recover from centuries of oppression and second-class citizenship. So, when organized resistance to these injustices began in the South during the 1940s and 1950s, bus boycotts, sit-ins, and organized nonviolent protests soon followed, thereby ratcheting up longstanding demands for true equality before the law. As Mark Newman observes, "placing black demands within the context of America's Judaeo-Christian tradition and the US Constitution, Martin Luther King and the SCLC were uniquely placed within the movement to articulate African American concerns and aspirations sympathetically to a white audience."[30]

Barack Obama carefully studied the speeches of Martin Luther King (along with those of many other civil rights leaders), and he eventually embraced the black church for its platform of social justice. He also read the narratives of slaves like Frederick Douglass. So steeped was he in this tradition that when he arrived in Chicago to begin organizing in poor neighborhoods, the "whistle of the Illinois Central" brought to his mind "the thousands who had come up from the South so many years before; the black men and women and children, dirty from the soot of the railcars, clutching their makeshift luggage, all making their way to Canaan Land."[31] From Malcolm X, Obama learned the art of "self-creation," and he grew to admire his words that "promised a new and uncompromising order."[32] In Louis Farrakhan, Obama noted the use of "sharply cadenced sermons." In Jeremiah Wright, he saw a man who could "hold together, if not reconcile, the conflicting strains of black experience," one who read Tillich, Niebuhr, and the black theologians.

In his 2005 remarks in honor of the sixty-fifth birthday of civil rights leader John Lewis, Obama uses many of the rhetorical devices noted above, for instance a cadence and repetition unique to preaching in the black church: "How far we've come from because of your courage, John. How far we've come from the days when the son of a sharecropper would huddle at the radio as the crackle of Dr. King's dreams filled his heart with hope." We also hear it in lines like these: "The road John chose for himself was not easy. But the road to change never is."[33] Hope and change are, of course, two themes closely associated with Obama's 2008 campaign. We also discover in these remarks by Obama a deliberate juxtaposition between the ideal and the status quo that defines the utopian impulse. I quote at some length here to allow that dialectical opposition to unfold completely:

> Today, we need that courage. We need the courage to say that it's wrong that one out of every five children is born into poverty in the richest country on Earth. And it's right to do whatever necessary to provide our children the care and the education they need to live up to their God-given potential.
>
> It's wrong to tell hardworking families who are earning less and paying more in taxes that we can't do anything to help them buy their own home or send their kids to college or care for them when they're sick. And it's right to expect that if you're willing to work hard in this country of American Dreamers, the sky is the limit on what you can achieve.
>
> It's wrong to tell those brave men and women who are willing to fight and die for this country that when they come home, we may not have room for them at the VA hospitals or the benefits we promised them. And it's right to always provide the very best care for the very best of America.
>
> My friends, we have not come this far as a people and a nation because we believe that we're better off simply fending for ourselves. We are here because we believe that all men are created equal, and that we are all connected to each other as one people. And we need to say that more. And say it again. And keep saying it.[34]

In addition to rhetorically contrasting a vision of a better America (the promise of the future) with the repudiation of the past, Obama references the Declaration of Independence and the moral precepts of Judeo-Christianity in a style very similar to Martin Luther King's "I Have a Dream" speech. Likewise, Obama also builds emotional tension that compels the listener with a sense of urgency reminiscent of the black preacher turned civil rights leader: "And we need to say that more. And say it again. And keep saying it." We also find in Obama's remarks a belief in the possibility for positive social change. As we look back to the eras of slavery,

Jim Crow, and the civil rights movement, it remains clear that blacks have yet to find true equality, but Obama suggests that the tangible proof of social progress is nevertheless clear from history. His rhetorical vision of a more perfect union is one of true racial equality.

Likewise, Obama's keynote address at the 2004 Democratic Convention in support of John Kerry contains many elements that would inform his own 2008 campaign rhetoric. In it, Obama offers his audience lessons drawn from American history, and then he lightly overlays a reference to himself in that historical continuum, to suggest that his American story fits here, too: "I stand here knowing that my story is part of the larger American story, that I owe a debt to all of those who came before me, and that, in no other country on earth, is my story even possible." Although Obama does not possess Dr. King's gift for imagery and metaphor, he does use simple, descriptive language to effectively evoke a universal yearning for a better day. Obama states, "It's the hope of slaves sitting around a fire singing freedom songs; the hope of immigrants setting out for distant shores; the hope of a young naval lieutenant bravely patrolling the Mekong Delta; the hope of a millworker's son who dares to defy the odds; the hope of a skinny kid with a funny name who believes that America has a place for him, too." These historical allusions in Obama's rhetoric of hope give it a practical grounding that more idealistic discourses sometimes eschew: "I'm not talking about blind optimism here — the almost willful ignorance that thinks unemployment will go away if we just don't talk about it.... No, I'm talking about something more substantial."[35]

Indeed, everywhere we turn in the rhetoric of hope we find a debt to the African American religious and political traditions that grew out of slavery, developed in the womb of the black church, and found expression in the art and culture of black America. Nowhere is this influence more apparent than in Obama's March 2008 "More Perfect Union" speech. In it, he has to distance himself from the Reverend Jeremiah Wright, who was something of a father figure to Obama in the absence of his own, but without divorcing himself from the African American traditions with which he increasingly identified throughout his college years. Obama explains:

> The man I met more than twenty years ago is a man who helped introduce me to my Christian faith, a man who spoke to me about our obligations to love one another, to care for the sick and lift up the poor. He is a man who served his country as a United States Marine; who has studied and lectured at some

of the finest universities and seminaries in the country, and who for over thirty years has led a church that serves the community by doing God's work here on Earth — by housing the homeless, ministering to the needy, providing day care services and scholarships and prison ministries, and reaching out to those suffering from HIV/AIDS.

As we saw in Chapter One, Obama faults Wright for failing to recognize that Americans can change, instead preferring to see "white racism as endemic." Obama's is a dazzling rhetorical act that at once cuts loose a former mentor and minister whose incendiary comments could have cost him the election, while at the same time embracing the black religious tradition that gave Wright, and other gifted individuals like King and Jackson, an opportunity to become community leaders.

Obama begins that race speech in a manner eerily similar to Martin Luther King, using a soft Lincolnian tone from which he will build to crescendo, all the while he employs references to the principles enshrined in the nation's founding documents:

> "We the people, in order to form a *more perfect union...*"
> Two hundred and twenty one years ago, in a hall that still stands across the street, a group of men gathered and, with these simple words, launched America's improbable experiment in democracy. Farmers and scholars, statesmen and patriots who had traveled across an ocean to escape tyranny and persecution finally made real their declaration of independence at a Philadelphia convention that lasted through the spring of 1787.

In the second paragraph of the speech, Obama modulates, from extolling the virtues of the Founding Fathers' work to noting the blot of slavery on that achievement: "The document they produced was eventually signed but ultimately unfinished. It was stained by this nation's original sin of slavery, a question that divided the colonies and brought the convention to a stalemate until the founders chose to allow the slave trade to continue for at least twenty more years, and to leave any final resolution to future generations."

The words on that parchment, Obama asserts, while grand, "would not be enough to deliver slaves from bondage, or provide men and women of every color and creed their full rights and obligations as citizens of the United States. What would be needed were Americans in successive generations who were willing to do their part — through protests and struggles, on the streets and in the courts, through a civil war and civil disobedience, and always at great risk — to narrow that gap between the promise of our ideals and the reality of their time." In this historical matrix, Obama locates his preacher in order to help the audience understand where Wright comes from, but at the very same time he distinguishes his own worldview from that of his one-time mentor. Employing biblical references to Ezekiel, David and Goliath, Moses and Pharaoh in the tradition of the black preacher and politician, Obama explains that to completely reject the Reverend Wright would mean turning away from much more than a single preacher at Trinity United Church of Christ:

> Like other predominantly black churches across the country, Trinity embodies the black community in its entirety—the doctor and the welfare mom, the model student and the former gang-banger. Like other black churches, Trinity's services are full of raucous laughter and sometimes bawdy humor. They are full of dancing and clapping and screaming and shouting that may seem jarring to the untrained ear. The church contains in full the kindness and cruelty, the fierce intelligence and the shocking ignorance, the struggles and successes, the love and, yes, the bitterness and biases that make up the black experience in America.

"I can no more disown him than I can disown the black community," Obama declares. Rather than choose between one or the other, a black America or a white America, Obama calls for unity, thereby distancing himself from race rhetoric that is divisive or from ideologies that distinguish based on color or creed. In closing this speech, one of the longest of his 2008 presidential campaign, Obama ends where he began, with a band of patriots who signed a document in Philadelphia that marked the beginning of a long process of perfecting the union.

George Washington, putting his own revolutionary beliefs into action, provided for the emancipation of nearly three hundred slaves upon his death. Sadly, he was the only one of the Founding Fathers to liberate his slaves in this manner (Jefferson freed only five house slaves—all relatives of Sally Hemings).[36] Perhaps the former slave William Grimes best illustrates the dialectical tension between the country's founding ideals and the harsh reality experienced by so many African Americans when he writes: "If it were not for the stripes on my back which were made while I was a slave, I would in my will, leave my skin as a legacy to the government, desiring that it might be taken off and made into parchment, and then bind the constitution of glorious happy and *free* America. Let the skin of an American slave, bind the charter of American liberty."[37] The liberty-based values that former slaves like Grimes expressed during

Reconstruction and afterwards would find expression in a distinct form of Christianity that Obama draws on in his rhetoric of hope.

In this chapter and the one that precedes it, we have noted how Obama references pivotal periods in American history to frame contemporary race relations in the United States. In appropriating the images, cadences, and tropes of both the founding documents and Judeo-Christianity, Obamian rhetoric essentially repackages proven techniques of persuasion for a twenty-first-century reality of continuing inequality. However, one of the things that distinguishes the rhetoric of hope from its historical and literary antecedents is its biracial messenger, who literally positions himself as a bridge between the black and white American experiences. Indeed, Obama lays claim to his black heritage, but as a self-styled prophet of the new millennium, his promise of equality extends beyond race and the borders of the United States.

In the next chapter, we move from the black experience in America to the role that three American presidents had on the formulation of the rhetoric of hope. What should become apparent as we proceed is that the rhetoric of hope is a tapestry comprising many individual threads woven so tightly together that when we tug on one thread, such the utopian tropes of Judeo-Christianity, others, like the idealism of the nation's founding documents or the hopes held by black slaves for emancipation, are sure to come along. This intertextuality is one of the most compelling features of Barack Obama's rhetoric of hope.

CHAPTER FOUR

The Legacy of
Three Great Presidents

We turn now to a thread in the rhetoric of hope that spans three centuries, and one which Barack Obama brings into the twenty-first. It represents a tradition of idealism in the American experience codified by Thomas Jefferson in the Declaration of Independence, invoked by Abraham Lincoln as he sought to preserve the union, and employed by Franklin Delano Roosevelt in the wake of the Great Depression. Since we have already considered the influence of the nation's founding documents on the Obamian rhetoric of hope, in returning to Jefferson in the initial section of this chapter, it is important to keep his utopian vision of the good society in focus. From Jefferson, we move on to Lincoln's rhetorical debt to the third president as he struggles to win the Civil War and then to Franklin Roosevelt's use of that tradition to inspire a country facing economic calamity. In each of these sections, we seek a common strand of idealism in American political rhetoric running through these three presidencies—one that Barack Obama draws from in his quest for that office more than two hundred years after Jefferson's election in 1800.

Thomas Jefferson left behind a voluminous body of work (including more than eighteen hundred letters) that the historian must parse in his quest for the sources of the ideal society. A man of extraordinary intelligence and wide-ranging interests, Jefferson studied subjects ranging from art and architecture to natural science and philosophy. If it is true that although "widely read and energetically curious, he was a brilliant adapter and interpreter of his era's ideas rather than a figure of towering creativity,"[1] then we should understand Jefferson as a syncretic thinker who drew ideas together from across time and culture to create a rhetorical vision of a better place. The historian's task in uncovering that vision of the ideal society is complicated by the fact that Jefferson often contradicts himself in his writing. He also led a life that left him open to the charge of not living up to the idealistic principles he espoused, most notably in terms of slavery. While ours is not to penetrate the enigma of his personality, nor to square his words with his actions, he did, according to his biographer R.B. Burstein, leave to posterity the notion that he was a man of ideas.

Just as Jefferson's idealism drew from many sources, President Obama's 2008 campaign rhetoric brings together disparate strands of idealism in Western history rather than creating something completely new. Even those features of Obama's rhetoric of hope that seem most unique (particularly the conflation of personal and national narratives and his creation of a prophetic persona) have clear historical and literary antecedents in American discourse. In adopting his ideas so freely, Barack Obama consciously places himself in a tradition of American idealism that Jefferson helped to formulate, but which has roots in Roman law, Judeo-Christianity, Scottish common sense, and an idealized view of English history.

Moreover, while Jefferson was a man of the Enlightenment, he was not one stymied by absolutist notions of the dominance of reason over other forms of knowing. Rather, like Thomas Paine, Joseph Priestley, Benjamin Franklin, and other American revolutionaries, Jefferson "believed that human redemption lay in education, discovery, innovation, and experiment."[2] We find in what Burstein calls the "key stars of Jefferson's constellation of revolutionary ideas" (independence, self-government, religious liberty, a virtuous and enlightened citizenry) an outline of his "vision of a good society, a happy and virtuous republic."[3] Some of the sources for his ideal republic include *Notes on the State of Virginia* in which Jefferson advocated agriculture "as the best way of life for free people wishing to remain free" and his proposals for revision of Virginia's harsh system of criminal law (based on the work of the Italian thinker Marquis Cesare de Beccaria).[4]

What one scholar calls Jefferson's "vaulting idealism" and another his "Romantic naturalism" inform his vision of a better place (utopia). Jefferson's ideal society also drew on the work of Francis Bacon and James Harrington, whose literary utopias were discussed earlier in the context of the nation's founding documents. As a demonstration of the power of that influence, Jefferson even borrows Bacon's classification of the faculties of the mind in cataloging his library.[5] Writing to Benjamin Rush, Jefferson declares that Bacon, together with Isaac Newton and John Locke, formed a "trinity of the three greatest men the world had ever produced."[6]

In mapping out his concept of the good society, Jefferson again drew on his own life experience. For example, the blessings of his domestic life in Monticello were welcome relief from the torments of his political life, so much so that his conceptions of home and world became reciprocal rhetorical constructions evoked at a distance from one another.[7] In Jefferson's view, therefore, that better place is agrarian (in direct contrast to the filthy cities he saw in Europe). "Noting how entrenched social differences damaged people's virtue, industry and happiness," Jefferson developed in Europe a deep compassion for the poor, and for the rest of his life warned his fellow countrymen not to move to the cities.

Because his ideal society was comprised of yeoman farmers who were self-sufficient and highly virtuous, adherence to a universal morality was the bedrock of that better place. His would not be a hereditary aristocracy but rather a meritocracy based on individual talent and virtue. Its citizens would reject manufactured luxury goods and commerce (for Jefferson's sojourns in London and Paris during the dawn of the Industrial Revolution convinced him of the advantages of simple living).[8] In sum, Jefferson's good society was established in dialectical contrast to the status quo that he saw in the Old World and fervently hoped would never contaminate the American experiment. From Jefferson and others, Barack Obama learns to critique the existing order by contrasting it with an ideal one. Obama carries this strategy into his 2012 campaign rhetoric, despite running as an incumbent.

In order to understand more about the moral values at the heart of Jefferson's good society, we turn to his book the *Life and Morals of Jesus of Nazareth* (completed by 1820 and published posthumously). Although Jefferson indicts institutionalized religion for supporting hereditary aristocracy, endorsing a deist worldview and rigorously defending the separation of church and state, he ultimately seeks to harmonize the Gospels with classical philosophy and ethics in order to promote Enlightenment and republican ideals.[9] Jefferson's stated goal in compiling the *Life and Morals of Jesus of Nazareth* was to separate the dross from the true moral teachings of Jesus. He interpreted this great teacher as an Enlightenment figure and social reformer. He strove to recover the historical Jesus freed from all distortions and found in the man a model of virtue. Because he taught duty and practiced charity toward others, Jesus became for Jefferson a kind of freedom fighter who provided "a genealogy for America's republican revolution." This reform impulse that Jefferson discovers in the teachings of Jesus represented for him "the true spirit of primitive, unadulterated Christianity."[10] He believed that Christianity could provide the simple moral code that the good society needed to flourish, were it shorn of its institutionalism.

Jefferson took evident glee in excising what he believed were the actual words of the historical Jesus, so much so that his *Life and Morals* likely says more about Jefferson than Jesus. He writes to John Adams that in extracting the "pure principles" that the prophet taught:

[W]e should have to strip off the artificial vestments in which they have been muffled by priests, who have travestied them into various forms, as instruments of riches and power to them. We must dismiss the Platonists and Plotinists, the Stagyrites and Gamalielites, the Eclectics the Gnostics and Scholastics, their essences and emanations, their Logos and Demi-urgos, Aeons and Daemons male and female, with a long train of Etc. Etc. Etc. or, shall I say at once, of Nonsense. We must reduce our volume to the simple evangelists, select, even from them, the very words only of Jesus, paring off the Amphibologisms into which they have been led by forgetting often, or not understanding, what had fallen from him, by giving their own misconceptions as his dicta, and expressing unintelligibly for others what they had not understood themselves. There will be found remaining the most sublime and benevolent code of morals which has ever been offered to man. I have performed this operation for my own use, by cutting verse by verse out of the printed book, and arranging, the matter which is evidently his, and which is as easily distinguishable as diamonds in a dunghill.[11]

Jefferson endeavored to attribute to Jesus only those words that were of "the utmost purity and simplicity." He aimed to humanize Jesus as an inspired man of integrity (though generally speaking Jefferson advocated a field of morality outside of religious practice).[12] This quality lends Jefferson's morality a universalism that Barack Obama references in his presidential campaign rhetoric.

Peter Onuf suggests that Jefferson's hope for the perfection of the union could be achieved only when freedom of the conscience was sanctioned through a synthesis of republicanism and Christianity.[13] "The true foundation of republican government," Jefferson asserts, "is the equal right of every citizen, in his person and property, and in their management.... I am not among those who fear the people.... But I know also, that laws and institutions must go hand in hand with the progress of the human mind. As that becomes more developed, more enlightened, as new discoveries are made, new truths disclosed, and manners and opinions change with the change of circumstances, institutions must advance also, and keep pace with the times."[14] In addition to demonstrating a firmly held belief in progress through social transformation, this passage speaks to Jefferson's generously optimistic view of human nature that undergirds his idealism. For instance, in a letter to Mann Page in 1795, Jefferson writes, "I do not believe that fourteen out of fifteen men are rogues: I believe a great abatement from that proportion may be made in favor of general honesty."[15]

As a result, Jefferson found that the "progressive development of society [was] the necessary precondition for the emergence of the modern individual in full enjoyment of his rights; by eliminating despotic rule of privileged classes, a republican government would secure national unity and facilitate individual 'pursuits of happiness' that in turn promote the community's prosperity and well being." While he looked to history for the justification of those rights, "the future was the screen upon which Jefferson projected his faith in the unfolding of the human potential under the conditions of freedom."[16] His foresight in dispatching Lewis and Clark to the unknown wilds of the West on an expedition of discovery, and the negotiation of the Louisiana Purchase, speak to Jefferson's fascination with the potential of the future. Obama borrows the ideal of continual and gradual progress toward "a more perfect union" directly from Jefferson.

So firm was Jefferson's belief in progress that he concluded that the United States Constitution should be amended as the times demanded. He even espoused a more radical view that the earth should belong only to the living generation and not to the dead through the power of inheritance (Jefferson was a lifelong opponent of primogeniture). In a well-known letter to James Madison written from Paris at the beginning of the French Revolution in 1789, he writes: "I set out on this ground which I suppose to be self evident, *'that the earth belongs in usufruct to the living'*; that the dead have neither powers nor rights over it. The portion occupied by an individual ceases to be his when himself ceases to be, and reverts to the society."[17]

Writing to William Smith in response to Shays's Rebellion in Massachusetts during the years 1786 and 1787, Jefferson betrays the extent of his revolutionary zeal: "God forbid we should ever be twenty years without such a rebellion.... What country ever before existed a century & a half without a rebellion? & what country can preserve its liberties if their rulers are not warned from time to time that their people preserve the spirit of resistance? Let them take arms. The remedy is to set them right as to facts, pardon & pacify them. What signify a few lives lost in a century or two? The tree of liberty must be refreshed from time to time with the blood of patriots and tyrants. It is it's natural manure."[18] Jefferson returns from France so infected with revolutionary fervor (all over again) that he brings with him "a conviction that the revolution of 1789 was the continuation and confirmation of 1776."[19] Jefferson was a radical prophet of progress who believed in constant revolution and held a firm conviction that government institutions should be challenged regularly lest they begin to accumulate power and infringe on the "self evident" rights of individuals.

Yet, despite this oft repeated reference to revolution and bloodshed, Jefferson asserted that the Enlightenment ideals of self-discovery and self-determination lead directly to social amelioration. As David Mayer explains, it was undoubtedly "Jefferson's comparatively optimistic view of human nature — his idea of natural society and the other premises associated with his concept of the self-government, such as the existence of a 'moral sense'— that underlay his confidence in the will of the majority."[20] Jefferson's optimistic idealism spilled over into his two-term presidency, which he initially won after thirty-six rounds of balloting in the fractious election in 1800 between Republicans and Federalists. Yet, rather than replace competent Federalist appointments made by his predecessor, Jefferson struck a note of conciliation in his First Inaugural Address in 1801:

> During the contest of opinion through which we have passed the animation of discussions and of exertions has sometimes worn an aspect which might impose on strangers unused to think freely and to speak and to write what they think; but this being now decided by the voice of the nation, announced according to the rules of the Constitution, all will, of course, arrange themselves under the will of the law, and unite in common efforts for the common good. All, too, will bear in mind this sacred principle, that though the will of the majority is in all cases to prevail, that will to be rightful must be reasonable; that the minority possess their equal rights, which equal law must protect, and to violate would be oppression. Let us, then, fellow-citizens, unite with one heart and

one mind. Let us restore to social intercourse that harmony and affection without which liberty and even life itself are but dreary things.... But every difference of opinion is not a difference of principle. We have called by different names brethren of the same principle. We are all Republicans, we are all Federalists.

Barack Obama skillfully turns this Jeffersonian political rhetoric into a clarion call for unity in his 2004 Democratic National Convention keynote address: "Now even as we speak, there are those who are preparing to divide us—the spin masters, the negative ad peddlers who embrace the politics of 'anything goes.' Well, I say to them tonight, there is not a liberal America and a conservative America — there is the United States of America. There is not a Black America and a White America and Latino America and Asian America — there's the United States of America." Like Jefferson's, Obama's is a vision of progress and betterment steeped in hope for the future. Jefferson once wrote, "My theory has always been, that if we are to dream, the flatteries of hope are as cheap, and pleasanter than the gloom of despair."[21]

Thomas Jefferson's idealism elicits jeers and condemnation from scholars like Conor Cruise O'Brien and Robert Tucker due to the fact that his attitudes about equality, for example, were not actualized in his own life. Of course, judging historical figures by the moral compass of the twenty-first century is a shabby and anachronistic way to gauge a man of ideas like Jefferson — although it is probably a good way to sell books. Not surprisingly, Barack Obama has likewise been charged with using idealistic rhetoric at odds with realistic assessments of policy, and while matching word and deed goes beyond the limits of this study, Peter Onuf's observations about Jefferson seem most applicable to President Obama: "Whatever else he was, Jefferson was no hypocrite in the conventional sense; as an exponent of 'natural speech' and 'self-evident' truths, he did not deploy glittering phrases with a cynical, instrumental disregard for what he took to be their meanings." This "disjunction of speech and act, so apparent to us," from the perspective of contemporary values, "does not necessarily reveal a flawed character."[22] It may also be that there is a bit of hypocrisy in every idealist, for often forward-looking ideas precede their historical realization.

On the other hand, Abraham Lincoln did not seem to consider him a hypocrite, despite the lofty idealism in Jefferson's rhetoric that was sometimes at odds with his actions. Politically speaking, Jefferson and Lincoln held different views about the progress of American society, but Lincoln's rhetorical debt to the Virginian is well documented. Lincoln wrote in 1859:

> All honor to Jefferson—to the man who, in the concrete pressure of a struggle for national independence by a single people, had the coolness, forecast, and capacity to introduce into a merely revolutionary document, an abstract truth, applicable to all men and all times, and so to embalm it there, that to-day, and in all coming days, it shall be a rebuke and a stumbling-block to the very harbingers of re-appearing tyranny and oppression.[23]

Perhaps, since Lincoln's own views on slavery evolved during his presidency, he understood that consistency was not necessarily the mark of a great mind, in Jefferson or in any other person. As Ralph Waldo Emerson famously stated in "Self-Reliance":

> A foolish consistency is the hobgoblin of little minds, adored by little statesmen and philosophers and divines. With consistency a great soul has simply nothing to do. He may as well concern himself with his shadow on the wall. Speak what you think now in hard words, and to-morrow speak what to-morrow thinks in hard words again, though it contradict every thing you said to-day.—"Ah, so you shall be sure to be misunderstood."—Is it so bad then to be misunderstood? Pythagoras was misunderstood, and Socrates, and Jesus, and Luther, and Copernicus, and Galileo, and Newton, and every pure and wise spirit that ever took flesh. To be great is to be misunderstood.[24]

Abraham Lincoln shares the honor of being misunderstood with Thomas Jefferson and these other progressive thinkers, though the myth of Lincoln that comes down to us (as Honest Abe the rail splitter) is a gentler one than that in currency about Jefferson as the slave-owning hypocrite. Sorting through these popular views does not directly concern us, however. Of more immediate concern is tracing that shared tradition of idealism that runs through the political rhetoric of Jefferson to Lincoln and that Barack Obama taps for his 2008 and 2012 presidential campaigns.

In the formulation of his political (some would say literary) persona, Abraham Lincoln draws upon the facts of his own upbringing in such a way as to put them in accord with dominant American mythologies that persist into our own time. The arc of these narratives was discussed in the introduction, but of course they include a pioneer spirit of hard work and self-reliance. Lincoln's 1859 autobiography, a marvel of concision at four paragraphs, was written with a mind toward making a run for the presidency in 1860. In it, Lincoln notes that he hails from "undistinguished families—second families" of Virginia and that his grandfather was "killed by Indians ... when he was laboring to open a farm in the forest" of Kentucky. A generation later, Lincoln tells us that his father moves the family to Indiana, which Lincoln describes as "a wild region, with many bears and other wild animals."

Like the narrative persona of Benjamin Franklin's *Autobiography*, Lincoln recounts raising himself out of poverty and obscurity despite a lack of educational opportunity. On the frontier, Lincoln explains, there "were some schools, so called; but no qualification was ever required of a teacher beyond '*readin, writin*, and *cipherin*,' to the Rule of Three." Of course, he explains, "when I came of age I did not know much. Still somehow, I could read, write, and cipher to the Rule of Three; but that was all. I have not been to school since. The little advance I now have upon this store of education, I have picked up from time to time under the pressure of necessity."[25] Lincoln notes that he "was raised on farm work, which I continued until I was twenty-two." Indeed this six-foot, four-inch giant of man did help his father clear forests, and he made extra money at odd jobs, including splitting rails. While this is factually accurate, Lincoln actually loathed this kind of mind-numbing, and backbreaking, labor.

In the autobiography, Abraham Lincoln explains that he relocated to Macon County in Illinois in his early twenties before settling in New Salem where he worked "as a sort of a clerk in a store." In 1832, he recounts volunteering for "the Black-Hawk War" fought against Native American tribes. Lincoln also notes being "elected a Captain of Volunteers—a success which gave me more pleasure than any I have had since." He then modestly recalls his first electoral defeat later the same year. Lincoln continues his brief autobiography with typical understatement and wry humor: "I am young, and unknown to most of you. I was born, and have ever remained in the most humble walks of life. I have no wealthy or popular relatives or friends to recommend me. My case is thrown exclusively upon the independent voters of the country; and if elected they will have conferred a favor upon me for which I shall be unremitting in my labors to compensate. But if the good people in their wisdom shall see fit to keep me in the background, I have been too familiar with disappointments to be very much chagrined."[26]

Although defeated in his first quest for elected office, Lincoln ran again and won election to the Illinois state legislature in 1834 (at the age of twenty-three). He enjoyed subsequent reelections to that post in 1836, 1838, and 1840. Lincoln won national election to the lower House of Congress in 1846, but he returned to law practice after deciding not to seek another term. He cites the repeal of the Missouri Compromise in 1854, which regulated slavery in the western territories, for firing his zeal to reenter politics and eventually seek the presidency. The fourth and concluding paragraph of Lincoln's autobiography highlights his use of ironic self-description and the adoption of a self-deprecating tone: "If any personal description of me is thought desirable, it may be said, I am, in height, six feet, four inches, nearly; lean in flesh, weighing on an average one hundred and eighty pounds; dark complexion, with coarse black hair, and grey eyes—no other marks or brands recollected."[27] Obama adopts a similarly modest and amused tone in his 2005 Herblock Foundation Annual Lecture (in honor of excellence in editorial cartooning): "Thank you for inviting me here tonight. It's been a pretty busy week, but I figured I'd better do my best to show up here since I can't think of an easier target for political cartoonists than a tall, skinny guy with big ears and a funny name."

As witnessed in these passages excerpted from his autobiography, Lincoln consciously cultivated the image of an ordinary person in his political rhetoric. William Gienapp notes that during the Lincoln-Douglas debates, Lincoln "traveled as a regular passenger, often alone, with only a bag containing a change of clothing. This mode of travel reinforced Lincoln's carefully cultivated image as a humble, self-made man, as did his decision to keep his aristocratic wife out of sight. His plain, well-worn clothing fostered this image as well." A contemporary in the audience at one of these debates remarked on his "course looking coat" with sleeves too short for the gangly arms that protruded out from it and baggy pants that failed to cover his boots.[28] When he ran for the U.S. presidency in 1860, Lincoln's campaign literature employed figures of "Honest Abe" and "The Railsplitter" to highlight his ordinary upbringing and portray him as "a symbol of democracy."[29] His consciously unpretentious and folksy manner helped Lincoln to win support of the general public. I contend that Barack Obama's careful study of Abraham Lincoln led him to deploy a twenty-first-century version of that life story in the rhetoric of hope. In it, Obama, the biracial son of a white woman from Kansas and a black father from Kenya, is depicted as rising from an undistinguished single-parent family. Through the force of hard work, he matriculates through the halls of some of our most prestigious institutions of higher learning to become the first black president of the United States.

From 1849 to 1854, Lincoln took little interest in politics until the passage of the Kansas-Nebraska Act repealed the aforementioned Missouri Compromise of 1820 and allowed settlers to decide on slavery in each territory. This act was widely seen as a tacit endorsement of the institution of forced bondage. Lincoln's 1854 Peoria speech marks a return to politics and represents a continual evolution in his thought on slavery. Although still advocating a policy of colonialism, which he later abandons, Lincoln declares: "My first impulse would be to free all the slaves, and send them to Liberia." Even so, he defends as "absolutely and eternally right" the doctrine of self-government. "If the negro is a *man*," argues Lincoln, "why then my ancient faith teaches me that 'all men are created equal'; and that there can be no moral right in connection with one man's making a slave of another." Many of Lincoln's speeches, like this one, make direct allusions to his beloved Declaration of Independence.

Focusing his keen powers of discernment on the Kansas-Nebraska Act itself, Lincoln asserts in the Peoria address: "I particularly object to the NEW position which the avowed principle of this Nebraska law gives to slavery in the body politic. I object to it because it assumes that there CAN be MORAL RIGHT in the enslaving of one man by another. I object to it as a dangerous dalliance for a few [free?] people — a sad evidence that, feeling prosperity we forget right — that liberty, as a principle, we have ceased to revere. I object to it because the fathers of the republic eschewed, and rejected it." Looking forward to a better future, and thereby creating a dialectic between the ideal and the status quo that we have seen defines utopia, Lincoln concludes: "Let us re-adopt the Declaration of Independence, and with it, the practices, and policy, which harmonize with it. Let north and south — let all Americans — let all lovers of liberty everywhere — join in the great and good work. If we do this, we shall not only have saved the Union; but we shall have so saved it, as to make, and to keep it, forever worthy of the saving. We shall have so saved it, that the succeeding millions of free happy people, the world over, shall rise up, and call us blessed, to the latest generations."[30]

Again following Jefferson, Lincoln often invoked higher principles and lauded reason in his speeches, the most famous example being his remarks to the Young Men's Lyceum of Springfield. A young man himself at the time of the speech, Lincoln observes that while passion helped to free the United States of America from the yoke of England in a time of revolution, "the pillars of the temple of liberty" must now be "hewn from the solid quarry of sober reason." Celebrating that singular principle of the Enlightenment from which the American experiment in democracy was born, Lincoln asserts: "Reason, cold, calculating, unimpassioned reason, must furnish all the materials for our future support and defense."[31] Lincoln's vision of the future, though differing considerably from that of Jefferson, has at its heart a similar universalism founded on rationality and a dedication to making word match deed in the fullness of time. Borrowing from Jefferson, Lincoln rhetorically contrasts the promise enshrined in the nation's founding documents with the status quo that fails to live up to it (just as Obama does in 2008 and 2012).

Perhaps at no time in American history has that gap between the ideal order and actual order been as more tightly drawn than during the Civil War, a conflict fought in part to free from bondage the most unfortunate in a land founded on the promise of equality. "It's not simply that a gap exists between our professed ideals as a nation and the reality we witness every day," Obama keenly observes more than a century and a half later, for in "one form or another, that gap has existed since America's birth. Wars have been fought, laws passed, systems reformed, unions organized, and protests staged to bring promise and practice into closer alignment."[32]

Over the course of his career, Lincoln so cultivated his crisp and lean prose style that it borders on the lyrical. His use of rhetorical anti-thesis (dialectical contrast between the ideal and actual), compression, aphorism, and figurative language and tropes reach an apex in the Gettysburg Address. Garry Wills, in his study of this landmark speech, declares: "By setting up this dialectic of the idea with the real, Lincoln has reached, already, the very heart of his Gettysburg Address, where a nation conceived in liberty by its dedication to the Declaration's critical proposition (human equality) must test that proposition's survivability in the real world of struggle." Wills goes on to trace this "dialectic of ideas struggling for their realization in history" to the German idealism that informed transcendentalism, a philosophical movement that Lincoln also knew well.[33] The entire address is cited below. Those of us who strive for concision in our own writing marvel at this dedication of a Civil War battlefield in 1863:

Four score and seven years ago our fathers brought forth on this continent, a new nation, conceived in Liberty, and dedicated to the proposition that all men are created equal.

Now we are engaged in a great civil war, testing whether that nation, or any nation so conceived and so dedicated, can long endure. We are met on a great battle-field of that war. We have come to dedicate a portion of that field, as a final resting place for those who here gave their lives that that nation might live. It is altogether fitting and proper that we should do this.

But, in a larger sense, we cannot dedicate — we cannot consecrate — we cannot hallow — this ground. The brave men, living and dead who struggled here have consecrated it, far above our poor power to add or detract. The world will little note, nor long remember what we say here, but it can never forget what they did here. It is for us the living, rather, to be dedicated here to the unfinished work which they who fought here have thus far so nobly advanced. It is rather for us to be here dedicated to the great task remaining before us— that from these honored dead we take increased devotion to that cause for which they gave the last full measure of devotion — that we here highly resolve that these dead shall not have died in vain — that this nation under God shall have a new birth of freedom — and that government of the people, by the people, for the people, shall not perish from the earth.[34]

The first paragraph of the Gettysburg Address, comprising a single sentence, invokes the promise of equality enshrined in the nation's founding documents. The second paragraph clearly frames the Civil War as a test of those founding ideals, while in the final paragraph, Lincoln inspires the living to undertake the "great task" of vigilantly keeping a government by the people alive and well.

The theme that Barack Obama adopts for his 2009 Inaugural Address, "A New Birth of Freedom," comes from the concluding paragraph of the Gettysburg Address, and it alludes directly to the ongoing nature of this "great task," as well as to his own inheritance of Lincoln's legacy of leadership. In Proclamation 8636, issued on March 4, 2011, Barack Obama writes: "President Lincoln reminded us in his Inaugural Address that America's Union was much older than the Constitution itself, and that our national fabric had been stitched together by shared memories and common hopes. As we observe the 150th anniversary of his Inauguration, we reflect on his unceasing belief and our enduring faith that we remain one Nation and one people, sharing a bond as Americans that will never break."

Barack Obama also took from Lincoln a belief that clarity is the hallmark of good writing, and while his prose style lacks the crisp leanness of his idol's, Obama does seem to have taken to heart Lincoln's advice to a young attorney (as reported by his law partner and biographer William Herndon): "Billy, don't shoot too high — aim lower and the common people will understand you. They are the ones you want to reach — at least they are the ones you ought to reach. The educated and refined people will understand you any way. If you aim too high your ideas will go over the heads of the masses, and only hit those who need no hitting."[35] Barack Obama's books and speeches also make use of ordinary language as the vehicle for profound ideas. As Wills observes, concerning the rhetoric of both presidents: "In his prose, Obama of necessity lagged far behind the resplendent Lincoln. But what is of lasting interest is their similar strategy for meeting the charge of extremism. Both argued against the politics of fear. Neither denied the darker aspects of our history, yet they held out hope for what Lincoln called here the better 'lights of current experience'—what he would later call the 'better angels of our nature.' Each man looked for larger patterns under the surface bitternesses of his milieu. Each forged a moral position that rose above the occasions for their speaking."[36]

By the time of Lincoln's Second Inaugural Address on March 4, 1865, delivered only weeks before his assassination in the waning days of the Civil War, Lincoln, although a product of the Enlightenment and a champion of rationality, had learned to pepper his speeches with biblical passages as a method of teaching through stories and fables. Many years earlier, he had effectively used scripture as a means of persuasion in his address to the Republican State Convention, "A House Divided," titled after a passage in Matthew 12:25.[37] That speech contains Lincoln's core justification for resolving the issue of slavery in the ideal of perpetual union at the heart of the country's founding documents: "I believe this government cannot endure, permanently half *slave* and half *free*. I do not expect the Union to be *dissolved*—I do not expect the house to *fall*—but I *do* expect it will cease to be divided. It will become *all* one thing or *all* the other."

In his Second Inaugural, Lincoln employs the trope of the vengeful God of the Old Testament to suggest that the suffering the Civil War caused was rooted in the original sin of the country, slavery:

> The Almighty has his own purposes. "Woe unto the world because of offenses! for it must needs be that offenses come; but woe to that man by whom the offense cometh." If we shall suppose that American slavery is one of those offenses which, in the providence of God, must needs come, but which, having continued through his appointed time, he now wills to remove, and that he gives to both North and South this terrible war, as the woe due to those by whom the offense came, shall we discern therein any departure from those divine attributes which the believers in a living God always ascribe to him?

While Lincoln expresses hope for a speedy end to the war, he employs powerful biblical imagery and figurative language to reinforce war as punishment for the sin of forced bondage in United States. Lincoln concludes, however, on a note of reconciliation and promise for the future:

> With malice toward none; with charity for all; with firmness in the right, as God gives us to see the right, let us strive on to finish the work we are in; to bind up the nation's wounds; to care for him who shall have borne the battle, and for his widow, and his orphan — to do all which may achieve and cherish a just, and lasting peace, among ourselves, and with all nations.[38]

On April 14, 1865, just a few weeks after delivering this speech, this colossus of a man died tragically at the hand of an actor and Confederate sympathizer. The United States would have to chart the waters of Reconstruction without the moral compass of his leadership.

Throughout his life, Lincoln advocated (and tried to model) the values of modesty, truthfulness, and a refusal to judge others. During the Civil War, Lincoln's basic character manifested good will and decency in his dealings with others. He displayed a genuine humility that combined with a strong self-confidence made him generous to his political rivals. Moreover, he demonstrated an even-keeled temperament that made him quite patient.[39] As George Anastaplo asserts, Lincoln routinely brought to public matters a moral focus "without becoming either stodgy or self-righteous."[40] The same can be said for Barack Obama's assertions of the centrality of values to his vision of progress. Following Lincoln, Obama also constructs a persona out of his own life story and emphasizes moral action in the pursuit of social amelioration and self-improvement in the rhetoric of hope.

So central are moral values to Lincolnian rhetoric that they are at the very heart of the ideal of government by the people that distinguishes American democracy. In a real sense, Lincoln saw himself as the defender of the perpetuity of the union against an illegal rebellion, which threatened to tear that union asunder. As one scholar observes, "Lincoln's understanding of the significance of the Civil War as a test of the effectiveness of democratic government" was not original but rather "the idea of the United States as a model democracy, with a moral obligation to demonstrate that democratic republicanism is practical as a form of government, dates back to the Founding."[41] This point reinforces Lincoln's admiration for, and appropriation of, central principles in Jefferson's work.

As one scholar of Lincoln correctly asserts, a political and idealistic thread unites Jefferson and Lincoln with Franklin Delano Roosevelt. For instance, the Republican Party to which Lincoln belonged during the 1860 presidential campaign emphasized his image as the "Great Commoner" by drawing on Lincoln's pioneer background. During the 1930s and 1940s, FDR's liberal left coalition of egalitarians actually seized on Jefferson's idealistic rhetoric and attempted to impress him in the campaign for FDR. Michael Lind claims that "New Deal liberals sought to enlist Lincoln as a political ancestor as well," a tactic by which they lured many progressive Republicans into the Democratic Party.[42]

FDR became the dominant president of the twentieth century, not only through the impact of his many achievements, but also simply because of his longevity (FDR will likely remain the only American president to give four Inaugural Addresses). He was also more tested in both war and peace than Abraham Lincoln. As with Lincoln, who also died in office, tens of thousands of people lined the railroad tracks to pay their last respects when the train carrying FDR's body passed through town after town.[43] So, what were FDR's leadership qualities that so endeared him to the ordinary citizen, and what were the progressive and idealistic (some might say utopian) principles that informed the New Deal? What were FDR's methods of persuasion? Which of those methods does Barack Obama appropriate in his rhetoric of hope? To those questions the remainder of this chapter is dedicated.

Like Abraham Lincoln's, Franklin Delano Roosevelt's was a rhetorical presidency. Through the skillful use of emerging media, FDR made himself into a symbol of hope and optimism for the American people during the Great Depression and later a model of courage after the surprise Japanese attack on Pearl Harbor on December 7, 1941. Although born to landed American gentry possessing great wealth and influence, Roosevelt would champion a "New Deal" for ordinary Americans and in doing so make himself a traitor to his class in the eyes of many elites. Yet FDR forever changed the relationship between the United States government and the individual by means of persuasion, one of his greatest political assets. He cultivated a cheerful persona full of camaraderie and sympathy, and he used it to champion welfare programs, such as Social Security, that are still with us today.

While most scholars agree that the New Deal programs do not constitute a single body of thought, they grew out of universal principles, such as the Golden Rule, and aimed at social amelioration in a time of

economic crisis. At the heart of FDR's vision of America is not a complicated political philosophy but a set of moral goals. His was an honest creed
spoken in plain language that skillfully mixed metaphor, figures of speech,
and anecdote. Paul Conklin compares Roosevelt to an artist who "loved
to mold and form" the voters (his artistic medium) "into a pattern of his
own choosing, yet be willing to choose a pattern in terms of his limited
and unalterable subjects. As all successful artists, he was able to effect
many of his designs, even when they proved poor ones. Persuasion was
his brush and chisel." At once, he could be a coach giving a pep talk, a
preacher with a simple but pointed moral message, or a military com-
mander encouraging weary troops.[44]

Like Lincoln and Jefferson before him, FDR was an idealist who used
the power of the nation's highest office in new ways so as to make manifest
his vision of a better America. The presidencies of these three men, in
their focus on equality and shared prosperity, provided Barack Obama
with a template for a uniquely American idealistic political discourse with
which to align his rhetoric of hope. Like FDR's New Deal rhetoric,
Obama's rhetoric of hope is grounded in moral principles that, if acted
upon by government, are said to move the country toward the promise of
a more perfect union enshrined in the nation's founding documents. This
aspect of FDR's forward-looking idealism is clearly discernible in New
Deal legislation, so much so that FDR was accused of being a socialist and
communist in his own lifetime for advocating a larger role for government
in protecting the welfare of American citizens. So widespread was this
notion that a young reporter once asked him:

"Mr. President, are you a Communist?"
"No."
"Are you a Socialist?"
"No," he said, with a look of surprise as if he were wondering what he was
     being cross examined about.
The young man said, "Well what is your philosophy then?"
  "Philosophy?" asked the President, puzzled. "Philosophy? I am a Christian
and a Democrat — that's all."[45]

In a 1932 presidential campaign speech delivered before the Commonwealth Club in San Francisco, FDR strikes not a communist but a
post-partisan stance, declaring: "I want to speak not of politics but of government. I want to speak not of parties, but of universal principles."

Because the "issue of government," FDR explains, "has always been whether individual men and women will have to serve some system of government of economics, or whether a system of government and economics exists to serve individual men and women." Speaking during a low point of the economic depression, he references the dream of the Industrial Revolution "to raise the standard of living for everyone" and contrasts it with the status quo: "A glance at the situation today only too clearly indicates that equality of opportunity as we have known it no longer exists."

Referring to the country's founding traditions, FDR explains in his Commonwealth Club address that while Alexander Hamilton "believed that the safety of the republic lay in the autocratic strength of its government," for Thomas Jefferson government "was a means to an end, not an end in itself; it might be either a refuge and a help or a threat and a danger, depending on the circumstances." By evoking this famous divergence of views, and the contested election of 1800, FDR aligns himself more with a Jeffersonian tradition in American political discourse. "As I see it," FDR explains, "the task of government in its relation to business is to assist the development of an economic declaration of rights, an economic constitutional order. This is the common task of statesman and business man. It is the minimum requirement of a more permanently safe order of things."[46]

In asserting that the government "must be swift to enter and protect the public interest," Roosevelt invokes the idea of social contract that inspired the Declaration of Independence, Constitution, and Bill of Rights. Note also that FDR adopts a highly idealistic tone by way of conclusion. He declares that we shall fulfill that contract "as we fulfilled the obligation of the apparent Utopia which Jefferson imagined for us in 1776, and which Jefferson, Roosevelt and Wilson sought to bring to realization." Failure, FDR reminds his audience, "is not an American habit; and in the strength of great hope we must all shoulder our common load."[47] Of course, "utopia" and "hope" are keywords that feature prominently in Obama's campaign rhetoric as well.

In his First Inaugural Address, in 1933, FDR returns to these idealistic themes and again grounds them in moral precepts. He begins with a recognition of the magnitude of the challenges facing the country and its new leader: "This is preeminently the time to speak the truth, the whole truth, frankly and boldly." Employing biblical allusion to attack the business and industry leaders for greed, Roosevelt explains that the light of the financial crisis chased these "money changers [...] from their high seats in the temple of our civilization," so that we might "restore that temple to the ancient truths. The measure of that restoration lies in the extent to which we again apply social values more noble than mere monetary profit."

Invoking the Declaration of Independence, FDR asserts that "happiness lies not in the mere possession of money; it lies in the joy of achievement, in the thrill of creative effort. The joy, the moral stimulation of work no longer must be forgotten in the mad chase of evanescent profits." Here, one is reminded of Lincoln's advice to J. M. Brockman that "Work, work, work, is the main thing." Of course, this work ethic also has religious connotations, in addition to being the basis of an American belief in social mobility. However, Lincoln's development of a narrative persona who through a process of self-education rises from obscurity to national power was a way to make his life story a part of the American mythology. As we shall see in Chapter Seven, Barack Obama will, like Franklin Roosevelt, borrow this rhetorical technique from Lincoln's political playbook.

Franklin Roosevelt suggested that his New Deal legislation emerged out of a "recognition of the old and permanently important manifestation of the American spirit of the pioneer." This aspect of the American mythology provided hope to a nation eager for any sign of action and of change. The New Deal, claims FDR, "is the way to recovery. It is the immediate way. It is the strongest assurance that recovery will endure." Although the United States Congress would rubber-stamp many of the New Deal bills during his first hundred days, FDR expanded the power of the presidency by sometimes challenging constitutional boundaries (as did Thomas Jefferson and Abraham Lincoln before him). For instance, FDR made the case that since "our constitutional system has proved itself the most superbly enduring political mechanism the modern world has ever seen," that he should be given "broad Executive power to wage a war against the emergency."[48] His stated concern was Congress not acting with all due and necessary speed in such a case.

Having fleshed out some of the moral and emotional appeals embedded in New Deal rhetoric, let us consider a few of the programs that emerged from it as a way to trace the concrete manifestations of FDR's idealism and to better appreciate his powers of persuasion. Some New Deal legislation, for instance, reflected the Jeffersonian ideal of true property and enterprise. The Farm Tenancy Act of 1937 created a program of land conservation and utilization that assisted with soil erosion, reforestation, and preservation of natural resources. It also provided credit to farmers to buy land. This act, like many others, represented an attack by Roosevelt "on entrenched privilege, on monopolistic wealth, on concentrated economic power, on unfair rules in the marketplace."

In addition to echoing progressive discourses of the day, acts such as this one exhibit a puritanical sense of broad opportunity and moral responsibility that lies at the heart of the American mind.[49] Agencies that came into being under the New Deal include the Agricultural Adjustment Administration of 1933 and 1938, which had helped to establish parity prices on basic commodities by reducing supply (first by paying farmers to reduce production and later by imposing a quota system), and the Works Progress Administration, which in 1935 attempted to address persistent unemployment by putting millions to work in labor-intensive projects (it even contained significant spending for the fine arts).

Among other noteworthy New Deal programs were the 1933 Public Works Administration designed to "prime the pump" of the economy by investing billions in the construction of roads, bridges, dams, schools, and hospitals. The Tennessee Valley Authority was "a vast scheme of regional development in one of the poorest parts of the United States," and the National Industrial Recovery Act allowed businesses to become more corporate, encouraged collective bargaining for unions, set up maximum work hours and wages, and outlawed child labor. A so-called second wave of New Deal legislation in 1935 was passed in response to Supreme Court invalidation of many early programs on constitutional grounds, as well as to help spur a flagging economy. Significant components of this second round of New Deal legislation included the National Labor Relations Act, the Social Security Act, the Banking Act of 1935, the Public Utility Holding Company Act, the Revenue Act of 1935 (which raised taxes on high incomes), and the aforementioned Works Progress Administration.[50]

The result of all of this New Deal legislation was the creation of a welfare state that is now conventional and orthodox in American politics (in the sense that certain expectations exist for the government to play a role in protecting and extending opportunity through social programs). What accounts for FDR's success in passing his legislative agenda? On the one hand, Herbert Hoover's failure to halt the Great Depression, despite several years of trying, can be attributed to that president's fatalistic view of the cyclic nature of economics. He was eventually convinced that there was little he could do but wait for an upward cycle. Hoover's pessimism was contrasted by FDR's contagious optimism and charm. Roosevelt's campaign theme song in 1932 was "Happy Days Are Here Again." The popular embrace of his New Deal rhetoric must be understood in the context of an electorate suffering the ever-compounding consequences of the worst economic depression in the nation's history. So the times were certainly on FDR's side (in much the same way that the economic recession in 2008 helped to propel Barack Obama to the White House). Ultimately, however, FDR's legislative success during his early years in office can be attributed to his legendary powers of persuasion.

If by rhetoric we mean the art of persuasive speaking, we should turn our attention to FDR's Third and Fourth Inaugural Addresses in pursuit of it. Although "a muted response to the war in Europe" delivered to a country very much in an isolationist mood (before Pearl Harbor), FDR's Third Inaugural in January 1941 attempted to outline "a philosophical treatment of domestic communal values."[51] Employing an extended simile, FDR asserted that the nation is "like a person," possessing a body, a soul, and a mind. He explains that all three components are important, but "if the spirit of America were killed, even though the Nation's body and mind, constricted in an alien world, lived on, the America we know would have perished." Roosevelt invokes the confluence of idealistic thought that for him defines the character of the nation:

> The democratic aspiration is no mere recent phase in human history. It is human history. It permeated the ancient life of early peoples. It blazed anew in the middle ages. It was written in the Magna Carta.
>
> In the Americas its impact has been irresistible. America has been the New World in all tongues, to all peoples, not because this continent was a new-found land, but because all those who came here believed they could create upon this continent a new life — a life that should be new in freedom.
>
> Its vitality was written into our own Mayflower Compact, into the Declaration of Independence, into the Constitution of the United States, into the Gettysburg Address.

Employing a rhetoric of action, FDR concludes, "We do not retreat. We are not content to stand still. As Americans, we go forward, in the service of our country, by the will of God."[52]

By the time of his Fourth Inaugural Address in 1945, FDR had all but won World War II. His health rapidly declining, he nevertheless looked to the future with characteristic optimism, yet he did so in a notably more somber tone. "In some respects," notes Halford Ryan, "FDR used his Fourth Inaugural as Lincoln did his Second Inaugural Address—to turn the audience's attention from the immediate situation of war to a philosophical discourse on the meaning of the war for the future."[53] Likely sensing his own impending death, Roosevelt confidently retained his notion of progress and amelioration. In the collective quest "for a just and honorable peace" (which the world so much needs even today), FDR espoused a doctrine of perfectionism that we have seen deployed in religious tropes of the New Jerusalem and in the secular documents of our nation founded on the promise of together forging a more perfect society. FDR declares: "We shall strive for perfection. We shall not achieve it immediately—but we still shall strive. We may make mistakes—but they must never be mistakes which result from faintness of heart or abandonment of moral principle."[54]

Like Jefferson, Franklin Roosevelt found that the strength of the nation derived ultimately from its ability to hold fast to the founding principles against the greed of the rich and powerful. Roosevelt believed that in "a free society, with beckoning opportunities, with no special privileges," each individual effort "to take advantage of existing opportunities was a lesson in responsibility, an inducement to good character, and a fulfilling experience. Such a simple but profound faith lay at the moralistic heart of American politics."[55] Roosevelt concludes his Fourth Inaugural with a homespun narrative refiguration of the Golden Rule:

> We have learned that we cannot live alone, at peace; that our own well-being is dependent on the well-being of other nations far away. We have learned that we must live as men, not as ostriches, nor as dogs in the manger.
>
> We have learned to be citizens of the world, members of the human community.
>
> We have learned the simple truth, as Emerson said, that "The only way to have a friend is to be one."
>
> We can gain no lasting peace if we approach it with suspicion and mistrust or with fear. We can gain it only if we proceed with the understanding, the confidence, and the courage which flow from conviction.
>
> The Almighty God has blessed our land in many ways. He has given our people stout hearts and strong arms with which to strike mighty blows for freedom and truth. He has given to our country a faith which has become the hope of all peoples in an anguished world.[56]

From the perspective of the early twenty-first century, we can see that Franklin Delano Roosevelt deployed a rhetoric that helped to transform the United States into a dominant late-twentieth-century superpower. Through the New Deal, he redefined the relationship between the national government and the American people. He extended regulations, built up a capital base, and constructed welfare policies that subsequent generations would take for granted.[57] While protections are still required today to prevent overreaching, the post–FDR federal government has largely been seen as a partner in both the protection of individual liberty and promotion of equal opportunity. We have seen Obama adopt a similar view of the role of government, one that slowly emerged from his experience with community organizing in Chicago, his embrace of the black church, and a careful study of American history.

Although Franklin Delano Roosevelt did not pursue one coherent program under the rhetorical umbrella of the New Deal, that failure had the happy consequence of allowing professionals in social welfare, academe, labor unions, newspapers, and architectural firms all to contribute to the New Deal: "Some were dreamers, even utopian dreamers."[58] As George McJimsey observes: "Roosevelt could not create a utopia of domestic and international peace and prosperity. But he could demonstrate the qualities needed to achieve them. No president in our history has faced such critical problems with the courage, vision, and stamina that Roosevelt displayed."[59] Like Roosevelt's, Obama's rhetoric of hope is also utopian and firmly grounded in moral principles. Although the economic problems that Barack Obama faced during his first years in office do not approach those of the Great Depression, one is struck by the historical correspondences of economic hardship, and the effectiveness of the hopeful rhetoric, that propelled each man to the presidency.

In this chapter, we have traced a long tradition of American idealism that runs through the rhetorical presidencies of Jefferson, Lincoln, and FDR. Barack Obama's 2008 and 2012 campaigns deftly wielded its tropes and memes. In making such an assertion, I do not mean to suggest that these three great presidents (in whose wake Obama styles his own narrative persona) shared a single coherent worldview, for they belong to different eras and faced unique historical circumstances. Rather, I simply point to a tradition of American idealism that emerges out of Enlightenment thought, becomes enshrined in the nation's founding documents, and is rhetorically deployed by Jefferson, Lincoln, and FDR. Obama taps the wellspring of this tradition in his rhetoric of hope. For the moment, I will forgo a more thorough analysis of the role that moral values and the content of character play in Obama's rhetoric of hope in favor of resuming it in Chapter Six. In the meantime, let us pursue another thread in the tapestry of the rhetoric of hope, the force of fiction, music, and popular culture.

CHAPTER FIVE

The Force of Fiction, Music and Popular Culture

Michiko Kakutani, writing in the *New York Times* on January 18, 2009, made the following observation about the new president: "Much has been made of Mr. Obama's eloquence — his ability to use words in his speeches to persuade and uplift and inspire. But his appreciation of the magic of language and his ardent love of reading have not only endowed him with a rare ability to communicate his ideas to millions of Americans while contextualizing complex ideas about race and religion, they have also shaped his sense of who he is and his apprehension of the world." This thoughtful insight at once acknowledges the power of Barack Obama's rhetoric of hope to persuade and locates the origin of that gift in the orator's broad reading. Obama's facility with language and ability to use it to communicate complex ideas to ordinary people does spring from his love of the written word. Even as a college student, Obama took his writing seriously; he signed up for creative writing courses, wrote short fiction, and even once considered a career as a writer.[1] So striking is his zeal for reading and writing that Michelle Obama asks others to follow Barack's example: "I want you all to open yourselves up to the entire college experience," she told a group of incoming freshman in Ghana. "Read lots of books. That's one thing Barack Obama does all the time. He reads everything."[2]

In his October 2008 essay "How to Read Like a President," Jon Meacham observes, "You can tell a lot about a president — or a presidential candidate — by what he reads, or says he reads." In addition to Hemingway, John McCain "loves the stories of W. Somerset Maugham, *The Great Gatsby, All Quiet on the Western Front* and James Fenimore Cooper's

Leatherstocking Tales, especially *The Last of the Mohicans*." By contrast, "When I asked him by e-mail to send a list of books and writers that were most significant to him, Obama offered American standards: The Federalist, Jefferson, Emerson, Lincoln, Twain, W.E.B. Du Bois's *Souls of Black Folk*, King's "Letter From Birmingham Jail," James Baldwin, and Toni Morrison's *Song of Solomon*. Meacham concludes, "Obama, unsurprisingly, appears to be more drawn to stories sympathetic to the working classes than is McCain."[3] Barack Obama also reads more African American literature than does McCain, though by no means does he limit himself to that tradition.

While diverse, the literary texts that Obama cites as influential on his own writing feature tropes of oppression and redemption, as well as share an emphasis on transgressing social and cultural boundaries in the pursuit of that redemption. As a result, they offer a response to injustice that ultimately moves a character, or society of characters, forward psychically or materially (and often both). Thus, much of the literature directly referenced in the rhetoric of hope evokes the classic utopian trope of progress from a bleak status quo to a more ideal social order. In the first section of this chapter, several works of literature cited by Obama himself (and by journalists and scholars writing about him) as instrumental in shaping "his sense of who he is and his apprehension of the world" are surveyed more or less chronologically (so that some sense of their grounding in American history can be preserved). We begin with Stowe's *Uncle Tom's Cabin* (1852) then move quickly on to Du Bois' *The Souls of Black Folk* (1903), Wright's *Native Son* (1940), Ellison's *Invisible Man* (1953), Faulkner's *Requiem for a Nun* (1951), and *Autobiography of Malcolm X* (1965). These books feature dark portrayals of life in America, and all of them belong to a literature of crisis that highlights the gap between the ideals upon which the nation was founded and the reality of political and economic exclusion historically faced by its minority classes. By giving voice to the voiceless, these texts insist on amelioration.

In *Uncle Tom's Cabin*, redemption from slavery in the antebellum South requires transgressing a rule of law that forced servitude on the historically disenfranchised. Written in the nineteenth-century sentimentalist mode, *Uncle Tom's Cabin* enjoyed tremendous success, selling more than 300,000 copies in its first year of publication. In her preface, Stowe plainly states that the "object of these sketches is to awaken sympathy and feeling for the African race" and to "show their wrongs and sorrows" under the institution of slavery.[4] It therefore had an unequaled influence on the abolitionist movements that sought an end to slavery in the United States. The plights of Eliza, a young mulatto woman, and Uncle Tom, a faithful and God-fearing man, as they endure the hardships of forced bondage allowed readers to sympathize with black slaves by humanizing them. Stowe's repeated assertion that the institution of slavery was incommensurate with the teachings of Christianity, a view highlighted by the fictional example of Uncle Tom, galvanized abolitionists and enraged southern slaveholders.

Harriet Stowe describes Uncle Tom as "a large, broad-chested, powerfully-made man, of a full glossy black, and a face whose truly African features were characterized by an expression of grave and steady good sense, united with much kindliness and benevolence. There was something about his whole air self-respecting and dignified, yet united with a confiding and humble simplicity."[5] She uses juxtaposition to contrast the cruelty of slavery with the spirit of Christianity. Just as he finishes his prayer meeting, Stowe has Eliza inform Tom that he has been sold by Mr. Shelby to cover mounting debts. Rather than fleeing to Canada himself, Tom insists that Eliza and her son (who has been sold as well) make for the border:

> "No, no—I an't going. Let Eliza go—it's her right! I wouldn't be the one to say no—'tan't in *natur* for her to stay; but you heard what she said! If I must be sold, or all the people on the place, and everything go to rack, why, let me be sold. I s'pose I can b'ar it as well as any on 'em," he added, while something like a sob and a sigh shook his broad, rough chest convulsively.

"Sobs, heavy, hoarse and loud," writes Stowe, "shook the chair, and great tears fell through his fingers on the floor: just such tears, sir, as you dropped into the coffin where lay your first-born son; such tears, woman, as you shed when you heard the cries of your dying babe."[6] At the end of the novel, Uncle Tom dies a death akin to that of an abused dog (for refusing to whip a fellow slave), yet he is given a divine vision of salvation so that despite his physical suffering, the reader understands that he reaches a spiritual freedom beyond the taint of the world.

In that scene, meant to evoke the passion of Christ, Uncle Tom commends his spirit to the Lord just before facing Simon Legree, his demonic master, who "foaming with rage, smote his victim to the ground." Here the pious narrator interrupts the action to drive home conflation of Tom and Christ: "But, of old, there was One whose suffering changed an instrument of torture, degradation and shame, into a symbol of glory, honor, and immortal life; and, where His spirit is, neither degrading stripes, nor blood, nor insults, can make the Christian's last struggle less than glorious."[7] As with Tom's salvific death that frees him from both slavery and his mortal coil, by the end of the novel Eliza and son are reunited with her husband George and flee to Canada. They thereby achieve a physical freedom that complements Uncle Tom's spiritual one. In this sense, the narrative arc of *Uncle Tom's Cabin* critiques slavery by contrasting it with the ideal condition of freedom on two distinct levels: the physical and spiritual that together make "life, liberty, and the pursuit of happiness" possible. We have seen Barack Obama repeatedly employ this same dialectic of bondage and freedom in the rhetoric of hope.

W.E.B. Du Bois begins his highly influential book *The Souls of Black Folk* (1903) with the recognition that "the problem of the Twentieth Century is the problem of the color-line." In it, Du Bois offers a sociological view of the African American experience following the Emancipation Proclamation and explores black life in its many permutations. He famously points to a double consciousness in the mind of the black American. Du Bois writes: "It is a peculiar sensation, this double-consciousness, this sense of always looking at one's self through the eyes of others, of measuring one's soul by the tape of a world that looks on in amused contempt and pity. One ever feels his twoness, — an American, a Negro; two souls, two thoughts, two unreconciled strivings; two warring ideals in one dark body, whose dogged strength alone keeps it from being torn asunder." For Du Bois, the history of black America is the history of "this longing to attain self-conscious manhood, to merge his double self into a better and truer self."[8] Such a state of unified consciousness can be brought about only through the fulfillment of the promises enshrined in the Declaration of Independence and the Constitution. For Du Bois, that meant education and training for blacks, equal representation at the ballot box, and, most importantly, "the freedom of life and limb, the freedom to work and think, the freedom to love and aspire."[9]

Du Bois goes on to explain that the teacher and the preacher in black America traditionally embodied these aspirational ideals and modeled them to the community. At the dawn of the twentieth century, Du Bois fretted presciently that instead of striving to fulfill them, "the danger is that these ideals, with their simple beauty and weird inspiration, will suddenly sink to a question of cash and a lust for gold." He wonders aloud what would happen "if the Negro people be wooed from a strife for righteousness, from a love of knowing, to regard dollars as the be-all and end-all of life?"[10] In answer to that question, Du Bois summons the so-called talented tenth of the population to come forth and lead the black people away from the lure of materialism and toward the ideals of freedom and equality enshrined in the founding documents. By contrast, Richard Wright and Ralph Ellison offer bleak answers to Du Bois' question about what happens when a desire for freedom turns into a thirst for money.

In Chapter Eight of *Dreams from My Father*, Barack Obama recalls his move from New York to Chicago's South Side to begin community organizing with local churches in the housing projects. As he approaches the city, Obama almost romantically imagines Frank Sinatra, Duke Ellington, or Ella Fitzgerald emerging from a gig "in front of the old Regal Theatre." Even the "mailman I saw was Richard Wright," Obama explains, "delivering the mail before his book sold."[11] He also sees in his mind's eye the tens of thousands of blacks who moved from the American South to the north following emancipation and later to escape Jim Crow. With them they would bring a dream for freedom and equality, only to have it deferred yet again. Langston Hughes asks, "What happens to a dream deferred? [...] Maybe it just sags like a heavy load./Or does it explode?" Richard Wright is unequivocal in his response: It explodes.

Wright's *Native Son* is set in the South Side of Chicago, where Obama worked after graduating from Columbia University. The title suggests that the murderous protagonist of the novel, Bigger Thomas, is a homegrown American whose violence stems from a lack of opportunity (even in the supposed Promised Land of the post–Reconstruction north). In an essay describing the origin of his main character, Richard Wright maintains that Bigger is a depiction of neither a communist nor a fascist, but rather he is "a product of a dislocated society; he is a dispossessed and disinherited man; he is all of this, and he lives amid the greatest possible plenty on earth and he is looking and feeling for a way out."[12] Wright explains that some blacks who suffered disenfranchisement "got religion" (like Uncle Tom, who became one of many stereotypes to emerge out of Stowe's novel). Such folks were convinced "that Jesus would redeem the void of living, [and] felt that the more bitter life was in the present the happier it would be in the hereafter." Wright responds to *Uncle Tom's Cabin*, and its kind-hearted and ever-suffering hero, by aligning Bigger instead with a spirit of rebellion and transgression against laws that served injustice by repressing and exploiting. "In many respects," explains Wright, Bigger's own "emergence as a distinct type was inevitable" in a country where the dispossessed "live amid the greatest possible plenty on earth."[13] Even in twenty-first-century America, this remains a salient, if bitter, observation concerning the gap between the wealthiest and most impoverished among us.

Bigger's inability to make anything of himself in the South Side ghetto of Chicago is dramatized in the opening scene. Bigger awakes in a single-room apartment that he shares with his mother and siblings. When a large rat scurries across the floor, he uses a kitchen skillet to kill the rodent intruder. Despite Bigger's success in killing the rat, his mother chides him for not contributing more to the family expenses: "We wouldn't have to live in this garbage dump if you had any manhood in you," his mother declares scornfully. Bigger, filled "with nervous irritation" after this humiliation, figures that he is "powerless to help them" or to relieve their suffering despite any effort he might make in that direction, so few opportunities does he perceive for someone like himself.

Tragically for Bigger, the very "moment he allowed what his life meant to enter fully into his consciousness" he "would either kill himself or someone else. So he denied himself and acted tough."[14] As this quotation presages, by the end of the novel Bigger has murdered two women, one white and the other black, in a failed attempt to fight off the conscious awareness of his lowly station in American society. In a well-known passage that speaks powerfully to his disenfranchisement, and his violent response to its conscious realization, Bigger and his friend Gus look up at the sky and see a tiny plane "leaving behind it a long trail of white plumage."

"Them white boys sure can fly," Gus said.

"Yeah," Bigger said, wistfully. "They get a chance to do everything."

"I could fly one of them things if I had a chance," Bigger mumbled reflectively, as though talking to himself.

Gus pulled down the corners of his lips, stepped out from the wall, squared his shoulders, doffed his cap, bowed low and spoke with mock deference:

"Yessuh."

"You go to hell," Bigger said, smiling.

"Yessuh," Gus said again.

"I *could* fly a plane if I had a chance," Bigger said.

"If you wasn't black and if you had some money and if they'd let you go to that aviation school, you *could* fly a plane," Gus said.

> For a moment Bigger contemplated all the "ifs" that Gus had mentioned. Then both boys broke into hard laughter, looking at each other through squinted eyes. When their laughter subsided, Bigger said in a voice that was half-question and half-statement:
>
> "It's funny how the white folks treat us, ain't it?"
>
> "It better be funny," Gus said.
>
> "Maybe they are right in not wanting us to fly," Bigger said. "'Cause if I took a plane up I'd take a couple of bombs along and drop 'em as sure as hell."[15]

This foreshadowing of murder, an act never justified in the novel, is presented in a context that nevertheless enables the reader to sympathize with the frustration of the repressed person when it boils over into violence.

There is "that American part of Bigger which is the heritage of us all," explains Wright. It is one "which we get from our seeing and hearing, from school, from the common people." It also comes from inheriting "an idealism that makes us believe that the Constitution is a good document of government, that the Bill of Rights is a good legal and humane principle to safeguard our civic liberties." The reality is that that dream, deferred for millions of African Americans over centuries, inspired the development of Bigger in fictional form at what Wright calls the intersection of "the springs of religion" and "the origins of rebellion."[16] We find acknowledgment of this historical condition in Obama's rhetoric of hope as well. In his 2008 speech on race, for instance, Obama admits that Trinity, his former church, "embodies the black community in its entirety — the doctor and the welfare mom, the model student and the former gang-banger." Like black churches everywhere, asserts Obama, Trinity "contains in full the kindness and cruelty, the fierce intelligence and the shocking ignorance, the struggles and successes, the love, and yes, the bitterness and bias that make up the black experience in America."[17]

If Bigger Thomas represents one response to Du Bois' problem of double consciousness, then the unnamed narrator in Ellison's *Invisible Man* answers Du Bois' conjecture about what happens to blacks who turn away from the pursuit of idealistic American values in favor of a simple "lust for gold." The plot of *Invisible Man* charts how a nameless narrator came to be holed up in a basement with "exactly 1,369 lights" that he wires to the ceiling in an act of sabotage against Monopolated Light & Power, a thinly veiled symbol of white hegemony. The narrator explains to the reader in the opening paragraph of the novel: "I was looking for myself and asking everyone except myself questions which I, and only I, could answer. It took me a long time and much painful boomeranging of my expectations to achieve a realization everyone else appears to have been born with: That I am nobody but myself. But first I have to discover that I am an invisible man!"[18]

Despite being literally and figuratively bathed in light, he remains an "invisible man." Attempting to explain what such an assertion means, he asks the reader to look beyond the darkness of his skin, and instead look to the force of perception for the answer: "Nor is my invisibility exactly a matter of a biochemical accident to my epidermis. That invisibility to which I refer occurs because of a particular disposition of the eyes of those with whom I come in contact. A matter of the construction of their *inner* eyes," he explains, "those eyes with which they look through their physical eyes upon reality."[19] In other words, his invisibility results not from being black per se, but from so many white folks refusing to see black people as human beings, but rather as stereotypes, if at all. The conscious realization of his own invisibility in a racist society occurs over the course of the novel, but in contrast to Wright's protagonist, Ellison's unnamed narrator articulates certain aspects of black consciousness that elude the slower-witted Bigger.

The first inkling of his invisibility comes to him as he graduates from a high school in the deep South. As one of the best students in the school, he earns the right to deliver a commencement speech, the subject of which he ironically bases on a supposition taught by white power: "humility was the secret, indeed, the very essence of progress" for blacks. His address, praised by every white authority in attendance, earns him another invitation to give a speech "at a gathering of the town's leading white citizens." However, when he arrives at the main hotel ballroom, he is unexpectedly asked to participate in a "battle royal to be fought by some of my schoolmates as part of the entertainment." Although unaware of it at the time, the narrator is being asked to run a gauntlet in return for the token rewards bestowed for obsequiousness toward prominent whites. Before they are made to fight one another, he and his fellow black students are subjected to the temptation of a naked white girl (with whom sexual congress represented the ultimate social transgression of white power). Some squirm to hide the visible signs of their arousal. After being taunted with this symbol of the pleasures that lay beyond their grasp, the blindfolded "shines," the "black sonsabitches" and "ginger-colored niggers," were made to box each other for the pleasure of the "bankers, lawyers, judges, doctors, fire chiefs, teachers, and merchants."[20]

In the ring, the blindfolded men fling and flail themselves about in increasingly vain attempts to knock out their peers and take the prize. After being severely beaten by his fellow blacks who all vie for the reward, the narrator fights to retrieve fake coins from an electrified rug (a scenario symbolizing Du Bois' warning against seeking the riches of whites over the ideals of hope and freedom). These repeated humiliations also reinforce power relationships akin to those between slave and master. Only after the narrator has endured repeated indignities is he given an opportunity (covered in gore though he is) to deliver his speech on the importance of humility for black people. For it, he is awarded "a scholarship to the state college for Negroes" (a derogatory reference to Tuskegee Normal and Industrial Institute and its founder Booker T. Washington, who advocated a slow road to equality and inclusion for blacks).

Through this, and a series of other conflicts over the course of the novel, the narrator of *Invisible Man* comes to understand his grandfather's dying words, which at one time had perplexed him (for his grandfather "had been a quiet old man" who never made any trouble): "Son, after I'm gone I want you to keep up the good fight. I never told you, but our life is a war and I have been a traitor all my born days, a spy in the enemy's country ever since I give up my gun back in the Reconstruction. Live with your head in the lion's mouth. I want you to overcome 'em with yeses, undermine 'em with grins, agree 'em to death and destruction, let 'em swoller you till they vomit or bust wide open." In the novel's epilogue, the narrator embraces his condition: "After years of trying to adopt the opinions of others, I finally rebelled. I am an *invisible* man."[21] Ralph Ellison explains that his novel reveals "the human universals hidden within the plight of one who was both black and American, and not only as a means of conveying my personal vision of possibility, but as a way of dealing with the sheer rhetorical challenge involved in communicating across our barriers of race and religion, class, color and region."[22]

Arguably, Barack Obama is unrivaled among contemporary politicians in formulating ways of communicating across such barriers in his rhetoric of hope. For instance, Obama cites another great American writer in the context of race relations in the United States. "William Faulkner once observed," Obama explains to his audience, that the "past isn't dead and buried. In fact, it isn't even past." The quotation comes from *Requiem for a Nun* (1951), a sequel to *Sanctuary* (1931). Faulkner's *Requiem* is a macabre multi-genre work that features the character Temple Drake, a young upper-class granddaughter of a local judge whose flirting and loose reputation results in her rape with a corncob by an impotent bootlegger. Eight years later, Temple Drake marries Gowan Stevens, the alcoholic who unwittingly compromised her safety years earlier. Together, they have two children, one of whom was murdered as an infant by the children's nurse. Both novels feature protracted court battles (through which Faulkner satirizes notions of southern justice and morality by revealing the rotting institutions that they support).

The passage quoted in Obama's race speech above, and incidentally in the 2004 preface to *Dreams from My Father* as well, comes from late in Act One in which Stevens and Temple, husband and wife, discuss their child's murder case (and indirectly the psychological effects of the rape years earlier). Although not culpable for her child's death, Temple nevertheless blames herself, and the circumstances of her past, for her present suffering. Note her double identity as the wild Temple Drake and the married society woman, Mrs. Gowan Stevens. The following exchange occurs between herself and her husband regarding facts in the murder trial:

STEVENS: You invented the coincidence.

TEMPLE: Mrs. Gowan Stevens did.

STEVENS: Temple Drake did. Mrs. Gowan Stevens is not even fighting in this class. This is Temple Drake's.

TEMPLE: Temple Drake is dead.

STEVENS: The past is never dead. It's not even past.[23]

Read in context, the implication of this exchange is clear. Temple Drake, who was raped and later sexually assaulted by a surrogate for her impotent abuser, can never completely die. The past remains part of her present, sometimes in ways that she is not fully conscious of. For Obama, "the past is never dead and buried" means that the "collective history" of humanity directly impacts every one of us today in "the underlying struggle — between worlds of plenty and worlds of want; between the modern and the ancient."[24] As David Frank explains, in terms of America, Obama believes that "there will be no collective understanding of why there is great anger, poverty, and despair in the black community" without historical context.[25] Yet, so incongruous is the original context of this quotation from Faulkner and the manner in which Obama uses it in the rhetoric of hope, one wonders if he knew the quotation from *Requiem for a Nun* or from popular usage. In any case, William Faulkner, like Mark Twain before him, was a keen observer of racism and social hierarchies of power in the United States, particularly in the South. As a result, both writers influenced Barack Obama.

However, in terms of race and the quest for equal rights from the Emancipation Proclamation through the 1960s (and continuing into the present day), the speeches and writings of Malcolm X are second only to those of Martin Luther King in their impact on Obamian campaign rhetoric. Malcolm X remains a controversial figure at the beginning of the twenty-first century, and some of his political rhetoric still bites at our social consciousness with all the sting of a determined gadfly. As a self-identified black man with the middle name Hussein running for the presidency of the United States in 2008, quoting an Islamic firebrand like Malcolm X would presumably not have been to Obama's advantage. However, journalists and historians have recognized the influence of Malcolm X on Barack Obama's intellectual life and his struggle with racial identity. Despite the fact that references to Malcolm X are rare in the rhetoric of hope, we nevertheless find a few, though not usually in the form of direct quotes from Malcolm X (which Obama might have made in that important speech on race, for instance).

In *Dreams from My Father*, which is an early formulation of what would become in the fullness of time a campaign rhetoric steeped in tropes of hope and idealism drawn from the American tradition, Obama discusses Malcolm X more openly. Obama writes that "in Bigger Thomas and invisible men, I kept finding the same anguish, the same doubt; a self-contempt that neither irony nor intellect seemed able to deflect." By contrast, Malcolm X's "repeated acts of self-creation spoke to me; the blunt poetry of his words, his unadorned insistence on respect, promised a new and uncompromising order, martial in its discipline, forged through the sheer force of will."[26] His talk of "blue-eyed devils and apocalypse" Obama neatly relegates to the "religious baggage" that Malcolm carried. The conciliatory ideas that Malcolm X develops at the end of his life resonated with the young Barry—and with equal force on the statesman Barack. Obama writes, "Toward the end of his life" Malcolm espoused a "hope of eventual reconciliation."

Alex Haley's *Autobiography of Malcolm X* (1965) challenged Obama to think in new ways as he worked in disadvantaged communities on

Chicago's South Side: "Ever since the first time I'd picked up Malcolm X's autobiography, I had tried to untangle the twin strands of black nationalism, arguing that nationalism's affirming message — of solidarity and self-reliance, discipline and community responsibility — need not depend on hatred of whites any more than it depended on white munificence."[27] The ideas behind the "affirming message" of black nationalism appealed to Obama and would later make their way into the rhetoric of hope, while the other "strand" of racial hatred Obama would outright reject, perhaps due to his biracial upbringing.

Malcolm X's pilgrimage to Mecca in 1964, a year prior to his brutal assassination, transformed his thinking from local to global. Malcolm reports: "It was there in the Holy Land, and later in Africa, that I formed a conviction which I have had ever since — that a topmost requisite for any Negro leader in America ought to be extensive traveling in the non-white lands on this earth, and the travel should include many conferences with the ranking men of those lands. I guarantee that any honest, open-minded Negro leader would return home with more effective thinking about alternative avenues to solutions of the American black man's problem." Elaborating on his newly acquired understanding, itself a necessary precursor to his "repeated acts of self creation," Malcolm explains:

> My pilgrimage broadened my scope. It blessed me with a new insight. In two weeks in the Holy Land, I saw what I never had seen in thirty-nine years here in America. I saw all *races*, all *colors*, — blue-eyed blonds to black-skinned Africans — in *true* brotherhood! In unity! Living as one! Worshiping as one! No segregationists— no liberals; they would not have known how to interpret the meaning of those words.[28]

This almost ecstatic religious awakening would speak to Obama's own struggle to come to grips with his biracial identity. Although direct references to Malcolm X drop off as Obama's rhetoric of hope develops, in contrast to those of Martin Luther King that proliferate, the values that Malcolm X endorsed of self-reliance and continual improvement, drive and discipline, temperance and hard work, all permeate Obama's campaign rhetoric. In many ways, these are quintessential American values enshrined in our national mythologies.

By way of example, Malcolm's insistence, in that fateful year 1965, on "truth, no matter who tells it" and his declaration that "I am for justice" both testify to the transformation of his thinking during the last months of his life. He explains: "Since I learned the truth in Mecca, my dearest friends have come to include all kinds— some Christians, Jews, Buddhists, Hindus, agnostics, and even atheists! I have friends who are called capitalists, Socialists, and Communists! Some of my friends are moderates, conservatives, extremists— some are even Uncle Toms! My friends today are black, brown, red, yellow, and white!"[29] Such a vision of racial integration and a synthesis of ideology corresponds with Obama's own ideas about multiculturalism and globalization (the subject of Chapter Eight).

Before he was assassinated, Malcolm X put his newfound belief in unity into practice by creating a new group that he called the Organization of Afro-American Unity. He became more open-minded as he grew older, telling one reporter, "I'm man enough to tell you that I can't put my finger on exactly what my philosophy is now, but I'm flexible." Even the multiplicity of names that Malcolm X used during his lifetime help the reader to chart his journey of continual self-creation: Malcolm Little, Big Red, Satan, Homeboy, El-Hajj Malik El-Shabazz,[30] among others. Furthermore, Malcolm X deploys the Judeo-Christian-Islamic tropes of the Promised Land that we also saw Obama use in Chapter One: "I believe in religion, but a religion that includes political, economic, and social action designed to eliminate some of these things, and make a paradise here on earth while we're waiting for the other."[31]

Manning Marable suggests that what made Malcolm X "truly original was that he presented himself as the embodiment of the two central figures of African American folk culture, simultaneously the hustler/trickster and the preacher/minister. Janus-faced, the trickster is unpredictable, capable of outrageous transgressions; the minister saves souls, redeems shattered lives, and promises a new world." Malcolm X also employed metaphors from black American folk culture, and in his speeches he "mesmerized audiences because he could orchestrate his themes into a narrative that promised ultimate salvation."[32] Similarly, Barack Obama, who we have seen make deliberate use of African American religious and literary traditions, also promises collective salvation in his 2008 rhetoric of hope, and it is a call that he repeated in 2012.

Just as Malcolm X drew from "the past experiences of his own life as well as from African American folklore and culture," so too does Barack Obama borrow from them in his rhetoric of hope. Obama writes that Malcolm deliberately "wove a narrative of suffering and resistance, of tragedy and triumph, that captured the imaginations of black people throughout the world."[33] In 2008, it was Barack Obama's narrative of hope that enchanted people, at home and abroad, so much so that he won the Nobel Peace Prize in 2009 "for his extraordinary efforts to strengthen international diplomacy and cooperation between peoples," an honor even Obama admits was largely undeserved. "I would be remiss," Obama explains in his Nobel lecture, "if I did not acknowledge the considerable controversy that your generous decision has generated. In part, this is because I am at the beginning, and not the end, of my labors on the world stage. Compared to some of the giants of history who've received this prize—Schweitzer and King; Marshall and Mandela—my accomplishments are slight." Yet, like Malcolm X, who "presented himself as vessel for conveying the anger and impatience the black masses felt,"[34] in the rhetoric of hope, Obama deliberately made himself into a receptacle for American (and world) frustration with the foreign policy of the Bush administration, which preceded his own.

Barack Obama and Manning Marable agree that Malcolm's great gift was self-reinvention. By the time of his death, Malcolm X was clearly headed away from the narrow stifling dogma that marked his earlier years as a leader in the Nation of Islam. We cannot help but wonder what avenues his keen and ever-opening mind would have traveled had not an assassin's bullet abruptly halted its transformations. Marable, in his insightful biography of Malcolm X, notes: "As his social vision expanded to include people of divergent nationalities and racial identities, his gentle humanism and antiracism could have become a platform for a new kind of radical, global ethnic politics."[35] Henry Louis Gates points out that Malcolm X possessed a profound "love of humanity and the humanities."[36] This process of self-education mirrors that of another of Obama's heroes as well: Abraham Lincoln. Perhaps, in some ways, Obama picks up where Malcolm left off, developing a vision of inclusivity in the pursuit of equality that has a global reach. Like Obama generations later, Malcolm sought a "fundamental restructuring of wealth and power in the United States—not a violent social revolution, but radical and meaningful change nevertheless."[37] I doubt very much if the writings of Malcolm X would have appealed to Obama had not this clear trend toward inclusion been present in the life and evolving thought of this seemingly fearless man.

In the final part of this chapter, we briefly consider the influence of American music and popular culture on the formulation of the rhetoric of hope, before moving on to the major role that moral values play in it in the following chapter. (The rhetoric of hope emerges at a historical moment when Republicans successfully beat the more pluralistically minded Democrats for a generation by deploying so-called family values.) During the 2008 campaign, much was made of Barack Obama's iPod playlist as revealed in an interview with *Rolling Stone*. A highly political listing, it may better indicate the demographics that the campaign targeted than represent the greatest musical influences on the author of the rhetoric of hope. Nevertheless, taken together with other interviews and excerpts from Obama's writings, we can construct a more meaningful list. After doing so, we will take a closer look at several musicians in search of themes and tropes that we have come to associate with his presidential campaign rhetoric.

Barack Obama's Facebook page lists some of his favorite musicians as Miles Davis, John Coltrane, Bob Dylan, Stevie Wonder, and Johann Sebastian Bach. The aforementioned *Rolling Stone* playlist includes Stevie Wonder, Bob Dylan, Bruce Springsteen, and Jay-Z, who all mingle effortlessly with Earth, Wind and Fire, Elton John, and the Rolling Stones. In *Dreams from My Father*, Obama cites Lena Horne, Mahalia Jackson, Marvin Gaye, Duke Ellington, and Ella Fitzgerald as being inspirational forces in his life. In August 2008, the *Telegraph* cited a list of Obama's "Top 10 Favorite Songs," one that features "Ready or Not" by the Fugees, "What's Going On" by Marvin Gaye, "I'm on Fire" by Bruce Springsteen, "Gimme Shelter" by the Rolling Stones, "Sinnerman" by Nina Simone, "Touch the Sky" by Kanye West, "You'd Be So Easy to Love" by Frank Sinatra, "Think" by Aretha Franklin, "City of Blinding Lights" by U2, and "Yes We Can" by will.i.am.[38] Curiously enough, this last title is an Emmy Award–winning track featuring inspirational passages from Obama's own speeches!

Indeed, the number of songs written about Barack Obama, such as "Yes We Can" by will.i.am, testifies to the power of the rhetoric of hope in American popular culture. They include: Jay-Z & Mary J. Blige's "You're All Welcome," Common's "The People," "Obamaway" by Ti$a (Taz Arnold), and Young Jeezy's "My President Iz Black." Moreover, the rhetoric of hope also inspired new music from artists around the world: Extra Golden's "Obama for Change," Cocoa Tea's "Barack Obama," Docta Musica WashiWara's "Barack Obama," and Mighty Sparrow's "Barack the Magnificent," to name but a few. Indeed, as Garrett Graff notes, during the 2008 presidential campaign Obama was "part preacher, part professor, and part movie star."[39] Confronted by such a diverse list of musical artists, let us focus upon a few whose social and political messages inform themes and tropes in the rhetoric of hope.

I have "probably 30 Dylan songs on my iPod," Obama claimed during the 2008 presidential campaign. Singling out "Maggie's Farm," he called it "one of my favorites during the political season." He explained that it "speaks to me as I listen to some of the political rhetoric."[40] Bob Dylan, himself part preacher and part rock star, wrote protest songs like "Maggie's Farm" to challenge the status quo. Dylan even performed at the March on Washington for Jobs and Freedom in 1963 where Martin Luther King delivered his legendary "I Have a Dream" speech, a rhetorical triumph that greatly impressed the young folksinger. Dylan performed three songs on that day: "Only a Pawn in Their Game," about the murdered civil rights activist Medgar Evers, "When the Ship Comes In," and "Keep Your Eyes on the Prize" (by Len Chandler). In "Only a Pawn," Dylan sings of the bullet that took Medgar Evers' life. Drawing to the fore the racial and economic injustices poisoning American society, Dylan indicts the structures of power that provide succor to that injustice.

"Maggie's Farm" often gets interpreted as a rejection of the 1960s folk music scene, which Dylan found increasingly restricting as he pushed into new, often electric, musical territory. Dylan's own growth as a musician parallels that gift for self-invention in Malcolm X that Obama so admired. Dylan began his musical career covering Woody Guthrie songs in Greenwich Village, yet in time he became a fiercely original singer and songwriter (and some would say national poet). The lyrics of "Maggie's Farm" speak to the economic exploitation of an underclass (both black and white) by elite owners of property and capital. The main refrain declares a refusal to work on the farm any longer. The labor-bound narrator has a head full of ideas, but on the farm there is no chance to develop them. Instead, he has to scrub the floor.

Dylan adeptly moves the target of each stanza to emphasize a break from all forms of exploitative power. One stanza insists on never working for Maggie's brother either, since he always finds a way to recoup salaries through fines and penalties. The third and fourth stanzas extend that refusal to be exploited to Maggie's father and mother as well. Mom may be the brains of the two, but at sixty-eight she's vain and vacuous, insisting absurdly that she's just twenty-four years old. Dylan even indicts the National Guard, which protects and legitimizes their power. The song's final stanza concludes by asserting the difficulty of achieving individuation in the face of these structures of power that crush creative expression. The narrator tries his best to be himself, but society insists on compliance.

This song, named by Obama as a favorite, is an indictment of all such distillations of power that demand social, intellectual, and artistic conformity.

A closer look at the structure of "Maggie's Farm" reveals a debt to American folk music, particularly to the spirituals sung by slaves in the South, and the gospel and blues music that emerged after the Civil War. In the Martin Scorsese documentary on Bob Dylan entitled *No Direction Home*, the Chicago-born singer Mavis Staples remarks that Dylan "was writing inspirational songs that inspire." They were the "same as gospel," she observes, in that "he was writing truth." Dylan, Staples suggests, sings truth to power. Like many blues lyrics, the words to "Maggie's Farm" are "extremely frank and almost exclusively concerned with the self, in relation to others." Rather than emphasizing a chronological narrative of events, "blues songs express feelings and emotions or describe actions based on them."[41] Dylan's lyrics also double the refrain at the beginning of each stanza, much like the rhymed couplet in the standard blues form.

During his election night victory speech in Chicago's Grant Park, Obama alluded to a similar refrain in a blues song by Sam Cooke, "A Change Is Gonna Come." Cooke sings about the slow nature of change but with an unsinkable optimism that it will come someday. Obama even employs the same rhetorical method of parallelism (isocolon) and refrain in this speech and in his other writings that collectively make up the rhetoric of hope. In his November 2008 victory speech, for example, Obama employs rhetorical figures common to blues music:

> It's the answer told by lines that stretched around schools and churches in numbers this nation has never seen [...]
> It's the answer spoken by young and old, rich and poor, Democrat and Republican, black, white [...]
> It's the answer that led those who've been told for so long by so many to be cynical and fearful [...]

Like a seasoned gospel or blues musician, Obama concludes his riff with a variation on the refrain while returning to the tonic chord to provide cadence and closure: "It's been a long time coming, but tonight, because of what we did on this date, in this election, at this defining moment, change has come to America."[42]

Several of Barack Obama's other favorite songs and songwriters, though by no means all of them, belong to a tradition that we may broadly term African American music (which includes the genres of jazz, rhythm and blues, soul, funk, hip-hop, and rap). Perhaps Obama's embrace of black music had something to do with his mother's encouragement to explore that aspect of his biracial identity. In *Dreams from My Father*, Obama reports that his mother, whom he calls "a lonely witness for secular humanism, a soldier for the New Deal, Peace Corps, [and] position-paper liberalism," instilled in him a message "to embrace black people generally. She would come home with books on the civil rights movement, the recordings of Mahalia Jackson, the speeches of Dr. King. Every black man was Thurgood Marshall or Sidney Poitier; every black woman Fannie Lou Hamer or Lena Horne. To be black was to be the beneficiary of a great inheritance, a special destiny, glorious burdens that only we were strong enough to bear." She used to remind him, "Harry Belafonte is the best-looking man on the planet."[43] Obama "recalls that he read Ralph Ellison, Langston Hughes, James Baldwin, Richard Wright and W.E.B. Du Bois when he was an adolescent in an effort to come to terms with his racial identity."[44] Yet, white American writers, like Harriet Beecher Stowe, Ralph Waldo Emerson, William Faulkner, and John Steinbeck, also helped to shape Obama's understanding of the American experience.

Since Barry Obama grew up with a white mother, grandmother, and grandfather, another way that he learned about black culture was through the mass media, specifically TV, movies, and radio. Obama explains: "Pop culture was color-coded, after all, an arcade of images from which you could cop a walk, a talk, a step, a style. I couldn't croon like Marvin Gaye, but I could learn to dance all of the *Soul Train* steps. I couldn't pack a gun like Shaft or Superfly, but I could sure enough curse like Richard Pryor." Marking an embrace of that new identity, Obama states flatly: "I decided to become part of that world." This desire to identify with his black heritage led him to the basketball court where a few black men on the team could teach him "an attitude that didn't just have to do with the sport." At one point, this youthful and exuberant embrace of African American culture made Obama reflect on the fact that he was "living out a caricature of black male adolescence, itself a caricature of swaggering American manhood."[45]

In this context, we turn to another tune that Obama identifies as a longtime favorite: Aretha Franklin's "Think." Franklin grew up singing gospel music in her father's Baptist church, and she performed "My Country 'Tis of Thee" at Barack Obama's inaugural in 2009. Although earning the moniker "the Queen of Soul" for her mastery of that genre, Franklin actually works in jazz, rhythm and blues, and even rock & roll, all of which spring from the black experience in America. "Think" opens with a counter-punctual repetition of the song's title. She sings of freeing the mind. In the lyrics, she asks her listener to consider how the self-awareness of difference creates a false sense of inferiority among oppressed people, and how they have been exploited as a result. "Think" also features the repetition of the word *freedom*, which we have seen associated with the rhetoric of hope in several other contexts.

Portia Maultsby points out that the sound of soul music "is characterized by a set of aesthetic features derived from the musical and preaching traditions of the Black folk church." Soul singers, in this sense, are secular counterparts of preachers. Aretha Franklin's musical delivery "reflects the dramatic performance style of Black preachers, who employ a range of improvisatory devices—vocal inflections, varying timbres, word repetition, and phrase endings punctuated by 'grunts,' 'shouts,' and moans, etc.— to gradually build the intensity to a level that transforms the sermon into quasi-song."[46] These devices also influence the tone and delivery of Obama's speeches, and it makes sense that his "ear" for such rhetorical patterns developed, not only by listening to black preaching, but also through soul, gospel, rhythm and blues, and other genres of African American music, including hip-hop and rap.

Tshombe Walker understands that since hip-hop "is a means of communicating the common experience of fighting against human exploitation and oppression," the "art form concerns itself with helping the community to transcend the negative aspects of living in an oppressive environment."[47] Like hip-hop, rap music reflects the society in which it is created. As Reginald Thomas asserts, "Some rap tries to elevate while other works serve only to hold a mirror to society and let the world know what that society looks like."[48] These functions of hip-hop and rap, to fight oppression, elevate, and accurately portray the status quo, mirror those of other African American art forms, including literature (as we saw above). Although he expresses dismay at the overt materialism of hip-hop culture, Obama acknowledged the power of the genre to shape the future in a 2008 interview with Jeff Johnson during Black Entertainment Television's political special *What's in It for Us?*: "Hip-Hop is not just a mirror of what is, it should also be a reflection of what can be." Obama offers a positive view of hip-hop's potential to bring about change: "Imagine communities that are not torn up by violence. Imagine communities where we are respecting women. Imagine communities where knowledge, and reading, and academic excellence are valued. Imagine communities where fathers are doing right by their kids. That's also something that has to be reflected. Art can't just be a rear view mirror. It should have a headlight out there pointing to where we need to go."

The Fugees, an innovative musical group that blends rap, hip-hop with soul and reggae, remains one of Obama's favorite bands. The second track on their album *Blunted on Reality* aims to frame the historical reality of racism and criticize the status quo that allows racism to continue, and seeks to elevate by citing the heroes in the struggle against it. It begins with the rapper Wyclef Jean asking why he is trapped in a metaphorical cage. This cry of social constraint is driven by heavy syncopated rhythms. The chorus, not unlike in gospel music, responds with a transgressive, yet hopeful, message that despite being held back, the "nappy heads" are making a move. Here again we find a dialectical tension between the ideal of equality and the actual world of discrimination. Jean chastises those who keep blacks in pain, and attacks Louis Armstrong for singing about a wonderful world, when blacks were out on the farm picking cotton. In contrast to Louis Armstrong, whom he depicts as an Uncle Tom figure (a common attack on the famed trumpeter), Jean invokes the great black leaders who fought the power (rather than become obsequious to it): Martin Luther King, Malcolm X, Frederick Douglass, and Harriet Tubman. The song closes seeking to inspire continual struggle for civil rights and to affirm black identity (much as the black power movement sought to do).

Writing in *The American Prospect* in early February 2008, Latoya Peterson calls Barack Obama "the first hip-hop presidential candidate." Peterson explains: "Hip-hop culture is a unifying force, a potent combination of entrepreneurship, community activism, creativity, and innovation that appeals to youth across the globe. Barack Obama is the hip-hop candidate, not because of his racial identity or his oratory skills, but because his policies and approach to politics demonstrate that he understands the needs and desires of the hip-hop community."[49] In much of the music that Obama reports to find meaningful, we discover tropes of suffering and redemption that are part of the African American experience.

In this chapter, we have considered the force of popular fiction and music on what would become the rhetoric of hope during the 2008 presidential campaign. Ours was necessarily a brief glimpse at but a few of the

American artists who helped to shape Obama's sense of identity and his worldview as a biracial individual growing up in the post–civil rights era. From *Dreams from My Father*, one understands that Barack Obama chose to identify himself with the black community partly due to the power of its art and religion. However, Obama is also half Caucasian and was raised by a white mother from Kansas, and so his tastes in literature and music reflect that part of his background as well. Indeed, "Obama's writings demonstrate conclusively that his ideas, like the ideas of all American thinkers worth studying, have been woven from many different sources."[50] As I noted at the beginning of the chapter, it is more useful to consider the social, cultural, and thematic commonalities among those works of literature and music favored by Obama, rather than to frame them purely in term of race and identity (as has been the tendency in Obama scholarship).

In many ways, the conclusion of this chapter marks a moment of transition. Up to now, our study of the rhetoric of hope has been historical and literary, indeed covering many centuries and revealing the utopian traditions in the West from which that rhetoric is drawn. In the next chapter, we pivot from tracing the antecedents of Obama's campaign rhetoric to a more sustained look at the role of values in that rhetorical vision. In Chapter Seven, we turn to the construction of Obama's narrative persona and explore how he deftly grafts it onto existing idealistic traditions in American culture. Chapter Eight demonstrates how that prophetic persona reinforces the universalist dimensions of the rhetoric of hope and culminates in a vision of a multicultural utopia. In the final two chapters, we consider Barack Obama's 2012 presidential campaign rhetoric and compare it with the rhetorical techniques employed in 2008.

CHAPTER SIX

Values and the
Content of Character

The first United States Secretary of War, Henry Knox, claimed in 1793: "It is the President's character, and not the written constitution, which keeps [the nation] together."[1] In the eighteenth century, the term "character" was synonymous with reputation, and as such it was something that could be acquired and enhanced.[2] Although specifically referring to George Washington, Knox gave expression to a higher truth about the relationship between the moral character of a leader and national unity. With the country still in its infancy, but finally free from the yoke of Great Britain, the United States could forge its own independent character by defining the values that would draw it together as a nation. George Washington presciently recognized the need for creating a new national identity. Like John Adams and James Madison, Washington engaged in a highly personalized "politics of character" in which his own character became a template for a national one. They all attempted to "construct character through particular forms of writing,"[3] and so theirs was ultimately a self-conscious rhetorical act of creation — one that involved both self and nation.

To some degree, all of the nation's founders "engaged in attempts to fashion a character for themselves, but none had been more successful than George Washington. The very titles he was known by — father to his country, Cincinnatus — attested to his success, revealing how thoroughly he managed to embody those roles."[4] Washington was aided in his endeavor (to shape a persona that could become a template for national character) by a widely read and highly influential book. In his *History of the Life and Death, Virtues and Exploits of General George Washington,*

Mason Locke Weems created an enduring image of the famed general that would make him the quintessential symbol of the new country. Weems attributes the rise of Washington from family farmer to the position of revolutionary general and then to the presidency of the United States to his "Great Virtues."[5] He writes, "To be truly great, a man must have not only great talents, but those talents must be constantly exerted on great, i.e., good actions—and perseveringly too—for if he should turn aside to vice—farewell to his heroism."[6] In this manner, Weems makes Washington an exemplar of the American character by portraying him as a self-made man who "could serve as a model for all Americans to emulate," a common man "who achieved greatness through his own efforts."[7] Washington's biography was framed as an American story made possible only through the adherence to the virtues of honesty, hard work, humility, courage, optimism, and duty to country.

Weems also aligns Washington with the positive moral values associated with Christianity. Writing in the exuberant and inflated style that characterizes his prose, he claims that Washington received a youthful revelation through his study of the "blessed gospel which contains the moral philosophy of heaven." In those pages, according to Weems, Washington

> learnt, that "God is love";—and that all he desires, with respect to men, is to glorify himself in their happiness; and since virtue is indispensable to that happiness, the infinite and eternal weight of God's attributes must be in favour of virtue, and against vice; and consequently that God will sooner or later gloriously reward the one, and punish the other. This was the creed of Washington. And looking on it as the only basis of human virtue and happiness, he very cordially embraced it himself, and wished for nothing so much as to see all others embrace it.[8]

As one can glean from this passage, the depiction of Washington borders on hagiography. By way of concluding Chapter Thirteen, for example, Weems notes: "Besides all those inestimable favours which he received from [religion] at the hands of her celestial daughters, the Virtues; she threw over him her own magic mantle of Character. And it was this that immortalized Washington." Chapters Fourteen, Fifteen, and Sixteen further expound the virtues of benevolence, industry, and patriotism present in Washington's character. Although prone to hyperbole, through this idealized biography Weems helped give shape to an enduring American mythology. Weems's was ultimately a "patriotic and didactic project of building the nation's character."[9]

The success of Weems' characterization extended Washington's own rhetorical construction of self. In his 1796 farewell address, a humble and unambitious Washington declines to seek a third term. He explains that his resolution to step down was not taken "without a strict regard to all the considerations" of a "dutiful Citizen to his country." While Washington acknowledges the force of patriotic obligation, he asks his countrymen not to disapprove of his determination to retire, and he thanks them for the honors that they have bestowed upon him. At this point in the farewell address, the beginning of the second paragraph, one might mistakenly assume that the famously taciturn Washington would have concluded it. Yet, it extends to thirty-two handwritten pages. Washington uses that additional space to construct a narrative persona that could serve as a moral model for the citizenry of his fledgling nation. For instance, Washington's decision not to seek a third term set a precedent that was largely honored (with the notable exception of FDR) until it was put into law by the Twenty-Second Amendment in 1951.

In those pages, Washington provided a list of thoughts that he explains were "the result of much reflection, of no inconsiderable observation, and which appear to me all important to the permanency of your felicity as a People." In passages that foreshadow the Civil War decades later, both North and South must cherish the union, rather than succumbing to petty regionalism. For Washington only a unified government could protect liberty, the very principle for which the nation fought a revolution. Respect for the authority of the federal government and "compliance with its Laws," cautions Washington, "are duties enjoined by the fundamental maxims of true Liberty."

George Washington returns repeatedly to the centrality of moral values to both individual freedom and American democracy. He calls "virtue or morality" the "necessary spring of popular government" and enjoins all Americans to "Observe good faith & justice towds all Nations. Cultivate peace & harmony with all." Washington believed that the United States, rightly led, should serve as a universal model of government based on virtue: "It will be worthy of a free, enlightened, and, at no distant period, a great Nation, to give to mankind the magnanimous and too novel example of a People always guided by an exalted justice & benevolence." Here, Washington ties the moral values of justice and benevolence directly to the success of the American experiment. "Can it be," Washington asks, "that Providence has not connected the permanent felicity of a Nation with its virtue?" Vice, Washington admonishes, renders that happiness impossible.

By way of concluding his farewell address, Washington again strikes a chord of humility: "Though in reviewing the incidents of my Administration, I am unconscious of intentional error—I am nevertheless too sensible of my defects not to think it probable that I may have committed many errors. Whatever they may be I fervently beseech the Almighty to avert or mitigate the evils to which they may tend." In addition to asking forgiveness for those decisions that carried unintended negative consequences, Washington gives voice to one last hope that the union will endure. "I shall also carry with me the hope that my Country will never cease to view them with indulgence; and that after forty five years of my life dedicated to its Service, with an upright zeal, the faults of incompetent abilities will be consigned to oblivion, as myself must soon be to the Mansions of rest."[10] The rhetorical acts of creation by Washington and his biographer provided a fledgling nation with an identity firmly grounded in what would evolve into a defining set of American values.

Because the idealistic traditions found in the United States drew on a heritage that reaches "back to the ancient Orient, classical Greece, medieval Christianity, and the threshold of the modern Western world," Americans hold a distinctively bright and hopeful view of the future promise of humanity. Endowed initially with plentiful natural resources and a relatively small population, "America invited faith in the ability of men and women to overcome the limitations that history and environment" placed on other nations and their people. The protection from invasion afforded by two oceans also "nourished this optimistic view of the new land and its happy implication for welfare, character, conduct, and fortune."[11] As a result, more than a decade into the twenty-first century, the American Dream remains "a major element of our national identity."[12]

Even before Washington and other Founding Fathers consciously helped to shape the contours of the American character, the Puritans bestowed upon the future nation a code of values (many of which are still enshrined in the myth of the American Dream). The New World beckoned to the Puritans as it would to countless millions over the following centuries. For them, the vast wilderness of American shores was literally a Promised Land. In point of fact, the Puritans believed "themselves to be literal and figurative descendants of the tribes who wandered the desert for forty years after leaving Egypt and founded the nation of Israel."[13]

Such an attitude eventually imbued the American Dream, and the values that undergird it, with a collectivist dimension (in addition to an individualist one grounded in salvation through grace or works). Although the Puritans were fiercely self-righteous, highly exclusive in terms of group membership, and murdered native inhabitants for their land, they nevertheless put stock in a particular set of values that included moral discipline, deferred gratification, duty, sobriety, and hard work. Their belief in worldly prosperity as a sign of adherence to those values evolved over time into the capitalistic impulse at the heart of American democracy.

Puritans and other Protestant groups that came to the New World (such as the Anabaptists, Baptists, Quakers, and Shakers) also brought with them a new conception of the relation of the individual to society, one which further developed over the course of time in the American colonies. Their sense of duty to the community was a practical necessity in the wilderness of the New World, but it also grew out of biblical traditions of exodus and redemption as well. For example, John Winthrop, a founder of the Massachusetts Bay Colony, envisioned a covenant between God and his fellow pilgrims to build a new society. In his 1630 thesis, *A Modell of Christian Charity*, Winthrop identifies the communal values that this new society would need to succeed. He writes:

> Wee must be knitt together, in this worke, as one man. Wee must entertaine each other in brotherly affection. Wee must be willing to abridge ourselves of our superfluities, for the supply of other's necessities. Wee must uphold a familiar commerce together in all meekeness, gentlenes, patience and liberality. Wee must delight in eache other; make other's conditions our oune; rejoice together, mourne together, labor and suffer together, allwayes haueving before our eyes our commission and community in the worke, as members of the same body. Soe shall wee keepe the unitie of the spirit in the bond of peace. The Lord will be our God, and delight to dwell among us, as his oune people, and will command a blessing upon us in all our wayes. Soe that wee shall see much more of his wisdom, power, goodness and truthe, than formerly wee haue been acquainted with. Wee shall finde that the God of Israell is among us, when ten of us shall be able to resist a thousand of our enemies; when hee shall make us a prayse and glory that men shall say of succeeding plantations, "the Lord make it likely that of New England." For wee must consider that wee shall be as a citty upon a hill.

In this utopian dream of the city on a hill, Winthrop evokes "a communitarian vision of American life."[14] For the Founding Fathers, who inherited such Protestant traditions from their religious forbears, the notion of communal responsibility would be translated into a recognition of the need for the government to protect individual rights.

So it was that these early settlers who sought religious freedom left future generations of Americans with a set of Protestant-inspired values (among them are work, sobriety, self-restraint, and a unique sense of individualism tempered by a notion of the common good). As we saw in Chapter Two, the framers of the United States Constitution and Bill of Rights mixed these religious values unreservedly with eighteenth-century Enlightenment thought. Historically speaking, the myth of the American Dream underwent further transformations during the American romantic movement in the nineteenth century, and while there were many contributors to it, none was more influential than Ralph Waldo Emerson.

Emerson had inherited a "basic postulate of the democratic faith" that affirmed that God had created a moral law for mankind on which to base his government, and that God also endowed human beings "with a conscience with which to apprehend it. Underneath and supporting human society, as the basic rock supports the hills, is a moral order which is the abiding place of the eternal principles of truth and righteousness."[15] As one scholar explains, in the early nineteenth century, Unitarianism attempted to reconcile Puritan theology "with Newtonian science, and to subdue to reason the thorny doctrine of the Trinity." Although Emerson distanced himself from its rationalist tradition, he was nevertheless sympathetic to the Unitarian movement. Morality remained a lifelong preoccupation for Emerson, and he invariably "sought a faith that would be a dynamism giving ethics significance" in American society.[16] Over the course of this study, we have seen how outstanding individuals, like George Washington, Benjamin Franklin, and Abraham Lincoln, all helped to create the ideal of upward mobility based on merit, virtue, and moral action at the heart of the American Dream. In place of that materialistic vision of the benefits of moral rectitude, Ralph Emerson would point instead to fixed eternal principles that undergird human society.

While it has become commonplace to attribute to Emerson a rejection of history as something to be bound by (so strong was his forward-looking idealism), he was actually influenced by the historical reform agendas of Protestant groups like the Quakers. Generally speaking, they emphasized liberty, universal brotherhood, and universal love, and from them sprang an inspired humanitarianism "that softened the individualism of the nineteenth century by adding to the responsibilities of the strong man the duty of aiding his less fortunate brother."[17] In his address to the Mechanics' Apprentices' Library Association in 1841, entitled "Man the Reformer," Emerson asks each person in the audience to "cast aside all evil customs, timidities, and limitations" and instead to become a "free and helpful man, a reformer, a benefactor" at the service of one's fellow citizens. Giving voice to an American creed of reinvention, Emerson wonders: "What is a man born for but to be a reformer, a Re-maker of what man has made; a renouncer of lies; a restorer of truth and good, imitating that great Nature which embosoms us all, and which sleeps no moment on an old past, but every hour repairs herself, yielding us every morning a new day, and with every pulsation a new life?"[18]

As Ralph Gabriel points out, Emerson was the chief prophet of the fundamental law of natural rights, and of the free individual, at the heart of the American doctrine of democratic faith. Emerson envisioned a nation of self-reliant individuals who "had a mission to stand before the world as a witness that free men can govern themselves without the aid of kings or of an hereditary aristocracy."[19] His best-known articulation of that American doctrine appears in the essay "Self-Reliance." Society everywhere, Emerson explains, "is in conspiracy against the manhood of every one of its members. Society is a joint-stock company, in which the members agree, for the better securing of his bread to each shareholder, to surrender the liberty and culture of the eater. The virtue in most request is conformity. Self-reliance is its aversion." The self-reliant person, for Emerson, is therefore a nonconformist freed from the burden of caring about what other people think of him. He does not require the approbation of his peers or the hollow praise of sycophants. The great man is "he who in the midst of the crowd keeps with perfect sweetness the independence of solitude." He speaks his mind regardless of the possibility of being misunderstood, and he does not apologize for changing his opinions as his understanding grows. "Let us never bow and apologize more," Emerson scolds, for greatness "appeals to the future."[20]

Here we find a dialectical tendency in Emerson's thought in which progress is made through contention with the existing order.[21] Such an assertion should not surprise as his championing of transcendentalism was marked by "a leap beyond the actualities of the social movement to a qualitatively different future." As Robert Milder aptly observes: "All revolutionaries are 'Utopians' in this Hegelian sense."[22] That is to say, the self-reliant and self-actualized person is characterized by an ability to perceive the next step in both the unfolding of the individual soul and in the progression of society. Emerson firmly believed that virtue must strive against entrenched power, a critical stance that further aligns him with the long tradition of utopianism in American thought.

In his essay, "The Transcendentalist," Emerson rejects the materialistic view of the world that those of his generation inherited from the eighteenth century. He writes:

> What is popularly called Transcendentalism among us, is Idealism; Idealism as it appears in 1842. As thinkers, mankind have ever divided into two sects, Materialists and Idealists; the first class founding on experience, the second on consciousness; the first class beginning to think from the data of the senses, the second class perceive that the senses are not final, and say, The senses give us representations of things, but what are the things themselves, they cannot tell. The materialist insists on facts, on history, on the force of circumstances, and the animal wants of man; the idealist on the power of Thought and of Will, on inspiration, on miracle, on individual culture.[23]

Thus, to Emerson "virtue is a reverence and delight in the presence of certain divine laws" that gives rise to an intuition of moral sentiment in the individual. The divine laws are eternal, "out of time, out of space, and not subject to circumstance," and they yoke together action and consequence. Here again, the perennial dialectical opposition between what Emerson calls "the force of circumstances" (the reality of the status quo) and the ideal of truth beyond the immediacy of the material world comes to the fore.

For both Emerson and his friend Henry David Thoreau, nature became the vehicle for a type of religious experience that claimed to radically transform the relationship between the individual and society. More specifically, nature offered the possibility of contact with an "infinite and immanent God that these transcendentalists call the Over-Soul."[24] For Emerson, an encounter with the Over-Soul resulted in a radical shift in attitude and perception in which the character of the individual is reconstituted with a less egocentric orientation. This transcendental experience, in which "every man's particular being" was seen to be "contained and made one with all other," became the basis of an idealized set of moral values eventually encoded in the American Dream (along with those of the Puritans and Founding Fathers that preceded them). These values directly emerged from Emerson's experience of nondualism at the heart of the transcendental religion. According to Emerson, every person is "at some time sensible" of that pure nature that lies within, for it is like a dust-covered diamond waiting to be polished back to its true luster. "It is undefinable, unmeasurable," he explains, and it "pervades and contains us."

In terms of the present study, the most significant consequence of this profound experience of unity that accompanies the realization of the Over-Soul is the resulting moral rectification that radiates outward from the individual to society. Emerson explains that when the experience of unity "breathes through his intellect, it is genius; when it breathes through his will, it is virtue; when it flows through his affection, it is love." Once the Over-Soul is encountered, "all right action is submission," and speech arises naturally from the quality of one's character. In unity with the Over-Soul, one's nature opens to the attributes of God: Justice, Love, Freedom, and Power.[25] By contrast, the individual who never realizes unity with the Over-Soul is endlessly stirred by passion, hatred, fear, admiration, and pity, all of which result in "competition, persuasion, cities and war."[26]

The excerpt that follows from Emerson's Divinity School Address succinctly outlines the moral values that take root in the individual who opens himself to the transcendental experience:

> Thus in the soul of man there is a justice whose retributions are instant and entire. He who does a good deed is instantly ennobled. He who does a mean deed is by the action itself contracted. He who puts off impurity, thereby puts on purity. If a man is at heart just, then in so far is he God; the safety of God, the immortality of God, the majesty of God do enter into that man with justice. If a man dissemble, deceive, he deceives himself, and goes out of acquaintance with his own being. A man in the view of absolute goodness, adores, with total humility. Every step so downward, is a step upward. The man who renounces himself, comes to himself.

By way of this simple formulation, Emerson directly connects the morality of the individual to the justness of society as a whole. As the individual seeks the Over-Soul, and is purified by the transcendental vision of unity that accompanies it, his relationships with others are transformed from competition and enmity to compassion and forbearance. "The perception of this law of laws," Emerson explains, also "awakens in the mind a sentiment which we call the religious sentiment, which makes our highest happiness." Crucially, for Emerson this "sentiment lies at the foundation of society."[27]

In this respect, the "Transcendentalists were also involved in more radical attempts to alter the American political and economic system by establishing new alternatives to it." In *Walden or Life in the Woods* (1854), Henry David Thoreau chronicles his two years of living as independently as possible by testing "the virtues of strict economy" and learning "the study of nature, and the contemplative life." Thoreau's experiment, although a solitary one, inspired others to establish intentional communities. In fact, it eventually gave rise to a proliferation of them in the United States during the late nineteenth century (from which point it fed the idealism of the Progressive Era). Brook Farm, for instance, was a utopian communal agricultural experiment that sought to "combine manual and intellectual labor" in an attempt to overcome "class divisions between the laborer and the intellectual."[28] The income needed to sustain the community came from the sale of hand-made goods and from a school that educated individuals of all ages. By the 1840s, the Brook Farm community adopted some of the ideas of the utopian socialist Charles Fourier. Although the community declined quickly after initiating the prerequisite reforms, it did serve as a model for many later communities in the United States that followed Fourier's general ideas.[29]

While the utopian impulse in America during the 1840s manifested itself "in the advocacy of Fourieristic communities," during the latter half of the nineteenth century and into the Progressive Era that impulse turned literary. More than forty utopian novels appeared between 1885 and 1900. Both Christians and utopian socialists alike "repudiated the doctrine of class struggle and maintained that collectivism could be realized through education and political and religious appeals" based on a shared belief in the goodness of human nature and the power of love to transform society. Perhaps none of these literary works was more popular than Edward Bellamy's *Looking Backward* (1887). As Merle Curti observes, no book "since *Uncle Tom's Cabin* had appealed so widely to the American idealism as Bellamy's romance."[30]

Readers familiar with the plot of *Looking Backward* will recall that Julian West falls asleep in 1887 and reawakens in the year 2000 to a radically transformed Boston, Massachusetts. Crime, war, class struggle, competition, and other social ills have been eliminated, and the state now "guarantees the nurture, education, and comfortable maintenance of every citizen from the cradle to the grave." The millennial Boston is a "new world blessed with plenty, purified by justice and sweetened by brotherly kindness."[31] With the abolition of social inequality, the innate goodness latent in human nature can find expression for the first time in history. All humankind comes together in a kind of Messianic brotherhood that requires duty and service to achieve a harmonious social order. "Humanity's ancient dream of liberty, equality, fraternity, mocked by so many ages," declares Mr. Barton in his Sunday sermon, "at last was realized."[32]

In the rhetoric of hope, Barack Obama makes masterful use of many of these idealistic traditions that on American soil were transformed into a powerful vision of social mobility based on the content of character and the force of shared values. Obama conflates individual and national character in a manner similar to Washington and other Founding Fathers in his campaign rhetoric. Indeed, Obama's rhetoric overflows with moral values traditionally associated with the myth of the American Dream, whether cited in the context of Judeo-Christian notions of a Promised Land, the nation's founding documents, or its slave narratives. The remainder of this chapter will be dedicated to examining the values at the heart of the rhetoric of hope in the context of the myth of the American Dream. Like Washington and Emerson before him, Obama maintains that just as the individual may transform himself through the force of moral values, likewise so must the nation. The relationship between the two is highly synergistic: individual morality advances social progress just as immorality conversely results in social decay.

Barack Obama often quotes Martin Luther King's belief that the "arc of the moral universe is long but it bends toward justice." This aphorism implies a shared hope in social amelioration, and it suggests that progress comes about when moral values are put into practice. Employing the religious language of the Pilgrims (who brought with them a dream of freedom and opportunity to the New World), Obama calls for "a new American social compact" that, if honored, would "point the way to a better future for our children and grandchildren." Like utopian thinkers throughout history, Obama recognizes a gap between the ideal and the actual, between "our professed ideals as a nation and the reality we witness every day."[33] Yet, rather than offering the moral imperatives and platitudes of the religious right and so-called compassionate conservatives, Obama roots his moral appeals in more widely held American values culled from its own past. We can easily recognize those Obamian values at this point in our study. In his own words, they are "self-reliance and self-improvement and risk-taking. The values of drive, discipline, temperance, and hard work. The values of thrift and personal responsibility."[34]

Obama's use of the term "self-reliance" deliberately evokes American icons, like Franklin and Emerson, just as "self-improvement," "discipline," "hard work" conjure those of Washington and Lincoln. Words like "temperance" and "risk-taking" deliberately allude to a Puritanical streak in the American consciousness still recognizable in some contemporary social-conservative movements. This adept use of both secular and religious values in the rhetoric of hope should not surprise, as the very nation itself was founded in the tension between church and state. The constitutional separation of these two impulses has resulted in a feeling of disenfranchisement among some religious conservatives that remains palpable even today. Indeed, the First Amendment Establishment Clause still creates controversy in American political life (for instance in the 2005 Supreme Court decision to ban a display of the Ten Commandments in Kentucky's McCreary County, while ruling concurrently that a similar one outside the State Capitol in Austin, Texas, could stand).

Perhaps as a result of his study of the law at Harvard University, the rhetoric of hope demonstrates Obama's keen understanding of the influence that religious and secular traditions had on the nation's founding documents and subsequent development. Indeed, in the rhetoric of hope, the idealized values that Americans share are portrayed as transcending sectarian political and religious ideology. Ideology, for Obama, tends to override "whatever facts call theory into question." In other words, ideology is blind to reality. Strict ideological adherence results in the "mind-forg'd manacles" that the great poet-painter William Blake referred to in his *Songs of Innocence and Experience* (1789–1794).

By contrast, Obama secularizes the "golden rule." That ethic of reciprocity becomes, for Obama, a "call to stand in somebody else's shoes and see through their eyes." Obama explains that the values he champions "are rooted in a basic optimism about life and a faith in free will," and that they demonstrate a uniquely American "confidence that through pluck and sweat and smarts, each of us can rise above the circumstances of our birth." Here we recognize the influence of the American Dream on the values lauded in the rhetoric of hope. Obama believes that "these values also express a broader confidence that so long as individual men and women are free to pursue their own interests, society as a whole will prosper."[35] Note here again Obama's conflation of individual natural rights with the prosperity of society (one which we have seen has clear antecedents in American history).

In the rhetoric of hope, Obama makes the case that the American system of self-government and its free market economy depend on the majority of Americans adhering to these shared values. He extends that argument further by asserting that the very "legitimacy of our government and economy depend on the degree to which these values are rewarded." American values like equal opportunity and nondiscrimination enhance rather than diminish the liberty by which the nation defines itself. Americans, Obama seems to suggest, simultaneously hold individualistic and communal values, in addition to those with religious and secular origins. These competing interests should be balanced.

The following passage from *Audacity of Hope* clearly explicates the tension between these poles of American experience: "Our individualism has always been bound by a set of communal values, the glue upon which every healthy society depends. We value the imperatives of family and the cross-generational obligations that family implies. We value community, the neighborliness that expresses itself through raising the barn or coaching the soccer team. We value patriotism and the obligations of citizenship, a sense of duty and sacrifice on behalf of our nation. We value a faith in something bigger than ourselves, whether that something expresses itself in formal religion or ethical precepts. And we value the constellation of behaviors that express our mutual regard for one another: honesty, fairness, humility, kindness, courtesy, and compassion."[36] By articulating this relationship between the individual and society, Obama recognizes that the positive values of self-reliance and independence can decay into selfishness, just as the healthy ambition needed to succeed can deteriorate into base greed when those shared values are abandoned in the quest for individual gain. Obama seeks equilibrium between the competing allegiances of the individual and the society in which he lives, although he realizes that "finding the right balance between our competing values is difficult."

This balancing of public and private interests, of the sacred and secular, defines the American experiment in democracy. The "promise of America — the idea that we are responsible for ourselves, but that we also rise or fall as one nation" remains, for Obama, a defining principle of the country. Indeed, this passage illustrates an interweaving of a rhetoric of individualism with that of biblical charity in Obamian discourse. Obama declares that together individual responsibility and mutual responsibility are "the essence of America's promise." Obama's use of the word "promise" here evokes both the religious conception of covenant as well as the promise of "life, liberty, and the pursuit of happiness" enshrined in the nation's secular founding documents.[37]

Although committed to a notion, which he inherited from Franklin Roosevelt, that government has a positive role to play in shaping American culture for the better, Obama nevertheless acknowledges the need to limit government intrusion into the lives of its citizenry. He admits that "this idea of communal values, our sense of mutual responsibility and social solidarity" should find expression "not just in the church or mosque or synagogue," or our workplaces and in our families, "but also through our government."[38] In his speech accepting the Democratic nomination for the presidency, entitled "The American Promise," Obama writes that what makes America exceptional is "that through hard work and sacrifice, each of us can pursue our individual dreams but still come together as one American family, to ensure that the next generation can pursue their dreams as well."[39] Likewise, in his victory speech in November 2008, Obama declares his election a shining example of American democracy in action. Deploying utopian rhetoric, he prophetically promises that through the adoption of shared values, "we as a people will get there."

The shared values of patriotism, service, responsibility, and opportunity for Obama constitute the foundation of an American form of democracy in which the strength of the nation lies not in military might but in moral rectitude. Augmenting those shared values in his subsequent January 2009 Inaugural Address, Obama cites the need for governmental justice, humility, and restraint alongside the individual altruistic values of kindness, selflessness, tolerance, and duty. "For as much as government can do and must do, it is ultimately the faith and determination of the American people upon which this nation relies. It is the kindness to take in a stranger when the levees break, the selflessness of workers who would rather cut their hours than see a friend lose their job, which sees us through our darkest hours. It is the firefighter's courage to storm a stairway filled with smoke, but also a parent's willingness to nurture a child, that finally decides our fate."[40]

Joel Kotkin, writing for *Forbes* just a few days after the election of Barack Obama in 2008, observes that for a generation, social conservatives "held a lock on the so-called 'values' issue. But Barack Obama is slowly picking that lock, breaking into one of the GOP's last remaining electoral

treasures."[41] The values-based appeals in the rhetoric of hope not only draw from American history, but put focus on that most besieged of American institutions: the nuclear family. In a Father's Day address at the Apostolic Church of God in Chicago, Obama notes that the family unit remains "the rock upon which we build our lives." Singling out the African American community, he notes that "children who grow up without a father are five times more likely to live in poverty and commit crime; nine times more likely to drop out of schools; and twenty times more likely to end up in prison." Obama asks black fathers to realize that it "is not the ability to have a child" that makes one a man, but "the courage to raise one." It remains up to parents to instill the American "ethic of excellence in our children." Parents must at once model and laud the values of "achievement, self-respect, and hard work."[42]

In the rhetoric of hope, Barack Obama insists that the principle of empathy must be passed along to the younger generation, for in it one finds the balance point between the needs of the individual and the welfare of society as a whole. "Not sympathy, but empathy — the ability to stand in somebody else's shoes" is required lest we embrace that American tradition of individualism too earnestly and learn to equate kindness with weakness. Individualism not firmly grounded in moral values degenerates into selfishness, avarice, and the exploitation of others for personal gain. Obama recounts his own realization of this shift in perception from the individual to the family (and by extension, the community): "When I was a young man, I thought life was all about me ... how do I become successful and how do I get the things that I want. But now," Obama explains, "my life revolves around my two little girls. And what I think about is what kind of world I'm leaving them."[43]

In this chapter, we encountered yet another unique feature of the rhetoric of hope: its equation of individual virtue with the advancement of society. As the individual turns from selfishness and cultivates empathy, an attitudinal transformation takes place and results in greater harmony within the family unit. That familial harmony, when informed by the proper values, radiates outward into one's immediate community. From there, it moves through society as a whole, and it eventually transforms the world. Such is the "soft power" of values in the rhetoric of hope. As Obama explains in his June 2006 address to the Call to Renewal conference, "The problems of poverty and racism, the uninsured and the unemployed, are not simply technical problems in search of the perfect ten

point plan. They are rooted in both societal indifference and individual callousness—in the imperfections of man."[44]

Since presidential elections are about character, they therefore ultimately concern the values that determine the content of it. In his rhetoric of hope, Barack Obama constructs a narrative of his own life that closely parallels aspects of the mythic stories the nation tells about itself. Speaking at the 2008 Democratic National Convention in Denver, Michelle Obama made this connection explicit. Using her husband as an example, she gave voice to the need for a set of individual values that are congruent with those necessary for social amelioration:

> Barack and I were raised with so many of the same values: that you work hard for what you want in life; that your word is your bond and you do what you say you're going to do; that you treat people with dignity and respect, even if you don't know them, and even if you don't agree with them.
>
> And Barack and I set out to build lives guided by these values, and pass them on to the next generation. Because we want our children — and all children in this nation — to know that the only limit to the height of your achievements is the reach of your dreams and your willingness to work for them.

The word "work" appears two times in this short excerpt. It is a term that we have seen associated with the values held by the first American settlers and passed down to future generations. When put into practice, those values bring with them the promise of equal opportunity in a society where advancement is based on merit.

In her convention address, Michelle Obama noted that her husband practices the values of community service and hard work that feature so prominently in his rhetoric of hope. Instead of "heading to Wall Street," she explains, Barack went "to work in neighborhoods devastated when steel plants shut down, and jobs dried up." Recounting a talk that he gave to these residents regarding the rebuilding of their communities, she notes the utopianism that even then filled his rhetoric:

> Barack stood up that day, and spoke words that have stayed with me ever since. He talked about "The world as it is" and "The world as it should be." And he said that all too often, we accept the distance between the two, and settle for the world as it is—even when it doesn't reflect our values and aspirations. But he reminded us that we know what our world should look like. We know what fairness and justice and opportunity look like. And he urged us to believe in ourselves—to find the strength within ourselves to strive for the world as it should be. And isn't that the great American story?[45]

Here again we encounter the utopian dialectic between the ideal and the actual—the dream and the stark reality in Obamian discourse. Indeed, the rhetoric of hope is steeped in idealistic traditions that were concretized in the nation's founding documents and are reiterated in the mythic stories that Americans identify with regarding social mobility, individual freedom, community obligation, and equal opportunity.

Sadly, it must be conceded that real life for many millions of American citizens does not remotely correspond to the ideal of prosperity and upward mobility found in the myth of the American Dream. In this context, I am reminded of Bigger Thomas' exchange with Gus in *Native Son*: "'I *could* fly a plane if I had a chance,' Bigger said. 'If you wasn't black and if you had some money and if they'd let you go to that aviation school, you *could* fly a plane,' Gus said." Too often in the history of the United States individuals such as Bigger have confronted the tragic irony of living in a country that promises equality and freedom but limits access to it. Moreover, having taught overseas for many years, I know firsthand the misplaced idealism that many people around the world have in the promise of freedom that for them defines the American experiment. Yet, even so, the founding principles of "Life, Liberty and the pursuit of Happiness" speak universally to humankind across the borders of race, religion, language, and geography. Before turning to that universalism, which the rhetoric of hope appropriates from the "great American story," let us consider the ways in which Barack Obama deliberately constructs a prophetic narrative persona and then overlays it onto American history.

CHAPTER SEVEN

Constructing the Narrative Persona

Just like any writing subject, Barack Obama creates an ideal image of himself for the reading public in the books and speeches that propelled him to the presidency in 2008. In *Dreams from My Father*, for instance, he brings together the events of his life through the power of memory and reconstitutes them as a meaningful narrative focused around an idealized self. For the purposes of persuasion, he models that persona after character types found in the tradition of American autobiographical writing and in the country's national mythologies. Obama's narrative persona also has prophetic dimensions, in that it constantly beckons toward the utopian promise of continual betterment celebrated in the nation's founding documents. During the 2008 presidential campaign, "Obama was new and he was hopeful and he projected change," but most importantly, "he had a better narrative" than John McCain.[1]

A carefully constructed narrative persona holds together the disparate ideological threads from which Obama's rhetoric of hope is woven. Traditionally, the term "persona" denoted a mask that an actor wore in ancient Greece to distinguish the roles that he would play on the stage. Although possessing nuanced meanings in disciplines such as literature, media studies, and psychology, today we generally understand persona to mean an idealized construction of one's self presented in spoken or written discourse. Persona can also be thought of as the image that we create of ourselves for public consumption. It is, as T.S. Eliot suggests, preparing "a face to meet the faces that you meet." During a job interview, for instance, one creates an idealized version of self by putting forward positive features and relegating to the background those that are less becoming. In this

124

sense, most of us adopt various personae for the many social contexts in which we find ourselves every day. At church or in temple, my public mask may denote sanctity or piousness, while out on the sports field a more aggressive and competitive self is on view.

As in all autobiographical writing, Barack Obama creates a narrative persona that embodies a set of beliefs encoded in a system of cultural values. We have seen that Abraham Lincoln and his biographers, for instance, constructed a narrative of success in which a stock American character type is grounded in larger cultural masterplots. This American type is heroic, successful, useful, moral, and future-oriented. In fact, autobiography has become "a characteristic form of American expression," one that can be traced back to early settlers like William Bradford and John Winthrop. Together with other influential autobiographers (Henry David Thoreau, Mark Twain, and Henry Adams, for example), these and other writers helped to construct an idealized version of the American character based on a mythic narrative of self-reliance.

Not surprisingly, American political autobiography (a tradition stretching from John Smith to Benjamin Franklin to Malcolm X) also tends to feature a "rise from the status of the unknown and inarticulate" to "the known individual that most Americans would like to be." As a result, one scholar suggests, such authors should be considered among the "leading architects of the American character."[2] Typically in political autobiography, the candidate was "born in poverty, rose up through hard work, knows the value of a dollar, yet is compassionate, cares for his mother, etc.—just the *type* you want in government. As always, there is a selection of *masterplots* to go with such types."[3] Masterplots are stories that we tell ourselves repeatedly, in a myriad of subtly different forms that connect with our deepest values, wishes, and fears. In American culture, the Horatio Alger narrative of success through hard work epitomizes such a master narrative. As a consequence, the American tradition of autobiography "renders in a peculiarly direct and faithful way the experience and the vision of a people, which is the same experience and the same vision lying behind and informing all the literature of that people."[4]

Obama's rhetoric of hope certainly features this kind of rise from obscurity to fame, and he further cultivates an image of goodwill toward the electorate by constructing a persona whose life story resembles quintessential American "masterplots" familiar to his implied audience. Political autobiographies by still active politicians, like those written by Obama, often feature a reconstruction of life events that seem too good to be true. This kind of overtly political life writing often excludes events in a politician's life that could contradict the desired image. Therefore, in order to be persuasive and effective in writing political autobiography, one must first establish narrative reliability. Out of the dustbin of memory, the author must reconstitute the events of his life into a compelling story and create an authoritative persona seen by the reader as possessing the values with which the country (rightly or wrongly) identifies itself. In this sense, life writing is always performative and truth gets refigured from the perspective of the speaking persona.

Politically motived autobiographical writing must be believable, or it risks being over-idealized and loses credibility. The reader will recall that slave narratives, a distinct form of American political autobiography, often employed paratextual materials (such as testimonials and historical documents) to enhance credibility. These slave narratives were also grounded in masterplots of Judeo-Christian deliverance from bondage and American ideals of freedom and equality. In the rhetoric of hope, Obama constructs his narrative persona based on features derived from stock literary types, and then he aligns that persona with broader cultural narratives for the purpose of persuasion.

A narrative persona is fictionalized in the act of sorting through the events of the past and selectively reconstituting them. Moreover, the story that the persona tells gets flattened (a normative function) in the retelling, which partly explains the experience of autobiography often seeming "too good to be true." Part of the challenge in writing political autobiography is to construct a persona, an idealized version of self, which is believable to a majority of the electorate. In the rhetoric of hope, Obama accomplishes this task by imparting to the reader the impression that he possesses a strong moral character through his association with virtuous goals, including the protection of the most vulnerable from exploitation by the rich and powerful through government regulation, moral striving for a better future, a fierce individualism tempered by an obligation to community betterment, and to liberty and justice for all.

Often in his writing, Obama describes himself as a biracial child, raised by a single mother, who through the force of hard work and moral fortitude becomes a United States senator before ascending to the presidency as the first African American to hold that post. In his politically motivated campaign book, *Change We Can Believe In*, Obama writes:

I know the toll that being a single parent took on my mother — how she struggled at times to pay the bills; to give us the things that other kids had; to play
all the roles that both parents are supposed to play. And I know the toll it took
on me. So I resolved many years ago that it was my obligation to break the
cycle — that if I could be anything in life, I would be a good father to my girls;
that if I could give them anything, I would give them that rock — that foundation — on which to build their lives. And that would be the greatest gift I could
offer.[5]

This "ethos" (the interplay of good sense, morality, and goodwill that an
audience attributes to the speaker) makes the persona believable and is
essential to effective persuasion. "Americans today," Jodi Cohen suggests,
"seem to rely on ethos more than on other dimensions of meaning."[6]
Obama puts shared values and goodwill toward others at the center of his
rhetoric of hope. Without question, one reason for the success of Obama's
2008 presidential campaign is his development of a persona interpretable
by the reader and listener as sympathetic to the core values of the national
community.

As noted in a previous chapter, Barack Obama has been an avid reader
of fiction since he was a young man. Perhaps he understood early in his
life the uniquely human need for narrative (and the ordering effect that
it brings with it). Indeed, this impulse is so strong that we arguably cannot
understand anything unless it is presented in the form of a story. Certainly
our national myths rely on this ordering effect, for they are formed through
the selection of certain memories from the nation's past (and the rejection
of others), and then they are re-presented in narrative form. A nation creates an idealized version of itself through its narratives. By way of example,
in *Dreams from My Father*, Obama explains that while working as a community organizer on the South Side of Chicago, he came to see that
"beneath the small talk and sketchy biographies and received opinions"
of everyday life, these "people carried within them some central explanation of themselves." Obama grasps immediately the fact that the "central
explanation of themselves" he was hearing from his constituents took narrative form. In time, he comes to call them "sacred stories" for they were
"full of terror and wonder, studded with events that still haunted or
inspired them." These were the stories that people told themselves over
the course of generations, and they shaped both individual and collective
identity.

One might therefore say that Barack Obama learned to come to grips with his own identity through the power of the story. While working as a community organizer, he unconsciously sought to create a persona that accounted for the various strands of his lived experience. At first, he felt that his own prior life at elite universities "would be too foreign for South Side sensibilities." Instead, he found that as people listened to his "stories of Toot or Lolo or my mother and father, of flying kites in Djakarta or going to school dances in Punahou, they would nod their heads or shrug or laugh, wondering how someone with my background had ended up, as Mona put it, so 'country-fied,' or most puzzling to them, why anyone would willingly choose to spend a winter in Chicago when he could be sunning himself on Waikiki Beach."

As Obama worked through the narrative of his own life, selecting and retelling aspects of it to others, he noticed his listeners would often offer a story "to match or confound" his own, and that that reciprocal narrative became "a knot to bind our experiences together — a lost father, an adolescent brush with crime, a wandering heart, a moment of simple grace." The effect of this discovery cannot be underestimated, for it culminates in a realization that had important implications for what would become the rhetoric of hope: "As time passed," Obama writes, "I found that these stories, taken together, had helped me bind my world together, that they gave me the sense of place and purpose I'd been looking for."[7] Obama learns, by writing out his own seemingly unique biography, that his story was actually very much an American one.

In arranging the elements of his own story, and constructing a narrative persona to tell it, Obama reaches back into his memories of childhood and adolescence. By 2004, in a preface to a new edition of *Dreams from My Father*, Obama can joke about himself without irony as a "black man with a funny name" who became only the third African American "since Reconstruction — to serve in the Senate." It is not just his decision to identify himself as black in this quotation, rather than as white or biracial, that is striking. Nor is it the fact that *Dreams from My Father* first appears in 1995 just as he begins his professional career, and therefore is self-consciously political (although to a lesser degree than *Audacity of Hope*). Rather, in that 2004 preface, Obama states that he originally wrote *Dreams* with the "belief that the story of my family and my efforts to understand that story might speak in some way to the fissures of race that have characterized the American experience."

The act of writing autobiography is one of self-creation. By writing,

Obama places his own story into a continuum of racial struggle for justice in American history. He discovers in the act of selecting and rejecting elements of his biography that he could simultaneously tap national narratives of American exceptionalism. He thereby overlays his own life story on top of the idealistic, even utopian, national myths that we have inherited. In this manner, he gains a powerful rhetorical tool by using common American tropes to persuade the electorate that he can be trusted, despite his "funny name." As the keynote speaker at the 2004 Democratic National Convention, Obama neatly summarized those aspects of his lived experience that he found accorded with the myth of the American Dream: "My father was a foreign student, born and raised in a small village in Kenya. He grew up herding goats, went to school in a tin-roof shack. His father — my grandfather — was a cook, a domestic servant to the British."

In this speech, Obama constructs a narrative frame that provides him with the lowly origin needed to tap the American myth of upward mobility. In doing so, he idealizes his own life based on recognizable types in American autobiography for the purpose of political persuasion. He does not acknowledge those aspects of his life story that would jeopardize that carefully cultivated image (for example that his father is actually "descended from a long line of Luo tribal warriors").[8] Instead, he chooses to focus on the idealism that this African grandfather possessed and that led him to labor incessantly to send his son (Barack's father) to the "Promised Land" of America to study. Obama explains, "my grandfather had larger dreams for his son. Through hard work and perseverance my father got a scholarship to study in a magical place, America, that shone as a beacon of freedom and opportunity to so many who had come before." Through such rhetorical devices, Obama deftly aligns his father, a Kenyan national, with the immigrant tradition on which the United States was founded.

In this context, Obama's 2004 keynote address is also important because it takes his book-length autobiography and distills it to an easily digestible meme designed to evoke key events in the American experience. It therefore reinforces his "American-ness." Obama explains that while studying in the United States, his father met his mother: "She was born in a town on the other side of the world, in Kansas. Her father worked on oil rigs and farms through most of the Depression. The day after Pearl Harbor my grandfather signed up for duty; joined Patton's army, marched across Europe. Back home, my grandmother raised a baby and went to work on a bomber assembly line. After the war, they studied on the G.I. Bill, bought a house through F.H.A., and later moved west all the way to Hawaii in search of opportunity." In this passage, Kansas evokes the traditional American values associated with the heartland, while references to the Great Depression, Pearl Harbor, and Patton all suggest shared historical suffering (despite the fact that these events took place before Obama's birth). Other references to the G.I. Bill and the pursuit of opportunity evoke the American promise of a "more perfect union."

In this speech, and in the rhetoric of hope more generally, Obama employs the signs and signifiers of certain strands of idealism found in the cultural myth of the American Dream. As one scholar explains, understanding "the variety of connections between signifiers and signifieds helps us realize the richness of meaning." Flags flying in the background as a president speaks, for example, have denotative and symbolic meaning. This process of making meaningful connections between flags and the patriotism of the person standing in front of them can happen either consciously or unconsciously.[9] In the passage above, Obama uses signs and signifiers, like the Great Depression and Pearl Harbor, to make symbolic connections between himself and American cultural myths of opportunity, morality, and freedom.

Weaving the facts of his life into a persuasive narrative, Barack Obama explains that his parents "shared not only an improbable love, they shared an abiding faith in the possibilities of this nation. They would give me an African name, Barack, or 'blessed,' believing that in a tolerant America your name is no barrier to success. They imagined — they imagined me going to the best schools in the land, even though they weren't rich, because in a generous America you don't have to be rich to achieve your potential." His story, he argues, is simply the American story rewritten for an age of multiculturalism and globalization. "I stand here knowing that my story is part of the larger American story, that I owe a debt to all of those who came before me, and that, in no other country on earth, is my story even possible."[10] In the rhetoric of hope, Obama deftly weaves the story of his own life, itself an act of narrative construction, out of fragments of memory (many of which were familial and handed down to him).

By way of illustration, in *Dreams from My Father*, Obama shares a collective memory that signifies "the morality tale that my father's life had become. According to the story, after long hours of study, my father had joined my grandfather and several friends at a local Waikiki bar." When someone complained of having to drink "next to a nigger," Obama's father, so the story goes, lectured, not fought the man. So convincing was this lesson that the offender reached into his own pocket and gave him "a hundred dollars," then paid the bar tab and the rent of the Kenyan student "for the rest of the month."[11] A tall tale, almost certainly, yet this inherited memory of an absent and little known father presented Obama with a story to use in the construction of his narrative persona. The signs and signifiers in this story suggest that although a self-identified black man, Obama prefers dialogue and rational discourse to a rehashing of the bleak legacy of racism in the United States. This passage also indicates Obama's understanding that his narrative persona should appear conciliatory and not angry or confrontational, since he was running for the presidency on a platform of hope and change.

Richard Wolffe has noted this tendency for Obama to string stories together in his rhetoric of hope. He observes that Obama's "narrative, his collection of people and their tales, seems to take the place of the stable family he never enjoyed" in his youth. Wolffe reports once overhearing Obama remark to a photographer: "All my life, I have been stitching together a family, through stories or memories or friends or ideas."[12] This insightful admission by Obama speaks at once to the force of the American stories that shaped his rhetoric of hope into an idealistic discourse with recognizable historical antecedents, as well as to the act of consciously constructing a narrative persona out of the fragments of his life story. That persona is tolerant and inclusive, good willed, steeped in the idealism that permeates the country's national myths, and it is constructed from a kaleidoscope of stories about progress toward individual and social perfectibility.

As Richard Sorabji points out, the idea of progress has appeal in religious as well as secular contexts and can be historically traced from Homer to the present day in the Western world.[13] In the rhetoric of hope, Obama's appropriation of American conceptions of progress and perfectibility following Jefferson, Lincoln, and Franklin Roosevelt allows him to fabricate a narrative persona that shares with his implied audience a pattern of national values that include forward-looking optimism and belief in a brighter tomorrow. Obama seems to have intuitively sensed early in his career that "the power of a story—or the combination of stories—would be central to his book writing and speechwriting."[14] In the course of time, he would learn to recontextualize American masterplots to create an idealized image of himself based on textually encoded possibilities.

By the time that he delivered his acceptance speech for the Democratic Party nomination for president in 2008, Barack Obama had long used speechwriters out of sheer necessity. Disappointed with a second draft submitted by them, he rewrote it over three nights to include the story that he wanted to tell.[15] It was one cobbled together from anecdotes told by those he met on the campaign trail and mixed with selected portions of his own biography. Obama found that the "sacred stories" he heard while canvassing actually corresponded with his own, so he made his campaign about "people from diverse backgrounds and unlikely places finding a common culture and a common set of values and ideals that make them American."[16] He constructed a narrative persona from the fractured elements of his life that implicitly embodied those American values. His biography became an American biography, and his persona gave shape to a new ideal of America for the twenty-first century. By highlighting "the fluid state of identity — the leaps through time, the collision of cultures — that mark our modern life," Barack Obama transforms his American story into a human one with universal dimension and appeal. Employing this idealized story of his life, Obama highlights the promise that America still holds at a time when its national narratives are increasingly globalized and collectivized.

The political consultant David Axelrod helped Obama to hone his political rhetoric to capture that life story. Axelrod noted immediately that Obama "embodied the impossible — a black community organizer who could rise up from obscurity and win a United States Senate seat." Moreover, his résumé included information "that would resonate with journalists and voters." About the time of his acceptance speech for that senate seat, the slogan "Yes We Can" crept into the rhetoric of hope, despite Obama's initial rejection of it as "a bit of a cliché."[17] However, "Yes, we can" would prove a clever turn of phrase that engaged his emerging rhetoric of hope in many ways. Two scholars of political rhetoric note the open nature of that trope, which invites, not closes, discursive possibility. Heavily citing Obama's speech conceding the New Hampshire primary to Hillary Clinton, they write:

> "Yes We Can" was the "spirit of a people" and the "creed written into the founding documents that declared the destiny of a nation"; it was the call of "slaves and abolitionists," workers, women suffragists, and immigrants. Recalling the

responses made to Senator Clinton's charges about the distinction between speech and action, "Yes We Can" was the "call of ... a president who chose the moon as our new frontier and a king who took us to the mountaintop." "Yes We Can" was "said" to justice, equality, opportunity, and prosperity. It was argued that "We Can" "heal this nation" and "repair this world"; "Yes We Can" was to be the rallying cry as "we" "begin the next great chapter in the American story."

By situating himself thusly "within historical narratives of progress and change in America," Obama rhetorically positions himself as an agent of transformation through the careful construction of a narrative persona.[18]

Kloppenberg also emphasizes the need to understand Obama as "an accomplished storyteller" whose facility with political rhetoric gradually made him "capable of bringing complex ideas to life by embodying them in narratives" about himself, those around him, and the country as a whole.[19] Kloppenberg repeatedly points to an "acute self-consciousness" in Obama's political writing that enables him to "interrogate his own convictions" in the "broader cultural and historical context by imaginatively scrutinizing them from a position centuries in the future."[20] This rhetorical stance brings to light the prophetic qualities of Obama's narrative persona in the rhetoric of hope. We saw earlier that Obama makes use of the forward-looking tropes in Judeo-Christianity to evoke a journey of collective moral striving that leads to a Promised Land. His narrative persona beckons to that future and promises a new order to replace the status quo.

Autobiography is therefore an attempt to make meaning out of one's life, to create one's own mythic tale, stocked full of themes that outline the writer's guiding philosophies, moral values, and worldview. It is an imaginative re-creation of the past using symbolic images that continue to live after the death of the author, and in this sense, autobiography constitutes a kind of posthumous propaganda. Nowhere is this truer than in political discourse like the rhetoric of hope. As a result, there exists "a considerable gap between the avowed plan of an autobiography, which is simply to retrace the history of a life, and its deepest intentions, which are directed toward a kind of apologetics or theodicy of the individual being."[21] In *Dreams from My Father*, *The Audacity of Hope*, and in a majority of the 2008 campaign speeches that make up the rhetoric of hope, Barack Obama forges a narrative persona that vindicates the ideal of American social justice. It embodies a set of natural rights and universal values set forth in the nation's founding documents.

By way of example, in his 2008 Super Tuesday address to supporters, Obama strikes a prophetic chord in the opening lines of his speech before reaching crescendo and declaring an apocalyptic shift in the American political landscape. Still awaiting the results of the California poll, but seemingly ever optimistic nonetheless, Obama declares "there is one thing on this February night that we do not need the final results to know—our time has come, our movement is real, and change is coming to America." In a voice reminiscent of one of his heroes, Martin Luther King, Obama surveys the transformative impulse for change from on high. He explains that what "began as a whisper in Springfield soon carried across the corn fields of Iowa, where farmers and factory workers; students and seniors stood up in numbers we've never seen." The voices of these earnest souls, his persona assures the audience, have "echoed from the hills of New Hampshire to the deserts of Nevada, where teachers and cooks and kitchen workers stood up to say that maybe Washington doesn't have to be run by lobbyists anymore. They reached the coast of South Carolina when people said that maybe we don't have to be divided by race and region and gender."

From this survey of the growing discontentment with the status quo, Obama looks to the future, and in doing so he outlines a utopian vision of America. Unlike political rhetoric of the past that promises much but delivers little, Obama assures his implied audience that he shares the values that are the vehicle for reaching that better place, and that he will deliver on his vision: When I am president, he declares, "we will put an end to a politics that uses 9/11 as a way to scare up votes, and start seeing it as a challenge that should unite America and the world against the common threats of the twenty-first century: terrorism and nuclear weapons; climate change and poverty; genocide and disease." Obama urges those skeptical of his lofty idealism to realize that through collective struggle and sacrifice, through ethical striving, a new social order can be brought about. "So tonight," declares Obama, "I want to speak directly to all those Americans who have yet to join this movement but still hunger for change—we need you. We need you to stand with us, and work with us, and help us prove that together, ordinary people can still do extraordinary things." In one of the most arresting aphorisms found in Obama's rhetoric of hope, he prophetically declares the coming of that new social order: "We are the ones we've been waiting for. We are the change that we seek."

In the final paragraphs of this speech, Obama employs the cadences

134

and rhythms that we saw emerge out of the black church in the United States: "We are the hope of the father who goes to work before dawn and lies awake with doubts that tell him he cannot give his children the same opportunities that someone gave him.... We are the hope of the woman who hears that her city will not be rebuilt; that she cannot reclaim the life that was swept away in a terrible storm.... We are the hope of the future; the answer to the cynics who tell us our house must stand divided; that we cannot come together; that we cannot remake this world as it should be."[22] Barack Obama's political rhetoric rests on a notion of collective ethical striving toward an ideal order, a better place. This dialectical tension between the ideal and the existing orders makes historical progress possible. By projecting his utopian vision into the future, Obama creates a rhetorical gap between the ideal and the actual by which he critiques the shortcomings of America at the dawn of the twenty-first century. This dialectic also speaks to a conception of utopia understood as an historical unfolding. It is a notion of historical progress made possible through the hard work of continual improvement toward a more perfect union. In making these rhetorical moves, Obama aligns his persona with a prophetic tradition in Judeo-Christianity recognizable to a large segment of the American electorate.

In the rhetoric of hope, Obama therefore casts himself as a prophet of change situated by virtue of his unique American story to usher in a new global order (which will finally replace the tired status quo). Such a rhetorical move is in line with his embrace of the black church and the customary role of its preacher. That tradition appropriates prophetic figures like Samuel, Jeremiah, Amos, and Ezekiel who spoke truth to power out of divine inspiration and moral conviction simultaneously. These were not men who simply pointed toward the future; they spoke against the corruption and decay of the existing order. Above all else, theirs was a call to justice and peace, so they were willing to stand up against repression wherever it was found. One of Obama's central themes in the rhetoric of hope is the need to rectify the racial and economic injustices that continue to plague the United States (despite the idealistic promises encoded in the country's mythologies). In insisting on amelioration, the rhetoric of hope beckons to a new American order in which ideology matches social reality.

In his "A More Perfect Union" speech, the prophetic dimensions of Obama's narrative persona come to the fore. In that address, "Obama conflates the past and present" and highlights their inextricable nature by "showing the ways in which past ghosts of structural and attitudinal racial inequality and oppression still manifest in the present." The present moment, in which the injustices of the past are still palpable, becomes for Obama "a fulcrum of action for changing the future and remedying the injustices of the past." In his campaign rhetoric, Obama insists that the time is now for hope to be made manifest. This idea of the present moment as a temporal fulcrum is idealized in the 2008 slogan "Change We Can Believe In."[23]

By positioning himself thusly using "temporality and spatial metaphors, Obama imbues the present moment with a sense of urgent importance and empowerment, situating himself as a figure capable of narrowing racial divides and connecting the current state of the Union with the ideals upon which it was founded; he becomes the bridge to the 'more perfect union.'"[24] This observation by Sarah McCaffery is borne out by this more extended study of Obama's political rhetoric. However, it is imprecise to assert that Barack Obama "becomes" the bridge between the injustice of the past and the promise of the future; rather, he skillfully constructs a narrative persona that becomes that link. This is a crucial distinction and one that highlights the strong intentionality in the rhetoric of hope.

In his study of the iconography of the 2008 campaign, Robert Spicer recognizes Obama's use of "religiofication," or the "art of turning practical purposes into holy causes." Not exactly the same as deification, religiofication resists attributing immortal characteristics to its subject (in this case Obama), but is nevertheless a "potent tool for harnessing the energy of the body politic" and transforming the "disconnected individual citizen" into a "true believer" in both the message and messenger. Spicer cites the "Obamamania" that swept through the country in 2008 as proof of the effectiveness of that rhetorical maneuver. The prevalence of the "Obama-as-messiah meme" extends political rhetoric into the realm of the religious mass.[25] In that meme, Obama is a prophetic figure whose appearance on the world stage augurs the coming of a new order.

As M. Cooper Harriss correctly asserts, Obama's 2008 campaign rhetoric "succeeded in representing both a metaphorical and a literal return to a centripetal orientation of 'America' by expanding the concept of nation" to include a greater number of people. For Harriss, Obama's campaign rhetoric is "textbook Wesleyan theology adapted to an electoral context, one in which the choice in the voting booth corresponds to choices of eternal consequence. The political choice resonates with eschatological urgency. The salvation at stake does not belong to the individual but to the nation."[26] Obama turns himself into a prophet of change in the rhetoric of hope by drawing simultaneously on secular and religious traditions embedded in American consciousness.

Like all political discourse, the rhetoric of hope is an apparatus of political authority. As H. Porter Abbott notes, "*everything* in the text contributes to its impact and our interpretation of it, and so everything has some rhetorical function." Therefore, it is "no exaggeration" to call narrative "an instrument of power."[27] Obama's political discourse aims to persuade his ideal audience that he possesses character, has the strength to lead, and that he shares the values by which the nation defines itself and from which its citizens derive their identity. To that end, both of his books and most of the 2008 campaign speeches are highly autobiographical and rely on a communicating persona that gives the written and spoken text power and authority. Along with its aforementioned intertextuality, this narrative persona is one of the most persuasive aspects of the rhetoric of hope.

As we have seen, autobiography is an act of self-creation and a bringing into consciousness, as much as it is a reconstruction of the past. In political autobiography the narrative persona tends to be even more highly idealized than in other forms of life writing. From the earliest iterations of the rhetoric of hope in *Dreams from My Father*, through the highly polemical *Audacity of Hope*, and into the 2008 and 2012 campaign speeches, Obama devises a persona that employs easily recognizable symbolic images of hope and national tropes of freedom. In doing so, he consciously places himself in an American masterplot of the self-made man who through hard work rises from obscurity into prominence where he can effect social transformation. Narratives such as these feature individuals who find success by reinventing themselves. In writing their new selves into existence, the Founding Fathers gave a fledgling nation a set of "sacred stories" about itself. The autobiographies of Franklin, Douglass, Malcolm X, and many more like them, helped to define the contours of the American experience by offering cultural narratives that are at once distinctive, yet also imply a form of universalism. In short, they offer direct access to that experience so that readers might share in their vision.[28]

Barack Obama reworks his own life story in the rhetoric of hope to correspond to easily recognizable American myths. By deploying a persona who shares a set of secular and religious beliefs and aspirations, Obama convinced an American electorate weary of wars in Iraq and Afghanistan to take a chance on a "black man with a funny name" in 2008. He combined his own personal story with American narratives as well as the anecdotes he acquired while campaigning. The result is a narrative persona that epitomizes American moral values and cultural myths in order to establish credibility and persuade. By way of illustration, Jonathan Alter notes the manner in which Obama skillfully deployed signs and signifiers from American history, specifically those of his hero Abraham Lincoln. During his inauguration, Obama "used the same train route to the capital as Lincoln had, swore the oath on Lincoln's Bible, and made sure the luncheon in the Capitol served the same menu served at the Inauguration of 1861" using "replicas of Mary Todd Lincoln's china." Obama's brief comments at the start of those inaugural ceremonies focused on unity and "the voices of men and women who have different stories but hold common hopes."

As Alter observes, Obama's "emphasis on storytelling and hope" has proven "remarkably consistent" since the beginning of his 2008 presidential campaign.[29] Obama uses the prophetic aspects of his narrative persona to beckon his audience toward the future with optimism and hope. In this sense, he makes himself a figure of transition from the status quo to that "more perfect" union of the future. Indeed, so remarkable is Obama's thematic consistency that his 2012 campaign rhetoric wields similar tropes and evokes similar themes based around hope and yearning. Before considering that speculation in more detail, let us turn now to the international reach of Obama's prophetic persona, for the rhetoric of hope offers not just national renewal—it promises a new global order.

CHAPTER EIGHT

Universalism, Globalization and the Multicultural Utopia

As the two previous chapters have shown, Barack Obama grounds the rhetoric of hope in moral values that have secular and religious roots in American history. Yet, the rhetoric of hope has intentional appeal beyond national borders, since it essentially extends the "American Promise" of freedom and equality to human beings the world over. With the benefit of hindsight, we see that Barack Obama was not only the clear choice for American voters in 2008, he was the candidate most favored by citizens and governments around the globe. One reason for this broad appeal lies in the universal dimensions of the rhetoric of hope.

Because Immigrants from countries around the world made the United States their home, the nation's mythologies of upward mobility and forward-looking optimism naturally grew out of their need to celebrate that mixed cultural and ethnic heritage. This emphasis on culture (over race or ethnicity) as the primary signifier of identity encourages inclusivity and increased representation for minorities. Unlike race and ethnicity, which tend to resist transformation, culture can be shared and transmuted since it does not define identity based on origin but rather on shared practice or social contract.[1] In the rhetoric of hope, Obama repeatedly points to this multicultural experience as a defining feature of the American experiment, and while he does not want to export American culture to the world per se, he does find in the proverbial melting pot a model for a new international status quo.

In the speeches that Barack Obama delivered during his highly publicized tour of the Middle East and Europe, we find the clearest articulation of Obama's vision of a multicultural utopia (a better world). During what was billed as his campaign "world tour" in late July 2008, Obama traveled to Iraq, Afghanistan, Jordan, Israel, the West Bank, Germany, France, and Britain in an attempt to burnish his foreign policy credentials. After first visiting troops in war-ridden Afghanistan and Iraq, he delivered brief remarks at a press conference in Amman, Jordan. Accompanied by Senators Jack Reed and Chuck Hagel, Obama discarded the soaring idealistic rhetoric that characterized his domestic discourse, and instead he opted for a more somber and presidential tone. Even so, he offers up a vision of a new global order, one that he implies will be realized following his election. Obama explains:

> If we responsibly end the war in Iraq, we can strengthen our military, step up our efforts to finish the fight against Al Qaida and the Taliban in Afghanistan, and succeed in leaving Iraq to a sovereign government that can take responsibility for its own future.
>
> In short, we can seize this moment to make America more secure, to focus on broader challenges, like defeating terrorism, reversing the spread of nuclear weapons and achieving true energy security, a challenge that I will discuss, among others, with some of our closest friends and allies in the days ahead.[2]

In the wake of the Bush administration's response to the attacks on September 11, this Obamian emphasis on multilateralism resonated across national boundaries made increasingly porous in a digital age.

Obama visited Israel the next day. In Sderot, on the Gaza border, he delivered prepared remarks against a backdrop of mortar shells and rockets that had fallen on the city. Anxious to appeal to Jewish voters back home, Obama explained that he brings "an unshakeable commitment to Israel's security. The state of Israel faces determined enemies who seek its destruction. But it also has a friend and ally in the United States that will always stand by the people of Israel. That's why I'm proud to be here today and that's why I will work from the moment that I return to America, to tell the story of Sderot and to make sure that the good people who live here are enjoying a future of peace and security and hope."[3] In this short passage, we recognize the importance of words and phrases like "good people," "future of peace," and "hope." By using them again in Israel, Obama offers the possibility of reconciliation to a region of the world torn by continuing sectarian strife.

After this somber and tempered start to the "world tour," in Berlin the next day Barack Obama let loose the full persuasive force and extended utopian reach of his rhetoric of hope. In a speech aptly entitled "A World

That Stands as One," Obama addresses a crowd swelling to two hundred thousand souls. Obamamania is sweeping through Europe as well the United States. Speaking in front of Victory Column in Tiergarten Park, he plays masterfully to the expectations of his audience: "Tonight," he begins, "I speak to you not as a candidate for President, but as a citizen — a proud citizen of the United States, and a fellow citizen of the world." In these opening lines, Obama establishes a nuanced continuity between the individual, the nation-state, and the global community that is developed in the remainder of the speech. He explains to his audience what they already know: he does not "look like the Americans who've previously spoken in this great city," and the journey that brought him to Berlin was an improbable one.

To reinforce the fantastic nature of his arrival in the upper echelon of political power, Obama returns to his life story. He underscores the fact that his grandfather was "a cook, a domestic servant to the British" and he thereby evokes a collective European experience with colonialism in Africa (and almost every other part of the world). Moving next to the end of the Cold War, Obama rehearses the history of the Soviet Union's "march across Europe." He emphasizes the collective struggle that eventually unified the city in 1989. "The only reason we stand here tonight," he asserts before that audience of Berliners, "is because men and women from both of our nations came together to work, and struggle, and sacrifice for that better life."

Exercising the prophetic aspects of his persona, Obama entreats all people around the world to "look at Berlin, where a wall came down, a continent came together, and history proved that there is no challenge too great for a world that stands as one." His is a rhetorical call for world unity that transcends national borders, cultural inheritance, socioeconomic class, and race. Noting the suspicions that have hindered foreign relations for centuries, Obama suggests solutions grounded in commonality: "Yes, there have been differences between America and Europe. No doubt, there will be differences in the future. But the burdens of global citizenship continue to bind us together."

He heralds the erasure of old schisms in Europe (and by implication around the world). Deploying symbolism derived from the partition that once divided East Germany from West Germany, Obama declares: "The walls between the countries with the most and those with the least cannot stand. The walls between races and tribes; natives and immigrants;

Christian and Muslim and Jew cannot stand. These now are the walls we must tear down." In this passage we recognize the collectivist appeal of the rhetoric of hope, only this time it is combined with a highly self-conscious universalism. Just as Americans must strive together to realize the promise of the "more perfect union" at the heart of the nation's founding documents, governments and individuals around the world need to share "the burdens of development and diplomacy; of progress and peace."

In a prophetic tone, Obama proclaims: "Now is the time to join together, through constant cooperation, strong institutions, shared sacrifice, and a global commitment to progress, to meet the challenges of the twenty-first century. It was this spirit that led airlift planes to appear in the sky above our heads, and people to assemble where we stand today. And this is the moment when our nations—and all nations—must summon that spirit anew." These themes of continual progress by way of shared sacrifice should be easily recognizable as we near the end of this study; what distinguishes this passage from previous Obamian rhetoric is its global reach.

Returning to the cadences and rhythms of the American black church, Obama uses the refrain, "This is the moment," to build towards a climax in Berlin. "This is the moment" when terror must be defeated and the world rid of nuclear weapons, when "every nation in Europe must have the chance to choose its own tomorrow." This is the moment when the world, not just the United States, must "build on the wealth that open markets have created, and share its benefits more equitably." Obama even anticipates the so-called Arab Spring that would begin just two years later: "This is the moment we must help answer the call for a new dawn in the Middle East." Repeating that refrain to a frenetic pitch, like a gospel singer or pulpit preacher, Obama portends the arrival of a moment pregnant with meaning, a pivotal intersection of historical trends that will lead to the creation of a new order from out of the ruins of the status quo. "This is the moment when we must come together to save this planet ... when we must give hope to those left behind in a globalized world." Expanding his ideal audience beyond European borders, Obama exclaims: "People of Berlin—people of the world—this is our moment. This is our time."

While Barack Obama frankly acknowledges the failure of the United States to live up to its best intentions, he finds something meaningful in that deficiency. It gives us something to work toward. The arc of history bends ever forward. Over "more than two centuries, we have strived," he explains, "to form a more perfect union; to seek, with other nations, a more hopeful world." Obama points to the pluralism among the American electorate and in American political discourse so as to provide a model for global progress. He asserts, "Every language is spoken in our country; every culture has left its imprint on ours; every point of view is expressed in our public squares." Obama's is a highly idealized reading of a twenty-first-century America, one in which someone like himself, who might never have even received an education in the era of the country's founding, can now gain access to the highest office in the land.

Next, Obama rhetorically conflates American values with those held by people around the world. He observes that the United States was founded on a "set of ideals that speak to aspirations shared by all people: that we can live free from fear and free from want; that we can speak our minds and assemble with whomever we choose and worship as we please." People from all nations on the earth, explains Obama, share these aspirations; they are universal human goals. In pursuit of them, Obama foresees that "a new generation — our generation — must make our mark on the world."

The closing paragraph of Obama's Berlin speech provides further evidence of the international scope of the rhetoric of hope. Like a biblical prophet, Obama announces a new dawn of cooperation: "The scale of our challenge is great. The road ahead will be long. But I come before you to say that we are heirs to a struggle for freedom. We are a people of improbable hope. With an eye toward the future, with resolve in our hearts, let us remember this history, and answer our destiny, and remake the world once again."[4]

When Barack Obama arrived in France on July 25, one day after his Berlin speech, President Nicolas Sarkozy welcomed him enthusiastically. They held a joint press conference (a gracious gesture by the French leader since such events were usually reserved for heads of state, not political candidates). In his brief remarks, Obama offers to those in attendance, and to those watching on television, a similar vision of global collaboration based on shared values that lead to tangible progress. He explains that "the United States and Europe can and will accomplish far more when we join in common cause." For the French president, who clearly enjoyed basking in the light of his political rock-star guest, Barack Obama represented the promise of American revitalization — precisely the image that Obama cultivated for himself in the rhetoric of hope.

Sarkozy begins his remarks at the press conference with earnest verve: "I want to say to Barack Obama that the French have been following with passion the election campaign in the United States, because the United States are a great democracy and that it's fascinating to watch what's happening there, and because America, the America that France loves, is an America that is farsighted, that has ambitions, great debates, strong personalities."[5] In the remainder of his comments, Sarkozy clearly juxtaposes the American status quo under the Bush administration with the forward-looking idealism of the country's founding documents. Sarkozy understood that being the biracial child of a white mother from the United States and a black father from Kenya made Obama a twenty-first-century embodiment of the American Dream. Combining that potent racial biography with the experience of growing up in Hawaii and later Indonesia, Obama now fashions himself into a messenger of a new world order based on the principle of gradual social amelioration. The French leader succinctly explains the biographical and narrative appeal of the rhetoric of hope: "Barack Obama's adventure is an adventure that rings true in the hearts and minds of the French and of Europeans."

Although Senator Obama went on to meet Gordon Brown in London on July 26, he returned to the United States the next day in time to make the rounds of the Sunday morning political talk shows. Without question, Obama's tour of the Middle East and Europe was a huge political success, but more importantly, it was a rhetorical coup that demonstrated the wide appeal of his carefully cultivated life narrative as an American native son turned politician, diplomat, and global leader. The new order that Obama promises to his foreign audiences derives from a unique American form of idealism that has historical antecedents in the classical world, Judeo-Christianity, the Age of Reason, the romantic movement, and the civil rights era.

In Obama's rhetorical portrait of the future, the United States no longer enjoys hegemony as the only global superpower; rather, power is shared among nations at a table of equals. He promises collective progress through shared values of equality and inclusion. These values are not uniquely American, but rather he claims that people in nations around the world hold them in esteem. The principles that Americans idealized (the cross-generational obligation of family, neighborliness, a sense of duty, honesty, and fairness), Obama suggests, are found everywhere that one looks in the world. Thus, the promise of the future rests on the adoption of an ideal form of global citizenship based on the universal human values that undergird his utopian vision of a multicultural world.

This nuanced understanding of multiculturalism, on display in the rhetoric of hope, has roots in the political theory that Obama encountered at Columbia and Harvard. According to James Kloppenberg, Obama learned from the American philosopher John Rawls to appreciate "the indispensable role played by communities" in the formulation of a theory of justice relevant to the current age. Obama also took from Rawls "a commitment to the dual importance of individual rights and equality," one which required minimizing the gap between the rich and poor. In time, Obama came to understand that the principles of justness and fairness require that a society (so formed) be comprised of free individuals who all possess equal basic rights and who enjoy an egalitarian economic system. Social cooperation is required in order for most citizens to live a decent life, and therefore the products of such a society should be shared equally. These "strong requirements of equality and reciprocal advantage are hallmarks of Rawls's theory of justice."[6]

Moreover, Obama took from Rawls "an awareness that these convictions do not descend directly from Reason or Natural Law but emerge from careful reflections on our own culture's particular historical experience." While Barack Obama makes thoughtful use of American history and culture to shape the substance of his rhetoric of hope, on the global stage, he widens its promise to include people of every culture and ethnicity. He embraces "community, liberty, equality, and historicism," which are values that one scholar reminds us are "often assumed to be in tension but, at least in Obama's writings, not only consistent but mutually constitutive."[7] In the rhetoric of hope, Obama cites "reformers, from Tubman to Douglass to Chavez to King," who championed the ideals of equality that "have gradually shaped how we understand ourselves and allowed us to form a multicultural nation the likes of which exists nowhere else on earth."

Obama also learned from Rawls to impress the language of religion into political discourse. For more than a generation before Obama entered politics, the Democrats remained reluctant to use overtly religious language due to their understanding of the separation of church and state set down in the nation's founding documents. Obama feels that progressives need to abandon their religious biases and recognize the "overlapping values" between the secular and nonsecular. He asks those who are religiously motivated to translate their concerns into "universal, rather than religion-specific, values." A pluralistic democracy, like that found in the United States and which Obama wants for the world, requires "a willingness to deliberate, and a commitment to compromise in order to reach provisional agreement."[8] What might be termed mainstream liberal universalism, built on the works of Rawls and other philosophers, defends the ideal of universal principles and minimal rights. Liberalism's response to all forms of diversity, as Laden and Owen explain, emphasizes "human equality as a result of human similarity" and therefore "advocates state neutrality and the protection of individual liberties as the just response to diversity."[9] Such a commitment requires "the adoption of an egalitarian liberal universalism."[10]

Obama champions the liberal principles noted above that emphasize social equality. They represent for him a more noble aspect of the American character than its ruthless capitalist individualism that too often slips into solipsism. He wants those liberal universal principles to be adopted across the globe. While Kloppenberg acknowledges that for Obama "the glittering idea of a universal principle of justice retained its seductive allure," he concludes that Obama largely rejects a "universalist vision of brotherhood."[11] This study of the rhetoric of hope shows, by contrast, that Obama does cherish a global vision of social solidarity based on universal principles. Obama clearly sees, in the study of human history, evidence of gradual but persistent social betterment (from improved race relations, to greater gender equality, to an increasing number of minorities in power).

All of these signs point toward a new global order, a universalist brotherhood, that is the rhetorical promise of the future. For Obama, the United States provides the world community with a unique model for social amelioration due to its ability to balance the tension between the "individualistic and the communal, autonomy and solidarity." For instance, while Europe struggled with the violent upheavals resulting from feudalism, the United States transformed itself over time from an agricultural to an industrial society by exploiting "the sheer size of the continent, vast tracts of land and abundant resources that allowed new immigrants to continually remake themselves."

Barack Obama's understanding of history as a process of transition and transformation toward betterment provides the philosophical basis for his rhetorical formulation of a multicultural utopia. In Obamian rhetoric, the world must be remade based on the principles of sustained work and collective sacrifice. By joining together "through constant cooperation, strong institutions, shared sacrifice, and a global commitment to progress," Obama believes that all nations can "meet the challenges of the twenty-first century."[12] His is a cosmopolitan vision grounded in an ideal model of global citizenship based on cooperation and equality. All of these rhetorical moves are in line with his articulated belief in the transformational quality of moral values, which for Obama radiate outward from the individual to the state, nation, and the world.

A multicultural utopia, like the one that Obama outlines in his rhetoric of hope, offers "a restructuring of intercommunal relations within and beyond the nation-state according to the internal imperatives of diverse communities."[13] In this restructuring of relations, Obama finds an increasing fluidity between personal, national, and global identity based on a widening series of affiliations from the individual to all of humanity. One of Obama's mentors at Harvard, Martha Minow, suggests that it is due to his unusual heritage and upbringing that Barack became "a universalist who doesn't deny his particularity." She understood that his "very special sense of universalism" would become part of his political message in later years.[14]

As Thomas McGovern aptly observes, this "fusion of self and society wrapped in religious metaphors is a recurring theme in American narrative,"[15] and it is a theme that Barack Obama deftly appropriates in his rhetoric of hope. One biographer suggests that in Obama's retelling, the civil rights movement became an "American moment of uprising and empowerment," and that impulse toward equality that led to the formation of the movement should be "understood as a universal one." Because the desire for equality is a universal and recurring impulse, in every generation individuals will stand for justice against the tyranny of oppression. Obama's story, therefore, is a "romantic (and partly romanticized) assertion of heroic continuity" from one generation to the next. Just as Martin Luther King was the prophet of the civil rights era, now the "politician of our age, who comes along to follow that prophet, is Barack Obama. Martin laid the moral and spiritual base for the political reality to follow."[16] This pattern of inheritance is also a defining feature of the Judeo-Christian prophetic tradition, and it once again highlights Obama's appropriation of religious rhetoric and symbolism for political purposes.

In the rhetoric of hope, Obama modeled his own life story on narratives of conversion and redemption, such as biblical stories and the autobiographies of American slaves. When speaking to citizens around the world, Obama uses that prophetic narrative persona to urge his audience to participate in the transition from national to global citizenship. He returns to metaphors of journeying to a "Promised Land." A prophet is a visionary leader or representative who advocates for a cause or principle, and he relies on the professed belief that a better place can be reached through sacrifice and a return to core values.

We have already noted how Obama "imbues the present moment with a sense of urgent importance and empowerment" through his use of spatial and temporal metaphors.[17] By creating this sense of urgency in the rhetoric of hope, he critically situates himself as the figure most capable of bridging the gap between the ideal and the actual. By virtue of his complex identity, he uniquely orients himself to navigate the waters of misunderstandings and inequities that characterize the global status quo. In the rhetoric of hope, Obama asks the people of the world to strive together to form a more perfect global union.

Here again we encounter the profound influence of Thomas Jefferson on the rhetoric of hope. Obama styles himself as the inheritor of the Jeffersonian mantle of universal rights. "What our deliberative, pluralistic democracy does demand," explains Obama in *The Audacity of Hope*, is that individual concerns be expressed through "universal, rather than religion-specific values." Obama suggests that if "universal strategies that target the challenges facing all Americans can go a long way toward closing the gap between blacks, Latinos, and whites,"[18] then global progress can be made in the same manner. Like Jefferson, who believed that he and his fellow Americans were not acting for themselves alone "but for the whole human race,"[19] Obama grounds his political rhetoric in values that transcend the barriers of race, culture, gender, or ethnicity.

Like Thomas Jefferson who believed that "the great principles of right and wrong" were "legible to every reader,"[20] Obama also emphasizes the need for the global adoption of "self evident" universal values and principles. Indeed, the right to speak our minds, worship as we wish, peaceably assemble, to be free from unreasonable search and seizure, are themselves a universal "codification of liberty's meaning."[21] In the rhetoric of hope, Obama uses American tropes of moral exceptionalism easily recognizable to the national electorate to win elections, but at the same time he infuses them with universal appeal. He argues that since American democracy is founded on the ideal of universal human rights, people everywhere should adopt them, especially those suffering under oppressive regimes. It is a message as revolutionary in some parts of the world today as it was in the American colonies in the eighteenth century.

While the values that made American democracy possible took shape in a unique historical and cultural context, Obama suggests that they are not culture-bound or culture-centric. That is to say, the adoption of American values is not synonymous with acculturation. Centuries earlier, Thomas Jefferson insisted that the "American Revolution was the forerunner of an age of democratic revolution that could conceivably embrace the globe."[22] Jefferson "trenchantly restated the view that the American Revolution was founded on universal principles, and was thus emphatically for export." It was simply "applicable to all men and all times."[23]

Through his study of history and the nation's founding documents, Obama came to believe that these Jeffersonian principles are nothing less than the "definitions and axioms of free society" everywhere.[24] All of his life, Thomas Jefferson remained passionately committed to one crowning idea: that his revolution was "universal, not limited to the American people or the American experience." Obama returns to this point repeatedly in the rhetoric of hope. Like many American presidents before him, in his election night victory speech in 2008, Barack Obama addressed not just the citizens of his nation but all of those listening around the world. Heralding "a new dawn of American leadership," Obama promises to simultaneously fight "those who would tear this world down" and support those who "seek peace and security." Reaching the height of his rhetorical powers, and summarizing the essential doctrines of the rhetoric of hope, Obama speaks directly to the citizens of the world whose view of America dimmed considerably during the eight-year Bush administration that preceded his own:

> And to all those who have wondered if America's beacon still burns as bright: Tonight we proved once more that the true strength of our nation comes not from the might of our arms or the scale of our wealth, but from the enduring power of our ideals: democracy, liberty, opportunity and unyielding hope.
>
> That's the true genius of America: that America can change. Our union can be perfected. What we've already achieved gives us hope for what we can and must achieve tomorrow.[25]

Through the rhetoric of hope, Obama sought to restore the glimmer that the word "America" evoked before the botched invasion of Iraq in

2003. He highlights those ideals and values that he knows will inspire people around the world. This conscious universalism gives the rhetoric of hope utopian dimensions that expand the compass of the idealistic traditions that the United States inherited.

This study defines the utopian impulse as one that critiques the status quo by offering an idealized vision of the future in which the ills of the day are ameliorated once and for all. If by "utopia" we mean the rhetorical construction of a better place, one that through its idealization critiques the status quo, then Obama's rhetoric of hope deserves the moniker (despite the term's pejorative popular connotation as something chimerical). For something to be utopian (whether political rhetoric, a literary text, or a painting), it must highlight the gap between the ideal and the actual. In political discourse, this means rhetorically constructing a vision of a better place, like Jefferson's "good society," Lincoln's "great task," or FDR's "new society." In this respect, Obama's rhetoric of hope is surely utopian, and one of the things that distinguishes it from other idealistic political discourse is its deliberate grounding in the religious, historical, and literary sources of idealism in the American, and broader Western, traditions from which it emerges.

For some this definition of the utopian impulse at the heart of the rhetoric of hope may seem like just another expression of the dubious doctrine of American exceptionalism. However, in Obama's formulation, this exceptionalism is extended to nations around the world, provided that they subscribe to its pluralistic doctrines. As Ruth Levitas explains, when something is utopian it "expresses and explores what is desired," and it often "contains the hope that these desires may be met in reality, rather than merely in fantasy."[26] As a result, utopian discourses point to the realm of the "Not Yet." A literary text or a painting, for instance, becomes utopian when that work portrays a society — earthly or otherworldly — which springs from a radical dissatisfaction with the imperfections of the world. This utopian impulse proclaims not perfection but simply the ongoing amelioration of society. Literary utopias, like those by Bacon, More, Harrington and others discussed in these pages, all emphasize this dialectical tension between the ideal order and status quo. Dystopian (or antiutopian) literature, by contrast, relies on a similar opposition between the status quo and a darker social vision, but to reinforce the notion that the current age is itself the best of all possible worlds (and to advocate the abandonment of the utopian project as unrealistic). Both utopia and dystopia refer back to the world of concrete acts and familiar experience that fantasy excludes.

During the 2008 presidential campaign, Barack Obama adroitly framed himself as a young insurgent candidate challenging the political status quo. He made himself into a biracial messenger of unity, highlighted America's capacity for change, and cultivated the cool-headed and calming persona of a "great unifier." He stirred a country divided ideologically between so-called red states and blue states to civic action, lauded public service, and affirmed the country's founding principles, and in doing so he dusted off an idealized version of America as a beacon of hope to the world. He called all Americans, conservatives and liberals, blacks and whites, men and women, to come together in common purpose, and he promised them that if they worked together, if they sacrificed in the short term, then together they could undertake the journey toward that more perfect union promised at the time of the country's founding (but as of yet not fully realized). In this sense, Obama simply promises us what our own American myths tell us is our due. Indeed, it is hard to argue with the rhetorical success of this strategy.

By using his own life story and overlaying it onto American history, Obama transformed himself into a prophet of change and a model of the ideal global citizen. "At the beginning of this young century, we face our own defining moment," he convinced us. "Every so often," Obama explained to us in the 2008 rhetoric of hope, "there are moments that define a generation." While the nation was embroiled in two foreign wars and facing a climate crisis and economic recession, he assured us that the United States could still reinvent itself—that it could change. He had "a vision for America grounded in the values that have always made America the last best hope of Earth-values," and he offered us the same old American myths, only made hip for the new century. He envisioned for us an "America where good jobs are there for the willing, where hard work is rewarded with a decent living, and where we recognize the fundamental truth that Wall Street cannot prosper while Main Street crumbles—that a sound economy requires thriving businesses and flourishing families."

In the rhetoric of hope, Barack Obama exploited the gap between an idealized future and the status quo, and to define that divide, he reached all the way back through American history to its Judeo-Christian and European origins. He showed us how the principles of freedom and equality in the nation's founding documents were the basis of a promise that can only be fully realized in the course of future history. He drew on the narratives of American slaves and evoked their Judeo-Christian religious vision of salvation in an attempt to beckon us ever onward. He placed himself in a biblical tradition of prophets and consciously emulated the rhetoric of Martin Luther King. In the rhetoric of hope, Obama aligned himself with the transformative presidencies of Jefferson, Lincoln, and FDR. He even deployed motifs, images, and tropes from popular culture to signal camaraderie with young people everywhere. In all of these ways, and more, Barack Obama persuaded a weary nation and a skeptical world to give him a chance in 2008. So, how does his campaign rhetoric change as he runs for reelection as an incumbent Washington insider in 2012? To that final question, we now turn.

CHAPTER NINE

Rhetoric and the Presidency

The sloganeering for Obama's final political campaign began to take shape more than a year and a half before the election. The phrase "winning the future," for instance, dates to January 2011 and was featured on the Whitehouse.gov website for about a year. In April, Barack Obama starts road-testing the slogan: "It begins with us." In the fall and winter, he embarks on a series of campaign-style speeches around the nation, in part to keep working out new material. It was during this period that the new campaign rhetoric began to take form. What follows is an analysis of several speeches delivered from September to December 2011 that together chart the development of Obama's 2012 campaign rhetoric (the subject of Chapter Ten).

During all of 2011, President Obama is shackled with unemployment, and as a consequence his approval ratings head steadily downward into the mid-forties. To compound these woes, the housing market remains stubbornly depressed and the economic prospects for millions of Americans are in decline. On the political front, things are not much better for the Commander-in-Chief. In May 2011, the Speaker of the House John Boehner, a Republican, announces that he cannot support raising the nation's debt ceiling without reductions in spending. Historically, raising the nation's debt limit was a pro forma act of Congress, but by midsummer, a showdown was brewing between the Speaker and the president. In the face of concerted Republican opposition, Obama is forced into a game of brinkmanship, which eventually ends with the downgrading of the nation's debt by Standard & Poor's (as well as the infliction of considerable political damage to both parties and their leaders).

At a White House press conference in July 2011, one reporter skeptically asks President Obama if he has any hope that the debt ceiling negotiations "might actually produce an outcome." Quickly donning his most winning smile, Obama quips: "I always have hope. Don't you remember my campaign? Even after being here for two and a half years, I continue to have hope. You know why I have hope? It's because of the American people." Even at the low point of his first term, Obama instinctually returns to a central theme of the 2008 campaign. His impromptu reappropriation of the forward-looking idealism that filled the 2008 rhetoric of hope signaled that Obama would not abandon it as a pipe dream in the face of the realities of Washington hardball politics. Obama returns to it, despite the fact that it leaves him open to charges of being a utopian dreamer, a champion of change who is unable to deliver it.

In the 2008 campaign, Obama established himself as a political outsider, which gave him an important vantage point from which to critique the record of his opponent, John McCain. This time around, he must reframe himself as an incumbent president running against a "do-nothing" Congress. Such a rhetorical move made good sense as Congressional approval ratings approached, and sometimes reached, the single digits in late 2011. Barack Obama's address before a joint session of Congress in September 2011 is a good example of his attempt to reposition himself for the general election contest. The address was originally scheduled for the seventh day of the month. Obama was humiliatingly forced to postpone it after a political fracas arose for scheduling it during one of sixteen Republican presidential debates leading up to the Iowa caucus. So, instead, the next evening Obama addresses Congress and the nation during prime time (and just before the kick-off of the National Football League season). As a result, more than thirty million Americans tuned in to hear the pitch for his American Jobs Act. Lacking a clear challenger to target in the increasingly factious race for the Republican nomination, Obama employs the rhetorical devices that served him so well just a few years earlier. Pandering hope and running against the political establishment is one thing as a little known junior senator from Illinois, but it is quite another when one is seen as complicit in the worst recession since the Great Depression. There is a delicate line between appearing stubbornly optimistic and supremely hypocritical, and Obama negotiated it carefully. In his address, he first asks the American electorate to continue the journey toward that "more perfect union" in 2012.

The president starts by noting the economic and political crisis confronting the nation. This rehearsal of the status quo allows him to appear engaged and to juxtapose the way things are now with a vision of a better future later in the speech. He explains that Republican opposition thwarts his repeated attempts to pass a jobs bill totaling over four hundred billion dollars in order to further stimulate the economy. For any other politician this would be dangerous political ground, because while the 2009 stimulus package may have saved the country from the brink of financial ruin, it remains widely unpopular and is often derided as ineffective in light of continued high unemployment and the slow pace of economic recovery.

Undaunted by that scorn, Obama asserts that it is the political pundits who remain obsessed with how his performance will affect his standing in the next election cycle. He claims, by contrast, to recognize the "real life" concerns of those who are looking for work. People who are doing "their best just to scrape by — giving up nights out with the family to save on gas or make the mortgage; postponing retirement to send a kid to college." This rhetorical move puts him in a position of strength as a champion of economic justice, and it makes him out to be the person most likely to push back against a Congress dedicated to protecting the interests of the wealthiest Americans. It helps to align him ideologically with the suffering of the oppressed and unemployed rather than with the privileged few.

Obama then evokes the myth of the American Dream and contrasts it with the status quo, a move straight out of his 2008 playbook: "The people of this country work hard to meet their responsibilities. The question tonight is whether we'll meet ours. The question is whether, in the face of an ongoing national crisis, we can stop the political circus and actually do something to help the economy. The question is— the question is whether we can restore some of the fairness and security that has defined this nation since our beginning." Attempting to distance himself from the economic crisis engulfing the nation, he acknowledges that politicians like himself cannot rescue the country alone. Instead, Obama insists that the government must work with business to restore American vitality. He therefore proposes the American Jobs Act to "put more people back to work and more money in the pockets of those who are working." He claims that it will "create more jobs for construction workers, more jobs for teachers, more jobs for veterans, and more jobs for long-term unemployed."

Adopting the dynamic phrasing and cadences of the black preacher,

Obama urges Congress to "pass this jobs bill—pass this jobs bill." He demands that Congress raise taxes on the wealthy. In doing so, he rhetorically defends the needs of ordinary Americans, and lets his Republican colleagues advocate for the elite who are responsible for the current economic crisis. Obama explains that under the current tax code the famed billionaire "Warren Buffett pays a lower tax rate than his secretary—an outrage he has asked us to fix. We need a tax code where everyone gets a fair shake and where everybody pays their fair share." Here, we recognize the heightened populist appeal of Obama's 2012 campaign messaging. Returning to the myth of American exceptionalism with which he peppered the rhetoric of hope in 2008, Obama panders to commonly held American beliefs: "Yes, we are rugged individualists. Yes, we are strong and self-reliant. And it has been the drive and initiative of our workers and entrepreneurs that has made this economy the engine and the envy of the world." Even as a Washington insider and weakened presidential incumbent, Barack Obama falls back on tropes of hope and change.

Obama cites Abraham Lincoln to give his argument additional force: "We all remember Abraham Lincoln as the leader who saved our Union. Founder of the Republican Party. But in the middle of a civil war, he was also a leader who looked to the future—a Republican president who mobilized government to build the Transcontinental Railroad—launched the National Academy of Sciences, set up the first land grant colleges." By referencing this legendary Republican at a time of great political divisiveness, Obama casts himself in the shadow of a great unifier. Obama also alludes to his own life story, one now so well known to the American public that he need not even contextualize it: "What would this country be like," he rhetorically asks, "if we had chosen not to spend money on public high schools, or research universities, or community colleges? Millions of returning heroes, including my grandfather, had the opportunity to go to school because of the G.I. Bill. Where would we be if they hadn't had that chance?" As in 2008, Obama employs a narrative persona that champions opportunity and inclusivity over exclusion.

He also reminds members of Congress of their obligation to their fellow citizens. He argues that despite the tradition of individualism that the country prides itself on, no "single individual built America on their own. We built it together. We have been, and always will be, one nation, under God, indivisible, with liberty and justice for all; a nation with responsibilities to ourselves and with responsibilities to one another." It is a collectivist appeal grounded in principles celebrated at the nation's founding. He references them to convince his audience that "now is the time" for Republican members of Congress to work with him. He closes by recognizing the scope of challenges facing the nation that need to be met head on. These are "difficult years," he concedes, but "we are Americans. We are tougher than the times we live in, and we are bigger than our politics have been." In addition to appealing to widely held American beliefs, Obama emphasizes the collective nature of the struggle toward a better future. He enjoins reluctant members of Congress, and his television audience, to "meet the moment. Let's get to work, and let's show the world once again why the United States of America remains the greatest nation on Earth."[1] As these passages from his address to a joint session of Congress indicate, Barack Obama's new campaign rhetoric looks, in some respects, strikingly similar to that of 2008.

In a speech delivered before the Congressional Black Caucus (CBC) Foundation's annual award ceremony on September 24, 2011, Obama returns to the religious tropes of a journey towards the Promised Land that featured so prominently in the previous campaign. Here again he employs an idealized version of his life story (carefully cultivated to highlight recognizable American themes of upward mobility, shared values, and an idealized reading of American history) in order to persuade. He opens by citing a biblical story of strife and connects it to the civil rights movement. In doing so, he establishes a shared experience with his audience (despite the fact that his generation's exposure to racism was radically different from previous ones). His linguistic accommodation to his CBC audience by employing African American vernacular English is also an attempt to establish credibility.

Stitching stories together from the campaign trail, Obama recounts hearing Dr. Joseph Lowery speak at Brown Chapel A.M.E. Church in Selma, Alabama (a starting point for marches that helped to facilitate the adoption of the Voting Rights Act of 1965). When Dr. Lowery took the pulpit, he told "the story of Shadrach and Meshach and Abednego" who stood up for God in the face of the threat of being burned alive. "I was running for president" at the time, Obama explains, and Dr. Lowery "turned to me from the pulpit, and indicated that someone like me running for president — well, that was crazy. But he supposed it was good crazy" (like the act of faith by the three men in the furnace). Obama interprets this biblical story as one about "faith, the belief in things not seen, the belief that if you persevere a better day lies ahead," and he points to his own improbable rise to the presidency of the United States as proof of the power of keeping that hope alive. For Obama, the CBC exemplifies the ideal of collective striving in the face of monumental difficulty. Just as African Americans endured unimaginable suffering on the road to equality, so must a nation struggling under the yoke of economic recession look forward to a brighter tomorrow.

Here, Obama pivots from the quest for liberty in American history to his own record as president of the United States. This is a common stratagem in the new campaign rhetoric, and one that marks a point of departure from 2008, when he had no such record. Obama acknowledges that the last few years have been difficult under his leadership. Americans have endured an economic crisis that "hammered" working families. The black community, he concedes, has been particularly hard hit, with a 17 percent unemployment rate (approximately two times that of the national average). Meanwhile, 40 percent of African American children continue to grow up in poverty. Obama confesses: "It's heartbreaking, and it's frustrating." Even so, he reminds those in the crowd that he sought the presidency to help more Americans reach the dream that Dr. King outlined for the nation: "To give every child a chance, whether he's born in Chicago, or she comes from a rural town in the Delta."

Putting the most positive spin on his own record, Obama reminds those in attendance that he never catered to the wealthiest Americans with tax breaks (an oblique reference to Bush-era tax policy): "We had a different vision and so we did what was right" by embracing an America "based on the idea that I am my brother's keeper and I am my sister's keeper, and we're in this together. We are in this thing together." This familiar allusion to shared kinship appears frequently in the rhetoric of hope, and here again it is imbued with the notion of collective ethical striving toward a new social order. Touting his record, and still using the collective pronoun to signal camaraderie, Obama claims, "We fought to extend unemployment insurance, and we fought to expand the Earned Income Tax Credit, and we fought to expand the Child Tax Credit — which benefited nearly half of all African American children in this country. And millions of Americans are better off because of that fight." In the paragraphs that follow, Obama highlights other achievements aimed at narrowing the gap between rich and poor, and he optimistically suggests that "in these hard years, we've won a lot of fights that needed fighting and we've done a lot of good. But we've got more work to do."

While Obama's CBC speech celebrates the social achievements of the civil rights movement, rhetorically it makes the Obama presidency a testament to historical progress. Interestingly, the media's reporting on the CBC address at the time focused instead on his perceived chiding of the black community. For the sake of example, the liberal-leaning *Huffington Post* featured a story with the awkward headline "Obama Congressional Black Caucus Speech: Stop Complainin' and Fight, " while the conservative mouthpiece Fox News opted for the more succinct "Obama Tells Congressional Black Caucus to 'Stop Complaining.'" In fact, media outlets like these were so caught up in parroting each others' headlines that no one noticed that Obama was borrowing central themes from his 2008 rhetoric of hope and refitting them for a run as an incumbent facing down a "do-nothing" Congress, a horde of Washington lobbyists, and the wealthy elite.

In returning to his own life story once more, Obama equates his own struggle with that of all people for the American Dream: "When Michelle and I think about where we came from — a little girl on the South Side of Chicago, son of a single mom in Hawaii — mother had to go to school on scholarships, sometimes got food stamps. Michelle's parents never owned their own home until she had already graduated — living upstairs above the aunt who actually owned the house. We are here today only because our parents and our grandparents, they broke their backs to support us." In this part of the speech, Obama positions himself as one who stands on the shoulders of giants and therefore sees the way forward in troubled times.

His rhetoric is steeped in myths of American exceptionalism recognizable to (and defended by) a large proportion of his audience and the broader electorate: "We're only here because past generations struggled and sacrificed for this incredible, exceptional idea that it does not matter where you come from, it does not matter where you're born, doesn't matter what you look like — if you're willing to put in an effort, you should get a shot. You should get a shot at the American Dream." By way of concluding this address that presages his rhetorical strategy for reelection, Obama harkens back to the struggles of the civil rights era. His speech therefore possesses a neat circularity, replete with familiar refrains and national tropes of progress. In the midst of troubled times, Obama emphasizes the gradual nature of social advancement: "Throughout our history, change has often come slowly. Progress often takes time. We take a step forward, sometimes we take two steps back. Sometimes we get two steps forward and one step back. But it's never a straight line. It's never easy. And I never promised easy. Easy has never been promised to us. But we've had faith. We have had faith. We've had that good kind of crazy that says, you can't stop marching."[2] Rhetorically, it is difficult to run for reelection in a time of crisis, on what is perceived to be a weak record, and yet to be able to position oneself as an agent of transformation. Nevertheless, he urges all those listening to "stop complaining, stop grumbling, stop crying" about what has not yet been accomplished and instead to set their sights firmly on the future. He asserts forcefully: "I expect all of you to march with me and press on."

This new campaign rhetoric even slips into Barack Obama's dedication to the Martin Luther King Memorial on October 16, 2011. Laura MacInnis and Lily Kuo, writing for the Reuters news agency, called it "a partisan-tinged speech" that "sounded at times like a sermon."[3] Having already charted the influence of Dr. King on Obama's writing, one that is derivative of his careful study of the African American experience more generally, we immediately recognize language in his dedication that Obama borrows from the 2008 rhetoric of hope. For instance, he describes King as someone who fits the American archetype of the self-made man. He was a "black preacher with no official rank or title who somehow gave voice to our deepest dreams and our most lasting ideals, a man who stirred our conscience and thereby helped make our union more perfect." Looking backward on the struggle for civil rights, Obama bears witness for the nation that social progress does happen, albeit sometimes gradually and painfully.

He notes that laws have changed to protect civil rights since the 1960s, but most importantly that "hearts and minds changed, as well." In a passage that encapsulates his notion of the dialectical nature of historical progress, Obama asks members of the audience to look not at the MLK monument itself, but "at the faces here around you," for in them "you see an America that is more fair and more free and more just than the one Dr. King addressed that day." Progress, Obama claims, expresses "itself in a million ways, large and small, across this nation every single day, as people of all colors and creeds live together, and work together, and fight alongside one another, and learn together, and build together, and love one another."

His injunction to love thy neighbor resonates with religious overtones appropriate to the occasion and to the legacy of a preacher turned social reformer.

While Barack Obama admits that he finds it fit and proper to sometimes "savor that slow but certain progress" the country has made, he recognizes the devastation that the financial crisis wrought on millions now "out of work" and "millions more just struggling to get by." Lest his audience forget the lessons of the past, the compass by which the future of the nation is to be charted, Obama again asks everyone to "remember that change has never been quick. Change has never been simple, or without controversy. Change depends on persistence. Change requires determination. It took a full decade before the moral guidance of *Brown v. Board of Education* was translated into the enforcement measures of the Civil Rights Act and the Voting Rights Act, but those ten long years did not lead Dr. King to give up. He kept on pushing, he kept on speaking, he kept on marching until change finally came." The implication of these remarks is clear. Although the country faces the wrath of a slow and bitter economic crisis, collective ethical striving will usher in a new era of prosperity and renewal. To make his point more salient and palatable to those facing economic duress, Obama explains that when he met with hardship and confronted disappointment, "Dr. King refused to accept what he called the 'isness' of today. He kept pushing towards the 'oughtness' of tomorrow." Martin Luther King sought the Not Yet, the promise of a better future. This dialectical tension, between the ideal and the actual, gives Obama's 2012 political rhetoric its utopian dimensions.

In dedicating the Martin Luther King Memorial, Barack Obama uses the overtly religious, values-based language that distinguished him from other Democrats of his generation in 2008. He tells participants that they should draw inspiration from Dr. King's "constant insistence on the oneness of man." His was an ideal "rooted in his Christian faith, that led him to tell a group of angry young protesters, 'I love you as I love my own children,' even as one threw a rock that glanced off his neck." If he were alive today, Obama conjectures, Martin Luther King would understand that "to bring about true and lasting change, there must be the possibility of reconciliation; that any social movement has to channel this tension through the spirit of love and mutuality." However, Obama acknowledges, "aligning our reality with our ideals often requires the speaking of uncomfortable truths and the creative tension of non-violent protest," an oblique allusion to the Occupy movements then spreading across the nation. For Obama, the legacy of Dr. King should "remind us that the unemployed worker can rightly challenge the excesses of Wall Street without demonizing all who work there; that the businessman can enter tough negotiations with his company's union without vilifying the right to collectively bargain." In this manner, he turns his dedication of the Martin Luther King Memorial into a highly political campaign-style address.

By way of concluding it, Obama posits that King's "life, his story, tells us that change can come if you don't give up." For this reason, Obama seems content to dedicate this memorial to someone "so quintessentially American — because for all the hardships we've endured, for all our sometimes tragic history, ours is a story of optimism and achievement and constant striving that is unique upon this Earth." America, he assures his audience, is still exceptional. Hitting full rhetorical stride, Obama conjures up a utopian vision of a better place: "And so with our eyes on the horizon and our faith squarely placed in one another, let us keep striving; let us keep struggling; let us keep climbing toward that promised land of a nation and a world that is more fair, and more just, and more equal for every single child of God."[4]

With his jobs plan still bogged down in the political mire during the waning months of 2011, Obama issues a series of executive branch actions to facilitate things like refinancing a home and to ease student loan repayment. In order to further pressure Congress to act, Obama travels to the western battleground states of Colorado and Nevada, as well as to less contested states like Texas. His campaign style addresses include the now familiar refrain "pass this bill," but also feature a newer one: "We can't wait." In this rhetorical formulation, Obama remains the agent of transformation and a vehicle for the realization of a better tomorrow — despite the fact that he has occupied the nation's highest office for several difficult years.

Speaking at Lab School at Eastfield College in Texas, Obama argues that his American Jobs Act will prevent the layoff of hundreds of thousands of teachers. In order not to seem aloof and detached, the president acknowledges early in his speech the serious difficulties being faced by ordinary Americans: "These are the toughest times we've been through since the Great Depression. And because the problems that led to the recession weren't caused overnight, they won't be solved overnight. That's the hard truth." He even calls out one member of the existing order by name, an unusual tactic in his condemnation of the status quo: "Yesterday, the

Republican Majority Leader in Congress, Eric Cantor, said that right now he won't even let this jobs bill have a vote in the House of Representatives." Adopting a familiar, and even folksy, tone to persuade, Obama continues his attack on the congressman from Virginia: "This is what he said. Won't even let it be debated. Won't even give it a chance to be debated on the floor of the House of Representatives. Think about that. I mean, what's the problem? Do they not have the time?" Eric Cantor must oppose rebuilding roads and bridges, giving tax breaks to small business, and funding veteran services, Obama implies.

Since the effectiveness of the rhetoric that Obama repackages for 2012 depends on opposition to a current social order, he points to the stonewalling and gamesmanship that continue unabated while the country wallows in the dregs of recession. He wants to act, he claims, but Republicans like Cantor stymie him at every turn. As everyone saw leading up to the debacle of raising the debt ceiling in 2011, he attempted to work with Congress. He was ready to compromise, but his Republican opposition, so the new narrative goes, thwarted him. Notice how stark Obama makes the contrast between his vision of a better America and the motives of his political opponents: "We've had folks in Congress who have said they shouldn't pass this bill because it would give me a win. So they're thinking about the next election. They're not thinking about folks who are hurting right now." Instead of resorting to innuendo, he directly accuses Republicans in Congress of not passing his jobs bill because it would give him a political victory before a national election. Obama lays it on thick: "Give me a win? Give me a break! That's why folks are fed up with Washington. This isn't about giving me a win. This isn't about giving Democrats or Republicans a win. This is about giving people who are hurting a win. This is about giving small business owners a win, and entrepreneurs a win, and students a win, and working families a win. This is about giving America a win."[5]

In late November 2011, with the election less than a year away, Obama ramps up his fund-raising and campaigning. Visiting Manchester High School Central in New Hampshire to deliver a fiery speech, he continues pressuring Congress to pass his jobs bill. Having astutely distanced himself from the work of the budget deficit "super-committee," he makes its failure yet another example of congressional intransigence. He challenges that unpopular institution to pass a payroll tax cut for middle-class families. Rather than the Washington insider responsible for the economic crisis,

Obama rhetorically positions himself as the person most likely to defend the interests of the majority of Americans.

Shrewdly, he begins his address at Manchester High anecdotally, by recounting a meeting over coffee with a math teacher from that school and his wife. Since his coffee companion and fellow educator had coincidently served in the military for more than twenty years (including tours in Iraq and Kuwait), relating this meeting at once allowed Obama to create intimacy with his audience and at the same time to tout the fact that all combat troops would leave Iraq by the end of 2011 (a promise from the previous campaign). Obama claims that "families like the Corkerys, families like yours, young people like the ones here today" are the reason that he ran for office in the first place. Following the pattern outlined above, he creates a bleak vision of the status quo in order to demonstrate an understanding of the plight of his audience despite his elevated position. Such a depiction also allows him to continue to portray himself as an agent of change battling the entrenched forces that buttress the current inequitable social order. "Today," Obama explains, "many Americans have spent months looking for work, and others are doing the best they can to get by. There are a lot of folks out there who are giving nights up — nights out, they just can't do that anymore because they've got to save on gas or make the mortgage."

This time Obama directly acknowledges the Occupy movements rather than allowing himself to become their target. He aligns himself with the "profound sense of frustration" that motivates its citizen protestors. Obama, more lucidly than any political pundit, attributes Occupy to a general exasperation that "the essence of the American Dream," which is that hard work leads to success, is "slipping away" for most people. The American Dream is what "we're fighting for. That's what is at stake right now." Despite the dire nature of the situation, Obama tells his audience that hope remains for a day when that promise of opportunity can be realized. In the bleakness of winter, Obama charts a rhetorical path to rejuvenation and future prosperity. He tells those desperate for relief that by working together "we're going to get it done. We're going to get there." Together we "can put our friends and neighbors back to work and help families like the Corkerys get ahead and give the economy the jolt that it needs." This is a "Yes We Can" moment, and implying it (rather than explicitly resorting to an old slogan) is a necessary strategy for a battered incumbent president seeking a second term.

During the remainder of his remarks in New Hampshire, Obama deftly juxtaposes congressional inaction with the hard work of everyday Americans. Obama's tone is again casual, colloquial, and familiar: "As I look around this room and I see these young people, but I also see their parents, I'm thinking, folks in Manchester, you guys work hard. You play by the rules. You're meeting your responsibilities. And if you're working hard and you're meeting your responsibilities, at the very least you should expect Congress to do the same." He returns to the values-based arguments that distinguished the 2008 rhetoric of hope, for it is those collectively held "values that built this country, those values that all of you represent, that's what we're fighting for." In closing, he invokes the American narratives of exceptionalism over which he so deftly laid his own biography in the previous campaign: "Our story has never been about doing things easy. It's been about rising to the moment when the moment is hard. It's about doing what's right. It's about making sure that everybody has a chance, not just a few." Unsurprisingly, he urges his listeners to move the nation forward, for he insists, "the best days of the United States of America are still ahead."[6] This is a powerful message in a time of crisis.

Throughout 2011, the one rhetorical move most at odds with the 2008 rhetoric (and the autobiographical writing that proceeded it) was Obama's impressing of Theodore Roosevelt into his campaign on December 6 in Kansas. The older cousin of Franklin Roosevelt (a Democrat), Teddy was not only a Republican leader, but unlike FDR he cultivated a manly outdoorsman persona and even owned a ranch in the Badlands. On the other hand, Obama's use of Theodore Roosevelt is a stroke of genius, for among his many other accomplishments Teddy broke corporate trusts with the Sherman Act and passed the Pure Food and Drug Act, which continue to protect consumers to this day.

Speaking at Osawatomie High School, President Obama explains that although Teddy Roosevelt was born into great privilege, he recognized that inequality and exploitation were not the necessary price of progress. Roosevelt knew "that the free market has never been a free license to take whatever you can from whomever you can." Teddy "understood the free market only works when there are rules of the road that ensure competition is fair and open and honest." Osawatomie may seem like a faraway place to deliver such a speech, but in 1910, Obama explains, "Teddy Roosevelt came here to Osawatomie and he laid out his vision for what he called a New Nationalism." His call was for "the triumph of a real democracy ...

of an economic system under which each man shall be guaranteed the opportunity to show the best that there is in him."

Making a clear allusion to the aspersions cast upon him by conservative pundits, Obama touts the fact the Teddy Roosevelt was called a socialist and communist for fighting to give ordinary Americans safeguards such as an eight-hour workday. Obama further contends that the current economic inequality in the United States actually distorts our democracy, because it "gives an outsized voice to the few who can afford high-priced lobbyists and unlimited campaign contributions, and it runs the risk of selling out our democracy to the highest bidder." Obama's is a clever rhetorical strategy timed to coincide with the apex of anticorporate sentiment in the aftermath of the 2008 economic recession. As this and other speeches show, Obama's rhetoric would be more overtly populist in 2012 than it was in 2008.

"In the final years of his life," Obama concludes, Teddy Roosevelt "took that same message all across this country, from tiny Osawatomie to the heart of New York City, believing that no matter where he went, no matter who he was talking to, everybody would benefit from a country in which everyone gets a fair chance." Like Roosevelt, who championed a square deal for the middle class, Obama makes himself into a twenty-first-century defender of the American Dream at a time when it is widely perceived to be under assault by corporate interests. Although much has changed since Roosevelt's day, Obama concludes, "What hasn't changed — what can never change — are the values that got us this far. We still have a stake in each other's success. We still believe that this should be a place where you can make it if you try."[7]

As we have seen in the foregoing analysis of several campaign speeches delivered in the closing months of 2011, Obama returns repeatedly to core themes from the 2008 rhetoric of hope. He crafts a message based on fairness, a belief in the value of shared prosperity, and above all on the proposition that we are all in this together. In fact, Obama's new campaign rhetoric falls into a pattern so easily discernible that one wonders why his political opponents did not try to undercut him with it more often. Perhaps hope is a hard thing to run against, especially when times are tough.

CHAPTER TEN

The 2012 Campaign

From January to November 2012, Barack Obama's political rhetoric would become increasingly populist, an inclination that also found voice in the president's policy speeches and political addresses. The 2012 State of the Union Address, for instance, is notable for its campaign-style flair. Obama begins his assessment by noting that for "the first time in nine years, there are no Americans fighting in Iraq," and perhaps more importantly, "for the first time in two decades Osama bin Laden is not a threat to this country." Politically speaking, starting with military accomplishments signals that he will not cede national security issues to Republicans during the general election.

After touting the other achievements of his administration, Obama returns to familiar tropes of the better place:

> Think about the America within our reach: a country that leads the world in educating its people; an America that attracts a new generation of high-tech manufacturing and high-paying jobs; a future where we're in control of our own energy; and our security and prosperity aren't so tied to unstable parts of the world. An economy built to last, where hard work pays off and responsibility is rewarded.
>
> We can do this. I know we can, because we've done it before. At the end of World War II, when another generation of heroes returned home from combat, they built the strongest economy and middle class the world has ever known.

Here again, Obama overlays his biography on American history by referencing his grandfather, "a veteran of Patton's Army" and his grandmother "who worked on a bomber assembly line."[1] He revisits the myth of the American Dream as a way to capture political turf traditionally held by religious conservatives, insofar as he lays claim to traditional American values and emphasizes the necessity of shared responsibility—all using folksy anecdotes. Sound familiar? It should.

After more than three years as president of the United States, Barack Obama is presiding over an anemic economic recovery, persistent high unemployment, and a devastated housing sector. Yet, he does not abandon the rhetoric of hope. Few political pundits would have predicted that Obama would recycle motifs of hope and change in 2012. Obama's decision is particularly surprising in light of the profound skepticism shared by conservatives and progressives alike concerning the nature of the change he promised in 2008 versus the reality of what he delivered. In 2010, in the middle of the economic recession, Sarah Palin famously quipped: ""How's that hope-y, change-y stuff working out for ya?"[2] In returning to the idealistic rhetoric of 2008 in his reelection campaign, Obama rhetorically confronts questions concerning the gap between the ideal and the actual in his own record. Hitting the campaign trail the day after his State of the Union Address, he urges a crowd at Conveyor Engineering and Manufacturing in Cedar Rapids, Iowa, to "work together and in common purpose" and to "build an economy that gives everybody a fair shot."[3]

In February, Obama submitted his budget request to Congress for the year. Jackie Calmes called it tantamount to his "agenda for a desired second term, with tax increases on the affluent and cuts in spending, especially from the military, both to reduce deficits and to pay for priorities like education, public works, research and clean energy."[4] In setting forth such a vision, Obama blurs the distinction between policy and the reelection campaign. On February 22, 2012, Barack and Michelle attend a groundbreaking ceremony at the new National Museum of African American History and Culture, and he uses the occasion to pitch to black voters (a demographic from which he enjoys unrivaled support). Hitting a key theme of the new campaign, he asserts that the museum "should stand as proof that the most important things in life rarely come quickly or easily. It should remind us that although we have yet to reach the mountaintop, we cannot stop climbing." Change, he concedes, does not often come quickly or easily. Drawing a familiar analogy to the odyssey African Americans endured to secure basic freedoms, he asserts: "I want my daughters to see the shackles that bound slaves on their voyage across the ocean and the shards of glass that flew from the 16th Street Baptist church, and understand that injustice and evil exist in the world. But I also want them to hear Louis Armstrong's horn and learn about the Negro League and read the poems of Phyllis [*sic*] Wheatley. And I want them to appreciate this museum not just as a record of tragedy, but as a celebration of life." Inside its walls, a history that is part of a larger American story will be told. It is the "history of a people who, in the words of Dr. King, 'injected new meaning and dignity into the veins of civilization.'"[5]

Moving slowly, yet deliberately, into full campaign mode, Obama addresses the United Auto Workers (UAW) Conference in Washington, D.C., at the end of February 2012 and uses the occasion to extol his efforts on behalf of labor and labor unions, a constituency essential to his reelection prospects. He rehearses the bleak reality faced by UAW members just a few years earlier: the disappearance of four hundred thousand jobs, the crush of the financial crisis, and the inability of the automotive industry to get the financial credit needed to keep it afloat. Without calling him out by name, Obama reminds the workers in his audience that some Republicans, that is, Mitt Romney, wanted to "let Detroit go bankrupt." By contrast, he notes that his politically unpopular decision to help the industry "retool and restructure" resulted in very positive outcomes just three years later: "GM is back on top as the number-one automaker in the world" with the "highest profits in its one-hundred-year history," and "Chrysler is growing faster in America than any other car company." Here again, Obama collectivizes the struggle for progress: "America is not just looking out for yourself. It's not just about greed. It's not just about trying to climb to the very top and keep everybody else down. When our assembly lines grind to a halt, we work together and we get them going again. When somebody else falters, we try to give them a hand up, because we know we're all in it together."[6] In the case of his remarks at the National Museum of African American History and Culture, and in this speech to the UAW, Obama uses the bully pulpit of the presidency to outline his perceived accomplishments and make the case for his reelection.

Through March and April 2012, President Obama pushes the theme of national renewal to the fore of his messaging. His campaign releases a documentary film covering his first four years in office with special trumpeting reserved for the killing of Osama Bin Laden, the mastermind of the September 11 attacks on the homeland. The film's title, *The Road We've Travelled*, alludes to a journey toward a better place, which we saw featured prominently in the 2008 rhetoric, and gives it a firm grounding in the utopian traditions of the West. In the film, important political figures and administration officials, such as Bill Clinton, Austan Goolsbee, David

Axelrod, Rahm Emanuel, and Joe Biden, testify to Obama's competence as president. The documentary film stands out not just for being an unusual medium for a campaign to employ, but because it was directed by Davis Guggenheim (of *An Inconvenient Truth* fame) and narrated by the popular actor Tom Hanks.

Hanks begins by asking the viewer, "What do we remember in November 2008?" Was it Barack Obama's election night victory, or the financial crisis that preceded it? "How do we understand this president and his time in office?" Offering viewers a clear rhetorical choice, Hanks continues, do "we look at the day's headlines or do we remember what we as a country have been through?" It's a critical question given the American tendency toward political amnesia, but even more so to the campaign, for if the answer is "the day's headlines," then Obama's chances at a second term are greatly diminished. For this reason, the film tries to remind viewers of the multitude of problems that Barack Obama inherited from the previous administration (most notably two wars in the Middle East and the worst recession since the Great Depression). Rahm Emanuel testifies that the "auto industry was literally days from collapse," and the financial sector was "frozen up" and "in cardiac arrest" when Obama came into office. The rapid decline in the value of the housing sector in 2009 was described in the film as "the biggest crash of household wealth that we've ever had in the United States."

Making a connection that was explored in considerable depth in Chapter Four, Tom Hanks declares: "Not since the days of Franklin Roosevelt had so much fallen on the shoulders of one president. And when he faced his country, who looked to him for answers, he would not dwell in blame or dreamy idealism." While Barack Obama arguably tends toward centrism and pragmatism in governing, his political rhetoric is steeped in an idealism enshrined in the country's national mythologies. Is it a "dreamy idealism"? Yes, by some measures, for the rhetoric of hope points towards a future time in which many of the ills of American society (and by extension the world) are ameliorated.

The pragmatic difficult decisions that the president had to make during his first year in office, Hanks explains, "would not only determine the course of the nation, they'd reveal the character of the man." In this passage, we find a familiar attempt in Obamian political rhetoric to persuade an ideal audience that he possesses an unusual strength of character. In this sense as well, the 2012 campaign builds upon the narrative persona developed in Barack Obama's early political writings, and it thereby extends the highly autobiographical nature of his campaign rhetoric. What one finds unique in the new campaign rhetoric is less of a focus on Obama's historic journey to prominence in American political life, and more on carefully reconstructing the seminal events of his presidency so as to frame them in the best possible light.

The Road We've Travelled lists the steps that the Obama Administration took to address the multiple crises it faced simultaneously: the Recovery Act to ease unemployment, retrain workers, and rebuild infrastructure; the unpopular automotive bailout that saved the industry; ending the war in Iraq after nine long years; bringing a new focus to Afghanistan and the elimination of Bin Laden as a threat to the United States; and the passage of the Affordable Care Act (widely and sometimes derisively known as "Obamacare") that addressed an issue "both parties had struggled with for more than three generations." The documentary ends by outlining further achievements that include Race to the Top, the Patient's Bill of Rights, the Consumer Protection Act, the Lilly Ledbetter Fair Pay Act, the creation of the Consumer Financial Protection Bureau, the repeal of Don't Ask Don't Tell, the appointment of two Supreme Court justices, and the creation of "over 3.5 million private sector jobs in two years." By Election Day, Barack Obama would be touting the creation of 5.5 million new jobs.

If, as many pundits have suggested, the president has been effective politically at the policy level but less so selling those policy achievements to the American people, this documentary aims to remedy that shortcoming. "Time and time again," Hanks offers, we can recognize the "rewards from tough decisions he had made," not for "quick political gain, but for long-term and enduring change." This evocation of change harkens back to the promises of the previous campaign. Although times are still tough, Team Obama suggests, the country is moving in the right direction; it is progressing. So, Hanks concludes, when we "consider this President, then and now, let's remember how far we've come and look forward to the work still to be done."[7]

In early April 2012, Obama takes off the gloves and starts hammering away at Mitt Romney by name, deriding him for supporting the budget proposed by Congressman Paul Ryan that would slash Medicaid and retirement benefits for federal workers while keeping taxes low on the nation's highest earners. At an Associated Press luncheon for the American Society of News Editors (ASNE) annual convention, President Obama mocked

Mitt Romney for calling the Ryan proposal "marvelous." He jokes that "is a word you don't often hear when it comes to describing a budget." Obama explains his agreement with Republicans to cut about one trillion dollars in annual spending in return for raising the debt ceiling in 2011, but he notes the new budget that Mitt Romney finds so "marvelous" would cut financial aid to college students and that "two hundred thousand children would lose their chance to get an early education in the Head Start program." In addition, hundreds of "national parks would be forced to close for part or all of the year," and we would lose "the capacity to enforce the laws that protect the air we breathe, the water we drink, or the food that we eat." It is a cutting argument, and one that highlights the strategy of the Obama campaign to frame Romney as a defender of the elite class. This position is in line with Obama's use of autobiography and a prophetic narrative persona in 2008, but it also makes sense in light of the 2011 Occupy protests discussed earlier.

In his ASNE speech, Obama calls the Republican budget, and by implication those who support it, essentially un–American:

> Disguised as deficit reduction plans, it is really an attempt to impose a radical vision on our country. It is thinly veiled social Darwinism. It is antithetical to our entire history as a land of opportunity and upward mobility for everybody who's willing to work for it; a place where prosperity doesn't trickle down from the top, but grows outward from the heart of the middle class. And by gutting the very things we need to grow an economy that's built to last — education and training, research and development, our infrastructure — it is a prescription for decline.

This reference to decline taps into an ongoing narrative concerning the loss of American hegemony in the world and an anxiety about increasing competition from countries like China, India, and Vietnam. Obama concludes his prepared remarks by returning to the myth of the American Dream. Americans have always held certain beliefs, he explains, including "that in order to preserve our own freedoms and pursue our own happiness, we can't just think about ourselves." We must, Obama offers, acknowledge "our fellow citizens with whom we share a community." Revisiting a variation of the red states and blue states argument that launched his national career at the Democratic National Convention in 2004, Obama declares: "This isn't a Democratic or Republican idea." It's patriotism. "And if we keep that in mind, and uphold our obligations to one another and to this larger enterprise that is America, then I have no doubt that we will continue our long and prosperous journey as the greatest nation on Earth."[8]

As April 2012 comes to a close, Helene Cooper reports that rather than depicting his opponent as a flip-flopper, senior administration officials, "along with Democratic and campaign officials, all say their strategy now will be to tell the world that Mr. Romney has a core after all—and it's deep red."[9] By framing his opponent as an extremist, rather than someone lacking substance, Mr. Obama can portray himself as the moderate in the 2012 race, a position that his campaign can easily reinforce due to Romney's move to the hard right during the Republican nomination process. Romney is no longer the presumptive nominee, but the party's official candidate. With him clearly in their sights, Team Obama announces the formal start date of its campaign (although the groundwork was quietly laid from January 2011 onward). On April 30, the Obama campaign begins test-driving its final slogan timed to coincide with another lengthy video release, entitled *Forward*.

On May Day 2012, the president arrives unexpectedly in Afghanistan to announce a new agreement that, in his words, "defines a new kind of relationship between our countries—a future in which Afghans are responsible for the security of their nation, and we build an equal partnership between two sovereign states; a future in which the war ends, and a new chapter begins." This dramatic visit to a war zone provides Obama with a telegenic platform for making good on a 2008 campaign promise to end both wars. Most of the American troops, he explains, are now scheduled to depart the country by 2014. Realistically, though, small numbers of soldiers and intelligence officers will "remain to accomplish two narrow security missions beyond 2014, counterterrorism and continued training." Connecting this announcement directly to the tragedy of September 11, 2001, Obama takes a moment, in an election year, to bolster his foreign policy and national defense credentials: "We broke the Taliban's momentum. We've built strong Afghan Security Forces. We devastated al-Qaida's leadership, taking out over twenty of their top thirty leaders. And one year ago, from a base here in Afghanistan, our troops launched the operation that killed Osama bin Laden. The goal that I set—to defeat al-Qaida, and deny it a chance to rebuild—is within reach." In closing he returns to central themes in the rhetoric of hope. "As we emerge from a decade of conflict abroad and economic crisis at home," he observes, "it is time to renew America. An America where our children live free from fear, and have the skills to claim their dreams. A united America of grit and resilience, where sunlight glistens off soaring new towers in downtown Manhattan, and we build our future as one people, as one nation."[10] It is a utopian vision.

On May 5, Obama held large rallies for enthusiastic supporters in the battleground states of Virginia and Ohio. Mark Lander writes that the president's rhetoric "signaled a new, more politically aggressive phase of the campaign and a sharpened critique of Mitt Romney."[11] Speaking before an audience of eight thousand supporters at Virginia Commonwealth University in Richmond, both Michelle and Barack home in on Romney and advance a depiction of the Republican opponent as elite and woefully out of touch. Michelle warms up the crowd and carefully sets up her husband's angle of attack. She argues that this election is about the "fundamental promise that no matter who you are or how you started out, if you work hard, you can build a decent life for yourself and yes, an even better life for your kids." Like her husband, she deftly employs her own biography to bolster her narrative reliability (and to heighten contrast with Romney's). She speaks of her father, who "was a blue-collar worker at the city water plant" and references "the very little apartment on the South Side of Chicago" where she grew up.

When she mentions her husband, she gives prominence to his modest upbringing: Barack Obama "is the son of a single mother who struggled to put herself through school and pay the bills. He's the grandson of a woman who woke up before dawn every day to catch a bus to her job at a bank." Glossing over the fact that Madelyn Lee Payne Dunham eventually became a vice-president for that local bank, she argues: "Barack Obama knows what it means when a family struggles" and "when someone doesn't have a chance to fulfill their potential" (a reference to the glass ceiling his grandmother hit at that financial institution). "Those are the experiences that have made him the man," she claims, "but more importantly, the President he is today."

When he takes the podium, Obama asserts that ordinary Americans are under attack and that his opponent represents the conservative forces responsible for it. It is a line of assault aimed at stinging the wealthy Romney for his pro-business stance. "The Republicans in Congress have found a champion," Obama suggests, and "they have found a nominee for president — who has promised to rubber-stamp this agenda if he gets a chance." Enlisting Bill Clinton to help define that Republican agenda as a conservative one "on steroids," Obama nails the opposition for wanting "even bigger tax cuts for the wealthiest Americans," and "even deeper cuts to things like education and Medicare and research and technology. This time, they want to give banks and insurance companies even more power to do as they please." He calls it a make-or-break moment for the middle class in America, and he implores his audience to give him more time to "move forward, to the future that we imagined in 2008."[12] Rather than running from the idealistic (and I argue fundamentally utopian) rhetoric of the last campaign, Obama continues to employ it.

On May 9, Barack Obama became the first sitting U.S. president to publicly endorse same-sex marriage. I'll resist the temptation to speculate too much about the timing for this declaration but rather simply note that the endorsement has few actual policy implications. The president's hand was seemingly forced by Joe Biden, who commented that he was "absolutely comfortable" with same-sex marriage just a few days earlier on the Sunday talk show *Meet the Press*. With the campaign already officially underway, Team Obama may have decided that the President's position had "evolved" enough on the issue to make a public announcement of his personal views on marriage equality. In moving from endorsing civil unions to full equality, Obama rehearses previous decisions of his that anticipated it, particularly the repeal of Don't Ask Don't Tell and the refusal to legally defend the Defense of Marriage Act.

Speaking to Robin Roberts of ABC's *Good Morning America*, Obama explains: "I've just concluded that—for me personally, it is important for me to go ahead and affirm that—I think same-sex couples should be able to get married. Now—I have to tell you that part of my hesitation on this has also been I didn't want to nationalize the issue. There's a tendency when I weigh in to think suddenly it becomes political and it becomes polarized." He is very careful to suggest that different states are coming to varying conclusions about same-sex marriage (North Carolina, for instance, was the thirtieth state to ban gay marriage), but he sees the country's view on the matter changing. Obama explains, "when I meet gay and lesbian couples, when I meet same-sex couples, and I see how caring they are, how much love they have in their hearts—how they're takin' care of their kids. When I hear from them the pain they feel that somehow they are still considered—less than full citizens when it comes to—their legal rights—then—for me, I think it—it just has tipped the scales in that direction." In keeping with the central message of the rhetoric of hope, and again adopting an unpretentious tone, Obama contends that "in this country we've always been about—fairness. And—and treatin' everybody—as equals. Or at least that's been our aspiration. And I think—that applies here, as well."[13]

By the end of May 2012, the Obama campaign heightens its attacks on Mitt Romney. Referring to negative advertisements that Team Obama stealthily prepared and tested months earlier, senior strategist David Axelrod concedes that in terms of tone, "we have to be very careful about the fact that the President does have standards and does have a brand that he feels strongly about." That "brand" is based on hope and a belief in gradual social amelioration. However, the hardball nature of presidential politics means that taking the high road or failing to respond to political attacks launched by opponents can result in defeat (the most obvious example being the "swift-boating" of John Kerry in 2004). Axelrod spins the Obama campaign's use of negative advertising this way: "I think it's possible to be tough and also fair, tough and also factual. And that's what we're going to do."[14] As the campaign ramps up to full speed, Peter Baker reports on the nineteen-hour days Obama is working and how his schedule is increasingly consumed by campaigning. Despite the demands on him, Barack Obama remains constantly engaged in the speechwriting process, much as he did in 2008. On one such occasion, Baker reports, Obama "spent the flight to Iowa editing speeches, scribbling in the margins."[15]

With the onset of summer, the Obama campaign attempts to frame the choice between the two nominees as either a return to the Republican policies of the previous administration that caused the economic collapse or continuance of the pro-growth policies of the current administration. Speaking at Cuyahoga Community College in Cleveland, Ohio, in the middle of June 2012, Obama refers to the stalemate in Washington that prevents further progress in improving the economy. He opens by reminding his audience of the Republican failure to "pay for the tax cuts and the wars" that "took us from record surpluses under President Bill Clinton to record deficits. And it left us unprepared to deal with the retirement of an aging population that's placing a greater strain on programs like Medicare and Social Security." By contrast, he claims that quick action resulted in economic growth just "six months after I took office and it has continued to grow for the last three years." He lists further accomplishments but acknowledges that they are not enough, for the country is still "digging out from an entire decade where six million manufacturing jobs left our shores; where costs rose but incomes and wages didn't; and where the middle class fell further and further behind."[16] By making the argument strongly and relatively early in the campaign season, the Obama team hoped to shift the narrative from a dark brooding over continued economic woe to a belief that at least things were going in the right direction: "Forward."

In what might be construed as another shrewd election year appeal to a crucial demographic, on June 15, 2012, Obama issues an Executive Order to permit nearly eight hundred thousand young migrants to remain in the United States. Under that order, if an illegal immigrant arrived in the country before age sixteen, resided here for five or more years, graduated from high school or served in the military, and has no criminal record, then he or she will no longer face deportation and will be allowed to work legally in the United States and apply for official documents such as driver's licenses. In his prepared remarks, Obama explains the rationale for his decision. These young people "are Americans in their heart, in their minds, in every single way but one: on paper. They were brought to this country by their parents—sometimes even as infants—and often have no idea that they're undocumented until they apply for a job or a driver's license, or a college scholarship." He makes clear that he is acting now because of Republican obstruction of the DREAM Act, which would have allowed young people like these a path towards citizenship. "In the absence of any immigration action from Congress," Obama asserts, this "temporary stopgap measure" allows "us to focus our resources wisely while giving a degree of relief and hope to talented, driven, patriotic young people." Falling back on his values-driven rhetoric, he concludes that taking this action was simply "the right thing to do."[17]

Later that same month, the Supreme Court upholds the Affordable Care Act, giving President Obama an unexpected victory just months before the election. Speaking from the White House, a triumphant yet modest Barack Obama sought to downplay the political dimensions of the decision: "Whatever the politics, today's decision was a victory for people all over this country whose lives will be more secure because of this law and the Supreme Court's decision to uphold it." Instead of parsing the rationale behind the court's decision, Obama lists the central benefits of the legislation: no more lifetime limits for coverage, insurance premiums cannot go up if one becomes ill, children with pre-existing conditions can no longer be discriminated against, young adults can stay on their parents' policy until twenty-six years of age, and thirty million uninsured Americans will soon have "an array of quality, affordable, private health insurance plans to choose from" through insurance exchanges. Obama ends his remarks with an allusion to his new campaign slogan: "But today, I'm as confident as ever that when we look back five years from now, or ten years from now, or twenty years from now, we'll be better off because we had the courage to pass this law and keep moving forward."[18]

As the hot and dry summer of 2012 progressed, the Obama campaign continued to hammer away at Mitt Romney in hopes of defining the discourse around him before he could introduce himself to the general electorate. Obama is impeded in making his case by a slowing economic recovery and stubbornly high unemployment at 8.2 percent — not an enviable place for an incumbent politician facing reelection. On the "Betting on America" bus tour through two swing states, Ohio and Pennsylvania, in early July 2012, Obama acknowledges as much. In a campaign speech at Carnegie Mellon University, he argues that the upcoming election is "about two fundamentally different visions of where we take America." He argues that the Republicans' "basic vision is one that says we're going to give five trillion of new tax cuts on top of the Bush tax cuts, most of them going to the wealthiest Americans" that would be "paid for by slashing education funding."

By way of juxtaposition, Obama outlines a vision of greater access to education, of investment in infrastructure and social protections, and even of high-speed rail and broadband Internet access across the country. Whereas Republicans like his wealthy opponent want to give top earners more tax breaks and relax regulations on business, Obama returns to the positive role that the American government can play in the lives of the majority of its citizens. Hoping to ride a wave of populist backlash against the so-called 1 percent, the Obama campaign launches attacks on Bain Capital, the company Romney ran through his tenure as chief executive of the 2002 Winter Olympics in Salt Lake City. In doing so, Obama attempts to put Romney's class and wealth on trial before the voters, rather than let Romney frame the debate around the weak state of the economy. By late July, those attacks had put Romney's campaign on the defensive about his time at Bain, particularly concerning the actual end date of his employment and how much outsourcing of American jobs the company did under his leadership. The Obama campaign also ratcheted up pressure on Mitt Romney to publicly release more than one or two years of his tax returns.

As August 2012 approached, Team Romney was clearly losing the rhetorical battle when conservative pundits like George Will suggested that since the high "cost of not releasing the [tax] returns are clear," by implication there must be still "higher costs in releasing them."[19] What was Romney hiding? Suddenly and unexpectedly, the political winds were shifting, putting Romney in the court of public opinion for his lack of transparency, record at Bain, and privileged upbringing. This portrayal of Romney is reinforced, as Richard Stevenson observes, by the candidate's own unfortunate choice of words: "Challenging a rival to a ten thousand dollar bet, citing friendships with Nascar owners, casually mentioning his ownership of 'a couple of Cadillacs' and asserting that 'corporations are people'—[these] have given Democrats ample fodder to portray him as detached from the anxieties of middle-class life."[20] The fight was on, and Obama was landing the early punches.

In late July and early August, the 2012 Summer Olympics took public attention away from politics and the presidential campaigns, but when they were over, there were less than one hundred days remaining until the election. On August 12, Mitt Romney announced congressman Paul Ryan of Wisconsin as his running mate. The Obama campaign seemed delighted by the choice, as earlier in the year it had pummeled Romney over his full-throated endorsement of the Ryan budget. Now, the assumption was that the choice of the young Congressman would prove an ideal target, as it would further tether Mr. Romney to an economic plan that would "voucherize" Medicare. David Axelrod awkwardly called the two of them the "Go Back Team." As he explained in a message to supporters on the day of the announcement:

> In Ryan, Romney has selected a running mate best known for designing the extreme GOP budget that would end Medicare as we know it, and—just like Romney's plan—actually raise taxes on middle-class Americans to pay for an additional $250,000 tax break for millionaires and billionaires. As a leader of the House Republicans and a Tea Party favorite, Congressman Ryan has led the relentless, intensely ideological battle for these kinds of budget-busting policies that punish seniors and the middle class.[21]

In this excerpt, Axelrod signals that the campaign felt it could attack Romney as a radical right-winger, a rhetorical position that it anticipated being able to defend with material from the Republican nominating process in which the governor had to get to the right of politicians like Newt Gingrich and Rick Santorum to win.

What Team Obama did not fully anticipate was how slippery Romney, a notorious flip-flopper, could be. President Obama would find out personally during the first presidential debate, in which he faced an opponent almost unrecognizably moderate, and one whom Obama was ill prepared to call out for changing positions with such fluidity. This lack of foresight, combined with perhaps some hubris on the president's part, would mean more than just squandering a lead in the polls. Barack Obama's first debate performance was so widely panned that the race would remain a virtual tie right up to Election Day. Despite his repeated declarations to the contrary, "Axe" could not have been pleased that what should have been an effective line of rhetorical attack was seemingly neutralized by the opponent during the first debate.

Immediately following the selection of Paul Ryan, Barack Obama hit the campaign trail in the Midwest. Speaking on August 14 in Iowa, the state that propelled his unlikely bid for the presidency in 2008 and one crucial to his reelection prospects, Obama explains to those gathered at the Nelson Pioneer Farm & Museum in Oskaloosa that a better tomorrow still lies beyond the horizon: "I'm back because our journey is not done. We're spending three days driving all the way across the state, just like we did in 2007 and 2008; we're going from Council Bluffs all the way to the Quads, Quad Cities, because once again you face a critical choice in November." Obama frames the choice between he and his opponent as one "between two fundamentally different visions of how America became great and how it's going to stay great, two fundamentally different visions of the path we need to take for the future of our kids and our grandkids."

Obama doubles down on a key theme from the 2008 campaign, that the "core idea" in the American way of life "says if you work hard in this country, you can get ahead; that if you take responsibility, then you can make it, and you can get into the middle class." Mitt Romney, by defending the interests of the elite and embracing the budget proposal written by Paul Ryan, stands directly in the way of the realization of that middle class aspiration. Obama calls Romney out for the "centerpiece" of his economic plan: "to give another five trillion tax cut on top of the Bush tax cuts that he's keeping." The Romney tax plan, Obama explains, "would actually raise taxes on middle-class families" in order "to pay for this big tax break that's going mostly to the wealthiest folks." Obama calls Romney a "pioneer of outsourcing" during his time in the private sector and accuses him of pandering the same "trickle down fairy-dust" of the Bush era.

By way of conclusion, Obama returns to a political autobiography virtually indistinguishable from that of 2008: "And when I think about my own life, when I think about Michelle's life — we didn't come from wealth. We didn't come from fame. But we were lucky enough to be born in a country where here, everybody gets a fair shot, everybody does their fair share, everybody plays by the same set of rules— no matter what you look like, no matter where you come from, no matter what your last name is, you can make it here if you try. That's the story of America. That's your story."[22] In other words, the rhetoric of hope had been repackaged for a new campaign, a new adversary, and to accommodate a less than ideal four-year record as president.

Leading up to the Democratic National Convention in September 2012, Helene Cooper notes that Obama was hitting the "four must-dos in every politician's instruction manual" with relative ease: display familiarity, display arcane knowledge, use an available prop, and show you have paid attention. One might take issue with Cooper's list of "must-dos," but she puts her finger on an important gift that the president has to socially and linguistically accommodate to his audience. She notes that Barack Obama opens his 2012 campaign speeches by "assuming the persona of wherever he happens to be, inserting place-specific asides." In New Hampshire he was "suddenly Mr. New England," noting that his daughters were "up here for camp for a month." By contrast, in Iowa a few weeks earlier "the president became Joe Six-Pack, talking about beer at every stop," while on a local college campus he "transformed into the graduate plagued by student loans" (by noting that he and Michelle did not pay off their student loans until eight years ago). Copper observes that by the end of that speech, Obama "was emoting into the microphone like a preacher."[23]

The 2012 Democratic National Convention featured many speakers, all of whom made the case for an Obama second term, but none of them did so more forcibly than Bill Clinton, who offered the most robust and systematic defense of the Obama presidency as anyone before or after him. This study of Obamian rhetoric is not the place to examine it in detail, but a few brief excerpts can capture the gist of Clinton's claim. After bashing the Republican agenda as "the same old policies that got us in trouble in the first place," the former president asserts: "I like the argument for President Obama's re-election a lot better. Here it is. He inherited a deeply damaged economy. He put a floor under the crash. He began the long, hard road to recovery and laid the foundation for a modern, more well-balanced economy that will produce millions of good new jobs, vibrant new businesses and lots of new wealth for innovators." He argues that "Obama's approach embodies the values, the ideas and the direction America has to take to build the 21st-century version of the American Dream: a nation of shared opportunities, shared responsibilities, shared prosperity, a shared sense of community." Concluding on a note that deliberately echoes the rhetoric of hope, Clinton insists the United States is "coming back" because "in the end we decide to champion the cause for which our founders pledged their lives, their fortunes, their sacred honor — the cause of forming a more perfect union."[24]

After Bill Clinton's fiery speech, Barack Obama's is more like dénouement. He opens with an allusion to his 2004 address before the same convention, one that launched him into the political limelight. Obama explains that, back then, he was "a Senate candidate from Illinois who spoke about hope, not blind optimism, not wishful thinking but hope in the face of difficulty, hope in the face of uncertainty, that dogged faith in the future which has pushed this nation forward." Eight years later, he admits, "that hope has been tested by the cost of war, by one of the worst economic crises in history and by political gridlock." After rehearsing his accomplishments, he concedes that a future shaped by the utopian principle of hope "will take more than a few years" and will "require common effort, shared responsibility, and the kind of bold, persistent experimentation that Franklin Roosevelt pursued during the only crisis worse than this one." The path he offers voters might be harder, "but it leads to a better place."[25] Writing in the *New York Times*, H. Samy Alim and Geneva Smitherman note central elements of what I call the rhetoric of hope in this 2012 speech, including Obama's "embrace of the black preacher tradition," and they marvel at his unrivaled "linguistic fluidity." Echoing one of the findings of this study, they conclude: "Mr. Obama's ability to bring together 'white syntax' with 'black style' played a critical role in establishing his identity as both an American and a Christian."[26]

Back on the campaign trail two days after the convention in the swing state of Florida, Obama assures anxious seniors that he will never turn Medicare into a voucher system. He embraces the term "Obamacare," and uses it to contrast himself and his opponent by noting flatly that the governor's vow to repeal it means "Romney doesn't care." In late September, Barack Obama is able to reinforce that point by referencing video secretly recorded at a private fundraiser in which Mitt Romney characterized

Obama voters as the 47 percent who rely on government handouts and do not pay taxes. At a campaign event in Milwaukee, Wisconsin, Obama sets up a new line of attack by returning to the change mantra that defined the 2008 race: "I've always said that change is going to take more than one term and one—more than one President, and it takes more than one party." However, that change can't happen "if you write off half the nation before you take office," Obama argues. "In 2008, forty-seven percent of the country didn't vote for me. But on election night I said to those Americans, I may not have won your vote, but I heard your voices, and I'll be your President, too."[27] Here Obamian political rhetoric is used to create contrast between the Democratic and Republican platforms, as well as the men representing them. This strategy of juxtaposition allowed Obama to open up an important lead in the polls just six weeks before Election Day— one that he was able to hold on to until Romney soundly bested him in the first presidential debate.

The Romney bounce that followed that debate meant that the race would remain virtually deadlocked up to Election Day. Despite two strong subsequent debate performances, Obama failed to regain the momentum that he enjoyed in September 2012. Speculation abounded in the media as to the causes of the first debate fiasco. Was Obama tired? Did he not prepare properly? Why did he arrive so late? Did the altitude of Denver affect him? Whatever the reason, Barack Obama underestimated his opponent. I'm reminded of a similar instance in January 2008 when then Senator Obama patronizingly quipped to Senator Clinton in the final debate of the New Hampshire primary: "You're likeable enough, Hillary." That comment, combined with an unexpectedly emotive response by Clinton to a question about how she dealt with the rigors of campaigning, contributed to Obama's loss in New Hampshire—a loss that would mean enduring an unusually drawn out nomination process. Now, once again, Barack Obama faced defeat by a political adversary whom he failed to properly size up.

In mid–October, the Obama team releases a short video narrated by the actor Morgan Freeman, entitled *Challenges*. It reinforces the slogan "Forward" by noting the progress made over the last four years. "Every president inherits challenges," Freeman explains, but "few have faced so many. Four years later our enemies have been brought to justice. Our heroes are coming home. Assembly lines are humming again—there are still challenges to meet, children to educate, a middle class to rebuild but the last thing we should do is turn back now." While the central elements of the rhetoric of hope are still apparent in Obama's political discourse, Ezra Klein points out that it lacks the audacity of 2008. He explains that this lack of daring is due to Team Obama research showing Americans "are tired of audacity and skeptical of big ideas. They're willing to believe Obama has done about the best job he could have been expected to do given the collapse of the global economy and the intransigence of the Republicans," but the campaign risks looking absurd if it hits the idealism too hard. As Klein succinctly puts it: "Better to underpromise and, if all goes well, overdeliver, than to overpromise and lose the election."[28]

So rather than outlining an agenda of big ideas in the waning days of the contest, Barack Obama continues to hammer away at Mitt Romney's lack of integrity by insinuating that the man will say anything to get elected. Speaking before an audience in Fairfax, Virginia, Professor Obama offers a diagnosis of his rival's incessant "backtracking and sidestepping." He declares, "I think it's called 'Romnesia.' That's what it's called. I think that's what he's going through." Obama taunts his opponent:

> I'm not a medical doctor, but I do want to go over some of the symptoms with you — because I want to make sure nobody else catches it. If you say you're for equal pay for equal work, but you keep refusing to say whether or not you'd sign a bill that protects equal pay for equal work — you might have Romnesia.
>
> If you say women should have access to contraceptive care, but you support legislation that would let your employer deny you contraceptive care — you might have a case of Romnesia.
>
> If you say you'll protect a woman's right to choose, but you stand up at a primary debate and said that you'd be delighted to sign a law outlawing that right to choose in all cases — man, you've definitely got Romnesia.[29]

It is a withering line of attack, and one that has been building to a crescendo since midsummer 2012. Note also the use of repetition, colloquial speech, and the cadences of the pulpit preacher examined in previous chapters of this study.

The slow formation of Hurricane Sandy, and its landfall on October 29, just a week before the election, gave President Obama unrivaled visibility, for Mitt Romney was forced to suspend his campaign. Governor Chris Christie, whose state of New Jersey was hit particularly hard by the storm, joined other Republicans in lauding the president for his leadership during a time of national crisis. When Obama and Romney returned to the campaign trail at the beginning of November, pundits were speaking about a "Sandy bounce" for the president. Perhaps in desperation at the end of a long race, the Romney team attempts to co-opt the change message that first propelled Barack Obama to the presidency. The implication was that Obama, after four years in office, represented the status quo. Writing for the *Huffington Post*, Jon Ward noted, "Romney's assertion of control over the 'change' label has irked the Obama campaign." When asked by the newspaper about the Romney move to "seize the change mantle," Ward observed that "Axelrod, the mild-mannered strategist, wrinkled up his nose in irritation," then asserted that they would confront such a "preposterous" proposition "head-on."[30]

Therefore, in his closing arguments of the 2012 campaign, President Obama pushes back on Romney's usurpation of the change message. Addressing a group in Las Vegas, Nevada, on November 1, Obama derides his Republican opponent for being disingenuous: "My opponent can talk about change, but I know what real change looks like because I've fought for it. I've got the scars to prove it." The more populist appeal of Obama's 2012 rhetoric of hope is on display in assertions such as this one: "folks at the very top in this country, they don't need a champion in Washington." It is ordinary "Americans whose letters I read late at night; the men and women I meet on the campaign trail every single day" who need an advocate. Obama adopts the tone a prophet leading his people to a better place, to a Promised Land. "We've come too far to turn back now. We've come too far to let our hearts grow faint, to go weary. Now is the time to keep pushing forward—to educate all our kids and train all our workers, to create new jobs and rebuild our infrastructure, to discover new sources of energy, to broaden opportunity, to grow our middle class, to restore our democracy—to make sure that no matter who you are, or where you come from, or how you started out, you can make it here in America. That's why we are moving forward."[31]

Speaking in the battleground state of Ohio on November 2, Obama reminds voters that he is running "because the voice of the American people" has been "shut out of our democracy for way too long by lobbyists and special interests; politicians who will do whatever it takes to keep things just the way they are. And over the last four years, you've seen it— the status quo in Washington has fought us every step of the way."[32] Despite his incumbency, Barack Obama continues to portray himself as an agent of social transformation. In this sense, the 2012 campaign rhetoric is a natural extension of that which came before it. With the contest too close to call, the Obama camp would have to wait for poll results on

November 6 to learn if its gamble of rhetorical continuity across two election cycles would pay off.

In his 2012 victory speech, delivered shortly after midnight on November 7, Barack Obama brings the rhetoric of hope to a close (for Mr. Obama claims this will be his last election). Not only does he revisit key themes from the 2008 campaign, at times he reaches further into the past in ways that have been discussed in the preceding pages. The opening line puts that rhetorical continuity into sharp focus: "Tonight, more than 200 years after a former colony won the right to determine its own destiny, the task of perfecting our union moves forward." The task of amelioration is gradual and requires collective effort. This country, Obama asserts, "moves forward because you reaffirmed the spirit that has triumphed over war and depression; the spirit that has lifted this country from the depths of despair to the great heights of hope — the belief that while each of us will pursue our own individual dreams, we are an American family, and we rise or fall together, as one nation, and as one people." The nation is on a journey to economic recovery that "has been long," but, he explains encouragingly, "we have picked ourselves up, we have fought our way back, and we know in our hearts that for the United States of America, the best is yet to come." The tacit assertion here is that speculation about an era of American decline is overstated.

Obama accepts the fact that in a country of three hundred million people democracy "can be noisy and messy and complicated." However, political arguments are worth having, for their very existence in factious times such as these "are a mark of our liberty." Besides, Obama points out, what the American people hold in common, their shared "hopes for America's future," trumps ideological division:

> We believe in a generous America; in a compassionate America; in a tolerant America, open to the dreams of an immigrant's daughter who studies in our schools and pledges to our flag. To the young boy on the South Side of Chicago who sees a life beyond the nearest street corner. To the furniture worker's child in North Carolina who wants to become a doctor or a scientist, an engineer or entrepreneur, a diplomat or even a President. That's the future we hope for. That's the vision we share. That's where we need to go. Forward. That's where we need to go.

Barack Obama is always beckoning to the future in the rhetoric of hope. He grounds his optimism for the "Not Yet" in the nation's past: "As it has for more than two centuries, progress will come in fits and starts.

It's not always a straight line. It's not always a smooth path." Despite "all the hardship we've been through, despite all the frustrations of Washington," Barack Obama has "never been more hopeful about our future," or about America, and he asks the country to "sustain that hope."

In concluding his 2012 victory speech, the president seeks to refute the notion that his rhetoric, which he claims matches his beliefs and informs his decision making, is utopian (in the pejorative sense of something chimerical). "I'm not talking about blind optimism — the kind of hope that just ignores the enormity of the tasks ahead or the roadblocks that stand in our path," he states flatly. "I'm not talking about the wishful idealism that allows us to just sit on the sidelines or shirk from a fight." Rather, he carefully defines the parameters his soaring idealism, which features so prominently in his campaign rhetoric: "I have always believed that hope is that stubborn thing inside us that insists, despite all the evidence to the contrary, that something better awaits us, so long as we have the courage to keep reaching, to keep working, to keep fighting."

In the final sentences of his 2012 victory speech, which would usher in his second term, Barack Obama returns to the motif of American unity that brought him to national prominence following a historic speech before the Democratic National Convention in 2004. In this sense, the rhetoric of hope contains a neat circularity that is the product of intentional design. For this reason alone, it seems fitting and proper to bring this study of presidential rhetoric to a close by citing the final passage of Obama's last acceptance speech for elected office. "I believe we can seize this future together," Obama declares, "because we are not as divided as our politics suggest; we're not as cynical as the pundits believe; we are greater than the sum of our individual ambitions; and we remain more than a collection of red states and blue states. We are, and forever will be, the United States of America. And together, with your help, and God's grace, we will continue our journey forward, and remind the world just why it is that we live in the greatest nation on Earth."[33]

Chapter Notes

Introduction

1. Ernst Bloch, *The Principle of Hope*, 3 vols. (Cambridge: MIT Press, 1995).

2. Martin Buber, *Paths in Utopia* (Boston: Beacon Hill, 1949), 7–8.

3. Nathaniel Coleman, *Utopias and Architecture* (New York: Taylor & Francis, 2005), 34

4. Karl Mannheim, *Ideology and Utopia: An Introduction to the Sociology of Knowledge* (New York: Harvest, 1985), 196.

5. United States Declaration of Independence, 1776.

6. Sculley Bradley, *American Tradition in Literature* (New York: Grosset & Dunlap, 1975), 236.

7. Walt Whitman. "Pioneers! O Pioneers!" *The Harvard Classics*, vol. 42, ed. Charles W. Eliot (New York: P.F. Collier & Sons, 1976), 54.

8. Ralph Waldo Emerson, *Emerson on Transcendentalism*, ed. Edward L. Ericson (New York: Ungar, 1986), 54–55.

9. Benjamin Franklin, *The Autobiography and Other Writings*, ed. Jessie L. Lemisch (New York: New American Library, 1961), 16.

10. John Seelye, "The Clay Foot of the Climber: Richard M. Nixon in Perspective," *Literary Romanticism in America*, ed. William L. Andrews (Baton Rouge: Louisiana State University Press, 1981), 110.

11. D. Merezhkovsky, *Tolstoi I Dostoevsky* (Moskva: Respliblika, 1995).

12. Henry David Thoreau, *Walden and Civil Disobedience*, ed. Owen Thomas (New York: W.W. Norton, 1966), 61.

Chapter One

1. Obama, Barack. *Dreams from My Father* (New York: Three Rivers Press, 2004), 133.

2. Ibid., 157.

3. Ibid., 122.

4. Barack Obama, *The Audacity of Hope: Thoughts on Reclaiming the American Dream* (New York: Vintage, 2008), 245–46.

5. Ibid., 134.

6. Jürgen Moltmann, *Theology of Hope* (New York: Harper & Row, 1965), 17.

7. Obama. *The Audacity of Hope*, 11, 22, 28, 113, 274.

8. Jill Abramson, V. Alabiso, T. Masuda, et al. *Obama: The Historic Journey* (New York: The New York Times, 2009), 109.

9. Mirian Eliav-Feldon, *Realistic Utopias: The Ideal Imaginary Societies of the Renaissance* (Oxford: Oxford University Press, 1982), 1.

10. Saint Augustine, *The Confessions of St. Augustine*, trans. J.M. Lelen (Totowa, NJ: Catholic Books, 1997), 346.

11. Martin Buber, *Paths in Utopia* (Boston: Beacon Hill, 1949), 7–8.

12. Ernst Bloch, *The Principle of Hope*, 3 vols. (Cambridge: MIT Press, 1995), 203.

13. Moltmann, *Theology of Hope*, 15–16.

14. Gerhard Von Rad, *The Message of the Prophets* (New York: Harper & Row, 1967), 207.

15. Roland DeVaux, "Jerusalem and the Prophets," *Interpreting the Prophetic Tradition*, ed. Harry Orlinsky (Cincinnati: Hebrew Union College Press, 1969), 277.

16. Gerhard Von Rad, *The Message of the Prophets* (New York: Harper & Row, 1967), 207.

17. Frank Kermode, *The Sense of an Ending: Studies in the Theory of Fiction* (Oxford: Oxford University Press, 1967), 14 and 100.

18. James Thurber Johnson, *The Bible in American Law, Politics, and Political Rhetoric* (Philadelphia: Fortress Press, 1985), 1.

19. James Darsey, *The Prophetic Tradition and Radical Rhetoric in America* (New York: New York University Press, 1997), 16 and 202.

20. Ibid., 203.

21. Paul Ricoeur, *Lectures on Ideology and Utopia* (New York: Columbia University Press, 1986), 278.

22. Ibid., 104–109.

23. Abramson, et al., *Obama*, 128–132.

24. Ibid., 220–21.

25. Ibid.

26. Ibid.

27. Obama, *Dreams from My Father*, 135.

28. Obama, *The Audacity of Hope*, 80.

29. David Remnick, *The Bridge: The Life and Rise of Barack Obama* (New York: Knopf, 2010), 19.

30. Obama, *The Audacity of Hope*, 274.

31. Obama, *Dreams from My Father*, 437.

32. Obama, *The Audacity of Hope*, 241.

33. Obama, *Dreams from My Father*, 294.

34. Remnick, *The Bridge*, 20.

35. Selma Voting Rights March Commemoration Speech, March 4, 2007.

36. Obama, *The Audacity of Hope*, 179 and 254.

37. Ibid., 253 and 256.

38. Obama, *Change We Can Believe In*, 246 and 259.

39. Ibid., 199–201.

40. Ibid., 193.

41. Ibid., 181.

42. Obama, 196.

43. Ibid., 1.

44. Abramson, et al., *Obama*, 235–36.

45. Obama, *Change We Can Believe In*, 180.

Chapter Two

1. David O. Stewart, *The Summer of 1787: The Men Who Invented the Constitution* (New York: Simon & Schuster, 2007), 45 & 235.

2. James T. Kloppenberg, *Reading Obama: Dreams, Hope, and the American Political Tradition* (Princeton: Princeton University Press, 2011), 151–52.

3. Ibid., 153–54.

4. Ibid., 161.

5. Francis Bacon, "The New Atlantis," *Three Early Modern Utopias: Utopia, New Atlantis, and Isle of the Pines*, ed. Susan Bruce (Oxford: Oxford University Press, 1999), 160.

6. Will Durant and Ariel Durant, *The Story of Civilization: Part VIII* (New York: Simon & Schuster, 1963), 179.

7. Nell Eurich, *Science in Utopia: A Mighty Design* (Cambridge: Harvard University Press, 1967), 141 and 166.

8. Carl L. Becker, *The Declaration of Independence: A Study in the History of Ideas* (New York: Knopf, 1964), 60.

9 Ibid., 26.

10. Winton U. Solberg, *The Constitutional Convention and the Formation of the Union* (Urbana: University of Illinois Press, 1990), xx.

11. Ibid., xx–xxi.

12. Ibid., xxii–xxiv.

13. Ibid., xxxv.

14. Ibid., xxxv.

15. Ibid., xxxiv–xxxv.

16. Walter B. Mead, *The United States: Personalities, Principles, and Issues* (Columbia: University of South Carolina Press), 76.

17. Solberg, *The Constitutional Convention and the Formation of the Union*, xxxvi.

18. Carl J. Friedrich and Robert G. McCloskey, eds., *From Declaration of Independence to the Constitution: The Roots of American Constitutionalism* (New York: Liberal Arts Press, 1954), x–xii.

19. Durant, *The Story of Civilization*, 581.

20. Becker, *The Declaration of Independence*, 57.

21. Solberg, Winton U. *The Constitutional Convention and the Formation of the Union* (Urbana: University of Illinois Press, 1990), xxxvii–xl.

22. Mead, *The United States: Personalities, Principles, and Issues*, 88.

23. Ibid., 81.

24. Solberg, *The Constitutional Convention and the Formation of the Union*, xliv and lv.

25. Barack Obama, *The Audacity of Hope: Thoughts on Reclaiming the American Dream* (New York: Vintage, 2008), 64–65.

26. Ibid., 111–13.

27. Becker, *The Declaration of Independence*, 5.

28. Ibid., 10 and 16.

29. Stewart, *The Summer of 1787*, 165.

30. Solberg, *The Constitutional Convention and the Formation of the Union*, ciii.

31. Mead, *The United States: Personalities, Principles, and Issues*, 89.

32. Obama, *The Audacity of Hope*, 275.

33. Heather E. Harris, et al., eds., *The Obama Effect: Multidisciplinary Renderings of the 2008 Campaign* (Albany: SUNY Press, 2010), 16–17.

34. Barack Obama, *Change We Can Be-*

lieve In (New York: Three Rivers Press, 2008), 207.

35. Gwen Ifill, *The Breakthrough: Politics and Race in the Age of Obama* (New York: Anchor, 2009), 52.

36. Obama, *The Audacity of Hope*, 104–05.

37. Ibid., 108.

38. Mary Frances Berry and Josh Gottheimer, *Power in Words: The Stories Behind Barack Obama's Speeches, From the State House to the White House.* Boston: Beacon Press, 2010), 205.

39. Kloppenberg, *Reading Obama*, ix and 43.

40. Ibid., 218.

Chapter Three

1. C. Eric Lincoln, ed. *The Black Experience in Religion* (New York: Anchor, 1974), 7–8.

2. Henry Lewis Gates and William Andrews, eds., *Pioneers of the Black Atlantic: Five Slave Narratives from the Enlightenment, 1722–1815* (Washington, DC: Counterpoint, 1998), 2–3.

3. Ibid., 369.

4. Ibid., 65.

5. Yuval Taylor, ed. *Growing Up in Slavery: Stories Told by Young Slaves as Told by Themselves* (Chicago: Lawrence Hill, 2005), 28–29.

6. Ibid., 126–27.

7. Ibid., xvi.

8. Charles T. Davis and Henry Louis Gates, *The Slave's Narrative* (Oxford: Oxford University Press, 1985), 149–51.

9 Yuval Taylor, *I Was Born a Slave: An Anthology of Classic Slave Narratives* (Chicago: Lawrence Hill, 1999), 539.

10. Ibid., 586.

11. Ibid., 715.

12. Taylor, ed. *Growing Up in Slavery*, 27.

13. Lincoln, ed. *The Black Experience in Religion*, 12–13.

14. Gaylaud S. Wilmore, *Black Religion and Black Radicalism* (New York: Doubleday, 1972), 18.

15. Barack Obama, *Dreams from My Father* (New York: Three Rivers Press, 2004), 437.

16. Wilmore, *Black Religion and Black Radicalism*, 36.

17. Eric C. Lincoln and Lawrence Mamiya. *The Black Church in the African American Experience* (Durham: Duke University Press, 1990), 200–03.

18. Ibid., 349.

19. Ibid., 17.

20. Ibid., 4–6.

21. Ibid., 234–35.

22. Barack Obama, *The Audacity of Hope: Thoughts on Reclaiming the American Dream* (New York: Vintage, 2008), 245.

23. Obama, *Dreams from My Father*, 134–35.

24. Heather E. Harris, et al., eds. *The Obama Effect: Multidisciplinary Renderings of the 2008 Campaign* (Albany: SUNY Press, 2010), 21 and 24.

25. James T. Kloppenberg, *Reading Obama: Dreams, Hope, and the American Political Tradition* (Princeton: Princeton University Press, 2011), 215–16.

26. Mary Frances Berry and Josh Gottheimer, *Power in Words: The Stories Behind Barack Obama's Speeches, From the State House to the White House.* Boston: Beacon Press, 2010), xxxi.

27. Richard. Wolffe, *Revival: The Struggle for Survival Inside the Obama White House* (New York: Crown, 2010), 23.

28. Lincoln, ed. *The Black Experience in Religion*, 77.

29. Mark Newman, *The Civil Rights Movement* (Edinburgh: Edinburgh University Press, 2004), 6–7.

30. Ibid., 69.

31. Obama, *Dreams from My Father*, 145.

32. Ibid., 86.

33. Berry and Gottheimer, *Power in Words*, 47.

34. Ibid., 49.

35. Abramson, et al., *Obama*, 69.

36. Joshua Brown, *Forever Free: The Story of Emancipation and Reconstruction* (New York: Knopf, 2005), 9–10.

37. Taylor, *I Was Born a Slave*, 232.

Chapter Four

1. R.B. Bernstein, *Thomas Jefferson* (Oxford: Oxford University Press, 2003), xiv.

2. Christopher Hitchens, *Thomas Jefferson: Author of America* (New York: HarperCollins, 2005), 43.

3. Bernstein, *Thomas Jefferson*, x.

4. Ibid., 38 and 50.

5. Adrienne Koch, *The Philosophy of Thomas Jefferson* (Chicago: Quadrangle, 1964), 105.

6. Bernstein, *Thomas Jefferson*, 95.

7. Peter S. Onuf, *The Mind of Thomas Jefferson* (Charlottesville: University of Virginia Press, 2007), 5.

8. Bernstein, *Thomas Jefferson*, 66.

9 Ibid., 29.

10. Ibid., 146.

11. Thomas Jefferson, *Writings* (New York: Library of America, 1984), 1301.

12. Koch, *The Philosophy of Thomas Jefferson*, 25 and 28.

13. Ibid., 147.

14. Jefferson, *Writings*, 1398–1401.

15. Frank Irwin, *Letters of Thomas Jefferson* (Tilton, NH: Sanbornton Bridge Press, 1975), 5.

16. Onuf, *The Mind of Thomas Jefferson*, 10–11.

17. Jefferson, *Writings*, 959.

18. Ibid., 911.

19. Hitchens, *Thomas Jefferson*, 73.

20. David N. Mayer, *The Constitutional Thought of Thomas Jefferson* (Charlottesville: University of Virginia Press, 1994), 104.

21. Koch, *The Philosophy of Thomas Jefferson*, 117.

22. Onuf, *The Mind of Thomas Jefferson*, 34.

23. Letter to Henry L. Pierce, April 6, 1859.

24. Ralph W. Emerson, *Selected Essays* (New York: Penguin, 1982), 183.

25. William E. Gienapp, *The Fiery Trial: The Speeches and Writings of Abraham Lincoln* (Oxford: Oxford University Press, 2002), 1–3.

26. Ibid., 7.

27. Ibid., 2–3.

28. William E. Gienapp, *Abraham Lincoln and Civil War America: A Biography* (Oxford: Oxford University Press, 2002), 62.

29. Ibid., 70.

30. Gienapp, *The Fiery Trial*, 31–34.

31. Ibid., 13.

32. Barack. Obama, *The Audacity of Hope: Thoughts on Reclaiming the American Dream* (New York: Vintage, 2008), 28.

33. Garry Wills, *Lincoln at Gettysburg: The Words That Remade America* (New York: Simon & Schuster, 1992), 103.

34. Abraham Lincoln, *Speeches and Writings 1859–1865* (New York: Library of America, 1989), 536–37.

35. Bernard L. Brock and Robert Lee Scott, et al., *Methods of Rhetorical Criticism: A Twentieth-century Perspective* (Detroit: Wayne State University Press, 1989), 60.

36. Garry Wills, "Two Speeches on Race," *New York Review of Books* 5.7 (2008): 4.

37. "A house divided against itself cannot stand."

38. Lincoln, *Speeches and Writings 1859–1865*, 686–87.

39. Gienapp, *Abraham Lincoln and Civil War America*, xi and 2–4.

40. George Anastaplo, *Abraham Lincoln: A Constitutional Biography* (New York: Rowman & Littlefield, 1999), 125.

41. Michael Lind, *What Lincoln Believed: The Values and Convictions of America's Greatest President* (New York: Doubleday, 2004), 279.

42. Ibid., 9–11.

43. Roy Jenkins, *Franklin Delano Roosevelt* (New York: Henry Holt, 2003), 1 and 166.

44. Paul Conkin, *The New Deal* (Arlington Heights: Harlan Davidson, 1975), 15–16.

45. Frances Perkins. *The Roosevelt I Knew* (New York: Penguin, 2011), 382.

46. Howard Zinn, ed., *New Deal Thought* (New York: Bobbs-Merrill, 1966), 45–52.

47. Ibid., 52.

48. Gordon Lloyd, *The Two Faces of Liberalism: How the Hoover-Roosevelt Debate Shapes the Twenty-first Century* (New York: M&M Scrivener, 2006), 160–164.

49. Conkin, *The New Deal*, 53.

50. Jenkins, *Franklin Delano Roosevelt*, 88–89.

51. Halford R. Ryan, *Franklin D. Roosevelt's Rhetorical Presidency* (New York: Greenwood Press, 1988), 92.

52. Franklin Delano Roosevelt, *Great Speeches* (New York: Dover, 1999), 101–103.

53. Ryan, *Franklin D. Roosevelt's Rhetorical Presidency*, 105.

54. Roosevelt, *Great Speeches*, 162.

55. Conkin, *The New Deal*, 52–53.

56. Roosevelt, *Great Speeches*, 161–62.

57. George McJimsey, *The Presidency of Franklin Delano Roosevelt* (Lawrence: University of Kansas Press, 2000), p. 296.

58. Conkin, *The New Deal*,48.

59. McJimsey, *The Presidency of Franklin Delano Roosevelt*, p. 295.

Chapter Five

1. David Remnick, *The Bridge: The Life and Rise of Barack Obama* (New York: Knopf, 2010), 105.

2. *The Obamas in the White House: Reflections on Family, Faith, and Leadership* (New York: *Time*, 2009), 44.

3. Jon Meacham, "How to Read Like a President," *The New York Times*, October 31, 2008.

4. Harriet Beecher Stowe, *Harriet Beecher Stowe: Three Novels* (New York: Library of America, 1983), 9.

5. Ibid., 34.

6. Ibid., 55.

7. Ibid., 480.

8. W.E. Burghardt Du Bois, *The Souls of Black Folk: Essays and Sketches* (New York: Bantam, 1989), 3.

9 Ibid., 8.

10. Ibid., 57.

11. Barack Obama, *Dreams from My Father* (New York: Three Rivers Press, 2004), 145–46.

12. Richard Wright, *Native Son* (New York: Harper & Row, 1940), xx.

13. Ibid., xiii and xx.

14. Ibid., 12–14.

15. Ibid., 19–20.

16. Ibid., xxiv–xxv.

17. Jill Abramson, V. Alabiso, T. Masuda, et al., *Obama: The Historic Journey* (New York: The New York Times, 2009), 106.

18. Ralph Ellison, *Invisible Man* (New York: Vintage, 1989), 15.

19. Ibid., 3.

20. Ibid., 17–21.

21. Ibid., 16 and 573.

22. Ibid., xxii.

23. William Faulkner, *Novels 1942–1954* (New York: Library of America, 1994), 535.

24. Obama, *Dreams from My Father*, x.

25. David Frank, "The Prophetic Voice and the Face of the Other in Barack Obama's 'A More Perfect Union,'" *Rhetoric and Public Affairs* 12.2 (2009): 182.

26. Obama, *Dreams from My Father*, 86–87.

27. Ibid., 197–98.

28. Alex Haley, *The Autobiography of Malcolm X* (New York: Ballantine, 1999), 395.

29. Ibid., 400 and 410.

30. Ibid., 467 and 495.

31. Manning Marable, *Malcolm X: A Life of Reinvention* (New York: Viking, 2011), 411.

32. Ibid., 11.

33. Ibid., 480.

34. Ibid., 480.

35. Ibid., 487.

36. Magnus Bassey, *Malcolm X and African American Self-Consciousness* (New York: Edwin Mellen, 2004), 43.

37. Marable, *Malcolm X*, 483.

38. Toby Harnden, "Top 10 Favorite Songs of Barack Obama and John McCain," *The Telegraph*, August 14, 2008.

39. Mary Frances Berry and Josh Gottheimer, *Power in Words: The Stories Behind Barack Obama's Speeches, From the State House to the White House* (Boston: Beacon Press, 2010), xxx.

40. "Inside Barack Obama's iPod," *Rolling Stone*, June 25, 2008.

41. Mellonee Burnim and Portia Maultsby, eds., *African American Music: An Introduction* (New York: Routledge, 2006), 84.

42. Berry and Gottheimer, *Power in Words*, 251.

43. Obama, *Dreams from My Father*, 50–51.

44. Michiko Kakutani, "From Books, New President Found Voice," *The New York Times*, January 18, 2009.

45. Obama, *Dreams from My Father*, 78–79.

46. Mellonee Burnim and Portia Maultsby, eds., *African American Music*, 279.

47. James L. Conyers, ed., *African American Jazz and Rap* (Jefferson, NC: McFarland, 2001), 214–15.

48. Ibid., 168.

49. Latoya Peterson, "Barack Obama, Hip-Hop Candidate," *The American Prospect*, February 4, 2008.

50. James T. Kloppenberg, *Reading Obama: Dreams, Hope, and the American Political Tradition* (Princeton: Princeton University Press, 2011), 253.

Chapter Six

1. David Kemper Watson, *The Constitution of the United States: Its History Application and Construction* (Chicago: Callaghan, 1910), 909.

2. Andrew S. Trees, *The Founding Fathers and the Politics of Character* (Princeton: Princeton University Press, 2004), 2.

3. Ibid., 3.

4. Ibid., 135.

5. Ibid., 137.

6. Mason Locke Weems, *A History of the Life and Death, Virtues and Exploits of General George Washington* (Philadelphia J.B. Lippincott, 1918).

7. Trees, *The Founding Fathers and the Politics of Character*, 139–40.

8. Weems, *A History of the Life and Death, Virtues and Exploits of General George Washington*.

9 Trees, *The Founding Fathers and the Politics of Character*, 140.

10. Excerpts from Washington's Farewell Address come from *The Papers of George Washington* at the University of Virginia, published online at http://gwpapers.virginia.edu/documents/farewell/transcript.html.

11. Merle Curti, *The Growth of American Thought* (New York: Harper & Row, 1964), 408–09.

12. Jim Cullen, *The American Dream: A Short History of an Idea That Shaped a Nation* (Oxford: Oxford University Press, 2003), 6.

13. Ibid., 16.

14. Ibid., 23.

15. Ralph H. Gabriel, *American Values: Continuity and Change* (Westport, CT: Greenwood Press, 1974), 6.

16. Ibid., 58–59.

17. Ibid., 34–36.

18. Ralph Waldo Emerson, *Selected Essays* (New York: Penguin, 1982), 130 and 142.

19. Gabriel, *American Values*, 95–96.

20. Emerson, *Selected Essays*, 178–85.

21. Joel Porte and Saundra Morris, eds., *The Cambridge Companion to Ralph Waldo Emerson* (Cambridge: Cambridge University Press, 1999), 66.

22. Ibid., 55.

23. Emerson, *Selected Essays*, 239.

24. Gabriel, *American Values*, 59.

25. Emerson, *Selected Essays*, 206–08.

26. Ibid., 211.

27. Ibid., 108–11.

28. Porte and Morris, eds., *The Cambridge Companion to Ralph Waldo Emerson*, Porte, 22.

29. Gregory Claeys and Lyman Tower Sargent, eds., *The Utopian Reader* (New York: New York University Press, 1999), 192.

30. Curti, *The Growth of American Thought*, 609–10.

31. Edward Bellamy, *Looking* Backward (New York: Dover, 1996), 43 and 160.

32. Ibid., 139.

33. Barack Obama, *The Audacity of Hope: Thoughts on Reclaiming the American Dream* (New York: Vintage, 2008), 221 and 28.

34. Ibid., 66.

35. Ibid., 66.

36. Ibid., 67.

37. Jill Abramson, V. Alabiso, T. Masuda, et al., *Obama: The Historic Journey* (New York: The New York Times, 2009), 130–131.

38. Obama, *The Audacity of Hope*, 77.

39. Abramson, et al., *Obama*, 128.

40. Ibid., 221.

41. Joel Kotkin, "Obama Family Values," *Forbes*, January, 20, 2009, http://www.forbes.com/2009/01/19/obama-family-religion-oped-cx_jk_0120kotkin.html.

42. Barack Obama, *Change We Can Believe In* (New York: Three Rivers Press, 2008), 234–238.

43. Ibid., 238–240.

44. Mary Frances Berry and Josh Gottheimer, *Power in Words: The Stories Behind Barack Obama's Speeches, from the State House to the White House* (Boston: Beacon Press, 2010), 79.

45. Michelle Obama, "Address at the Democratic National Convention in Denver," *American Presidency Project* [online].

Chapter Seven

1. Remnick, David. *The Bridge: The Life and Rise of Barack Obama* (New York: Knopf, 2010), 516.

2. James Olney, ed., *Autobiography: Essays Theoretical and Critical* (Princeton: Princeton University Press, 1980), 167–68.

3. H. Porter Abbott, *The Cambridge Introduction to Narrative* (Cambridge: Cambridge University Press, 2003), 131–32.

4. Olney, ed., *Autobiography*, 13.

5. Barack Obama, *Change We Can Believe In* (New York: Three Rivers Press, 2008), 236.

6. Jodi R. Cohen, *Communication Criticism: Developing Your Critical Powers* (Thousand Oaks: Sage, 1998), 155–57.

7. Barack Obama, *Dreams from My Father* (New York: Three Rivers Press, 2004), 190.

8. Peter Firstbrook, *The Obamas: The Untold Story of an African Family* (New York: Crown, 2010), 3.

9 Cohen, *Communication Criticism*, 46.

10. Barack Obama, 2004 Democratic National Convention Keynote Address, Americanrhetoric.com, July 27, 2004.

11. Obama, *Dreams from My Father*, 10–11.

12. Richard Wolffe, *Renegade: The Making of a President (*New York: Three Rivers Press, 2010), 32.

13. Richard Sorabji, *Self: Ancient and Modern Insights About Individuality, Life, and Death* (Chicago: University of Chicago Press, 2006), 178.

14. Wolffe, *Renegade*, 63.

15. Ibid., 220.

16. Ibid., 152.

17. Mary Frances Berry and Josh Gottheimer, *Power in Words: The Stories Behind Barack Obama's Speeches, from the State House to the White House* (Boston: Beacon Press, 2010), 27–28.

18. John M. Kephart and Steven F. Rafferty, "'Yes We Can': Rhizomic Rhetorical Agency in Hyper-Modern Campaign Ecologies," *Argumentation and Advocacy* 46 (Summer 2009): 6–20.

19. James T. Kloppenberg, *Reading Obama: Dreams, Hope, and the American Political Tradition* (Princeton: Princeton University Press, 2011), 82.

20. Ibid., 234.

21. Olney, ed. *Autobiography*, 39.

22. Barack Obama's Speech on Super Tuesday, February 5, 2008.

23. Heather E. Harris, et al., eds., *The Obama Effect: Multidisciplinary Renderings of the 2008 Campaign* (Albany: SUNY Press, 2010), 33.

24. Ibid., 33.

25. Ibid., 193 and 200.

26. Ibid., 127–28.

27. Abbott, *The Cambridge Introduction to Narrative*, 36.

28. Olney, ed., *Autobiography*, 13.

29. Jonathan Alter, *The Promise: President Obama Year One* (New York: Simon & Schuster, 2010), 101.

Chapter Eight

1. Grant Cornwell and Eve Stoddard, *Global Multiculturalism: Comparative Perspectives on Ethnicity, Race, and Nation* (New York: Rowman & Littlefield, 2001), 12.

2. "Obama's Speech in Amman, Jordan," *The New York Times*, July 22, 2008.

3. "Obama's Speech in Sderot, Israel," *The New York Times*, July 23, 2008.

4. "Transcript: Obama's Speech in Berlin," *PBS Newshour*, July 24, 2008.

5. "Obama and Sarkozy's News Conference in Paris," *The New York Times*, July 25, 2008.

6. Leif Wenar, "John Rawls," *Stanford Encyclopedia of Philosophy* (Fall 2008).

7. James T. Kloppenberg, *Reading Obama: Dreams, Hope, and the American Political Tradition* (Princeton: Princeton University Press, 2011), 140.

8. Ibid., 144.

9 Anthony Simon and David Owen, eds.,

Multiculturalism and Political Theory (Cambridge: Cambridge University Press, 2007), 9.

10. Ibid., 15.

11. Kloppenberg, *Reading Obama*, 149.

12. "Transcript: Obama's Speech in Berlin," *PBS Newshour*, July 24, 2008.

13. Cornwell and Stoddard, *Global Multiculturalism*, 14.

14. David Remnick, *The Bridge: The Life and Rise of Barack Obama* (New York: Knopf, 2010), 195.

15. Thomas McGovern, *Memory's Stories: Interdisciplinary Readings of Multicultural Life Narratives* (New York: University Press of America, 2007), 60.

16. Remnick, *The Bridge*, 20–21 and 24.

17. Heather E. Harris, et al., eds., *The Obama Effect: Multidisciplinary Renderings of the 2008 Campaign* (Albany: SUNY Press, 2010), 33.

18. Barack Obama, *The Audacity of Hope: Thoughts on Reclaiming the American Dream* (New York: Vintage, 2008), 259 and 295.

19. David N. Mayer, *The Constitutional Thought of Thomas Jefferson* (Charlottesville: University of Virginia Press, 1994), 125.

20. Adrienne Koch, *The Philosophy of Thomas Jefferson* (Chicago: Quadrangle, 1964), 137–138.

21. Obama, *The Audacity of Hope*, 103.

22. R.B. Bernstein, *Thomas Jefferson* (Oxford: Oxford University Press, 2003), xii.

23. Christopher Hitchens, *Thomas Jefferson: Author of America* (New York: HarperCollins, 2005), 3.

24. Bernstein, *Thomas Jefferson*, 198.

25. "Obama's Victory Speech," *The New York Times*, November 5, 2008.

26. Ruth Levitas, *The Concept of Utopia* (Syracuse: Syracuse University Press, 1990), 221.

Chapter Nine

1. Address by the President to a Joint Session of Congress, Whitehouse.gov, September 8, 2011.

2. "Transcript: President Obama's Speech at the CBC Foundation Gala," *The Grio*, September 24, 2011.

3. "Obama Likens Civil Rights to Economy Fight at Memorial," *Reuters*, October 16, 2011.

4. "Full Text: President Obama's Speech at the MLK Memorial Dedication," *The Grio*, October 16, 2011.

5. President Barack Obama's Speech on the American Jobs Act Impact on Teachers in Mesquite, Texas, October 4, 2011.

6. "Transcript of President Obama's address in Manchester," *Union Leader*, November 22, 2011.

7. Remarks by the President on the Economy in Osawatomie, Kansas, Whitehouse.gov, December 6, 2011.

Chapter Ten

1. "State of the Union 2012: Obama Speech Transcript," *Washington Post*, January 24, 2012.

2. "Sarah Palin Gave a Campaign Speech," *The Atlantic*, February 6, 2010.

3. "Transcript: President Obama's Remarks in Cedar Rapids," *The Gazette*, January 25, 2012.

4. "Military Cuts and Tax Plan Are Central to Obama Budget," *The New York Times*, February 13, 2012.

5. President Obama Speaks at the National Museum of African American History and Culture Groundbreaking, Whitehouse. gov, February 22, 2012.

6. Remarks by the President to UAW Conference, Whitehouse.gov, February 28, 2012.

7. The Road We've Traveled, Barack obama.com, March 2012.

8. "Transcript of Obama's Remarks to Newspaper Editors," *Wall Street Journal*, April 3, 2012.

9 "In Strategy Shift, Obama Team Attacks Romney from the Left," *The New York Times*, April 20, 2012.

10. Remarks by President Obama in Address to the Nation from Afghanistan, White house.gov, May 1, 2012.

11. "Obama Formally Kicks Off Campaign in Ohio and Virginia," *The New York Times*, May 5, 2012.

12. Remarks by the President and the First Lady at a Campaign Event: Virginia Commonwealth University, Richmond, Virginia, Whitehouse.gov, May 5, 2012.

13. "Transcript: Robin Roberts ABC News Interview with President Obama," ABC News, May 9, 2012.

14. "Aggressive Ads for Obama, at the Ready," *The New York Times*, May 8, 2012.

15. "Obama Finds Campaigning Rules Clock," *The New York Times*, May 28, 2012.

16. "Full Transcript of Obama's Speech on the Economy in Cleveland, Ohio," *Washington Post*, June 14, 2012.

17. Remarks by the President on Immigration, Whitehouse.gov, June 25, 2012.

18. Remarks by the President on Supreme Court Ruling on the Affordable Care Act, Whitehouse.gov, June 28, 2012.

19. "What's Romney Hiding in His Tax Returns?" *Bloomberg BusinessWeek*, July 17, 2012.

20. "On Tricky Terrain of Class, Contrasting Paths," *The New York Times*, July 7, 2012.

21. The Go Back Team, Barackobama. com, August 11, 2012.

22. Remarks by the President at a Campaign Event — Oskaloosa, Iowa, Whitehouse. gov, August 14, 2012.

23. "Relaxed and Loose, Candidate Obama Hits His Mark," *The New York Times*, August 27, 2012.

24. "Transcript of Bill Clinton's Speech to the Democratic National Convention," *The New York Times*, September 5, 2012.

25. "Transcript: President Obama's Convention Speech." Npr.org, September 6, 2012.

26. "Obama's English," *The New York Times*, September 8, 2012.

27. President Obama's Remarks at Milwaukee Theater Campaign Event, DailyKos. com, September 22, 2012.

28. "Why Obama Abandoned Audacity," *Washington Post*, September 30, 2012.

29. Remarks by the President at a Campaign Event — Fairfax, VA, Whitehouse.gov, October 19, 2012.

30. "Obama Campaign Irked by Romney Attempt to Seize 'Change' Mantle," *Huffington Post*, November 3, 2012.

31. Remarks by the President in Las Vegas, NV, Whitehouse.gov, November 1, 2012.

32. Remarks by the President at a Campaign Event — Hilliard, OH, Whitehouse.gov, November 2, 2012.

33. Remarks by the President on Election Night, Whitehouse.gov, November 7, 2012.

Selected Bibliography

Abbott, H. Porter. *The Cambridge Introduction to Narrative*. Cambridge: Cambridge University Press, 2003.

Abramson, Jill, V. Alabiso, T. Masuda, et al. *Obama: The Historic Journey*. New York: The New York Times, 2009.

Alter, Jonathan. *The Promise: President Obama Year One*. New York: Simon and Shuster, 2010.

Anastaplo, George. *Abraham Lincoln. A Constitutional Biography*. New York: Rowman & Littlefield, 1999.

Augustine, Saint. *The Confessions of St. Augustine*. Trans. J.M. Lelen. Totowa, NJ: Catholic Books, 1997.

Bacon, Francis. "The New Atlantis." *Three Early Modern Utopias: Utopia, New Atlantis, and Isle of the Pines*. Ed. Susan Bruce. Oxford: Oxford University Press, 1999.

Bassey, Magnus. *Malcolm X and African American Self-Consciousness*. New York: Edwin Mellen, 2004.

Becker, Carl L. *The Declaration of Independence: A Study in the History of Ideas*. New York: Knopf, 1964.

Bellamy, Edward. *Looking Backward*. New York: Dover, 1996.

Bernstein, R.B. *Thomas Jefferson*. Oxford: Oxford University Press, 2003.

Berry, Mary Frances, and Josh Gottheimer. *Power in Words: The Stories Behind Barack Obama's Speeches, From the State House to the White House*. Boston: Beacon Press, 2010.

Bloch, Ernst. *The Principle of Hope*. 3 vols. Cambridge: MIT Press, 1995.

Bradley, Sculley. *American Tradition in Literature*. New York: Grosset & Dunlap, 1975.

Brock, Bernard L., Robert Lee Scott, et al. *Methods of Rhetorical Criticism: A Twentieth-century Perspective*. Detroit: Wayne State University Press, 1989.

Brown, Joshua. *Forever Free: The Story of Emancipation and Reconstruction*. New York: Knopf, 2005.

Buber, Martin. *Paths in Utopia*. Boston: Beacon Hill, 1949.

Burnim, Mellonee, and Portia Maultsby, eds. *African American Music: An Introduction*. New York: Routledge, 2006.

Claeys, Gregory, and Lyman Tower Sargent, eds. *The Utopian Reader*. New York: New York University Press, 1999.

Cohen, Jodi R. *Communication Criticism: Developing Your Critical Powers*. Thousand Oaks: Sage, 1998.

Coleman, Nathaniel. *Utopias and Architecture*. New York: Taylor & Francis, 2005.

Conkin, Paul. *The New Deal*. Arlington Heights: Harlan Davidson, 1975.

Conyers, James L., ed. *African American Jazz and Rap*. Jefferson, NC: McFarland, 2001.

Cornwell, Grant, and Eve Stoddard. *Global Multiculturalism: Comparative Perspectives on Ethnicity, Race, and Nation.* New York: Rowman & Littlefield, 2001.

Cullen, Jim. *The American Dream: A Short History of an Idea That Shaped a Nation.* Oxford: Oxford University Press, 2003.

Curti, Merle. *The Growth of American Thought.* New York: Harper & Row, 1964.

Darsey, James. *The Prophetic Tradition and Radical Rhetoric in America.* New York: New York University Press, 1997.

Davis, Charles T., and Henry Louis Gates. *The Slave's Narrative.* Oxford: Oxford University Press, 1985.

DeVaux, Roland. "Jerusalem and the Prophets." *Interpreting the Prophetic Tradition.* Ed. Harry Orlinsky. Cincinnati: Hebrew Union College Press, 1969.

Du Bois, W.E. Burghardt. *The Souls of Black Folk: Essays and Sketches.* New York: Bantam, 1989.

Durant, Will and Ariel. *The Story of Civilization: Part VIII.* New York: Simon & Schuster, 1963.

Eliav-Feldon, Mirian. *Realistic Utopias: The Ideal Imaginary Societies of the Renaissance.* Oxford: Oxford University Press, 1982.

Ellison, Ralph. *Invisible Man.* New York: Vintage, 1989.

Emerson, Ralph Waldo. *Emerson on Transcendentalism.* Ed. Edward L. Ericson. New York: Ungar, 1986.

_____. *Selected Essays.* New York: Penguin, 1982.

Eurich, Nell. *Science in Utopia: A Mighty Design.* Cambridge: Harvard University Press, 1967.

Faulkner, William. *Novels 1942–1954.* New York: Library of America, 1994.

Firstbrook, Peter. *The Obamas: The Untold Story of an African Family.* New York: Crown, 2010.

Frank, David. "The Prophetic Voice and the Face of the Other in Barack Obama's 'A More Perfect Union.'" *Rhetoric and Public Affairs* 12.2 (2009).

Franklin, Benjamin. *The Autobiography and Other Writings.* Ed. Jessie L. Lemisch. New York: New American Library, 1961.

Friedrich, Carl J., and Robert G. McCloskey, eds. *From Declaration of Independence to the Constitution: The Roots of American Constitutionalism.* New York: Liberal Arts Press, 1954.

Gabriel, Ralph H. *American Values: Continuity and Change.* Westport, CT: Greenwood Press, 1974.

Gates, Henry Lewis, and William Andrews, eds. *Pioneers of the Black Atlantic: Five Slave Narratives from the Enlightenment, 1722–1815.* Washington, DC: Counterpoint, 1998.

Gienapp, William E. *Abraham Lincoln and Civil War America: A Biography.* Oxford: Oxford University Press, 2002.

_____. *The Fiery Trial: The Speeches and Writings of Abraham Lincoln.* Oxford: Oxford University Press, 2002.

Haley, Alex. *The Autobiography of Malcolm X.* New York: Ballantine, 1999.

Harris, Heather E., et al., eds. *The Obama Effect: Multidisciplinary Renderings of the 2008 Campaign.* Albany: SUNY Press, 2010.

Hitchens, Christopher. *Thomas Jefferson: Author of America.* New York: HarperCollins, 2005.

Ifill, Gwen. *The Breakthrough: Politics and Race in the Age of Obama.* New York: Anchor, 2009.

Irwin, Frank. *Letters of Thomas Jefferson.* Tilton, NH: Sanbornton Bridge Press, 1975.

Jefferson, Thomas. *Writings.* New York: Library of America, 1984.

Jenkins, Roy. *Franklin Delano Roosevelt.* New York: Henry Holt, 2003.

Johnson, James Thurber. *The Bible in American Law, Politics, and Political Rhetoric.* Philadelphia: Fortress Press, 1985.

Kephart, John M., and Steven F. Rafferty. "'Yes We Can': Rhizomic Rhetorical Agency in Hyper-Modern Campaign Ecologies." *Argumentation and Advocacy* 46 (Summer 2009).

Kermode, Frank. *The Sense of an Ending: Studies in the Theory of Fiction*. Oxford: Oxford University Press, 1967.

Kloppenberg, James T. *Reading Obama: Dreams, Hope, and the American Political Tradition*. Princeton: Princeton University Press, 2011.

Koch, Adrienne. *The Philosophy of Thomas Jefferson*. Chicago: Quadrangle, 1964.

Levitas, Ruth. *The Concept of Utopia*. Syracuse: Syracuse University Press, 1990.

Lincoln, Abraham. *Speeches and Writings 1859–1865*. New York: Library of America, 1989.

Lincoln, C. Eric, ed. *The Black Experience in Religion*. New York: Anchor, 1974.

Lincoln, Eric C., and Lawrence Mamiya. *The Black Church in the African American Experience*. Durham: Duke University Press, 1990.

Lind, Michael. *What Lincoln Believed: The Values and Convictions of America's Greatest President*. New York: Doubleday, 2004.

Lloyd, Gordon. *The Two Faces of Liberalism: How the Hoover-Roosevelt Debate Shapes the Twenty-first Century*. New York: M&M Scrivener, 2006.

Mannheim, *Ideology and Utopia: An Introduction to the Sociology of Knowledge*. New York: Harvest, 1985.

Marable, Manning. *Malcolm X: A Life of Reinvention*. New York: Viking, 2011.

Mayer, David N. *The Constitutional Thought of Thomas Jefferson*. Charlottesville: University of Virginia Press, 1994.

McGovern, Thomas. *Memory's Stories: Interdisciplinary Readings of Multicultural Life Narratives*. New York: University Press of America, 2007.

McJimsey, George. *The Presidency of Franklin Delano Roosevelt*. Lawrence: University of Kansas Press, 2000.

Mead, Walter B. *The United States: Personalities, Principles, and Issues*. Columbia: University of South Carolina Press, 1987.

Merezhkovsky, D. *Tolstoi I Dostoevsky*. Moskva: Respliblika, 1995.

Moltmann, Jürgen. *Theology of Hope*. New York: Harper & Row, 1965.

Newman, Mark. *The Civil Rights Movement*. Edinburgh: Edinburgh University Press, 2004.

Obama, Barack. *The Audacity of Hope: Thoughts on Reclaiming the American Dream*. New York: Vintage, 2008.

_____. *Change We Can Believe In*. New York: Three Rivers Press, 2008.

_____. *Dreams from My Father*. New York: Three Rivers Press, 2004.

Olney, James, ed. *Autobiography: Essays Theoretical and Critical*. Princeton: Princeton University Press, 1980.

Onuf, Peter S. *The Mind of Thomas Jefferson*. Charlottesville: University of Virginia Press, 2007.

Porte, Joel, and Saundra Morris, eds. *The Cambridge Companion to Ralph Waldo Emerson*. Cambridge: Cambridge University Press, 1999.

Remnick, David. *The Bridge: The Life and Rise of Barack Obama*. New York: Knopf, 2010.

Ricoeur, Paul. *Lectures on Ideology and Utopia*. New York: Columbia University Press, 1986.

Roosevelt, Franklin Delano. *Great Speeches*. New York: Dover, 1999.

Ryan, Halford R. *Franklin D. Roosevelt's Rhetorical Presidency*. New York: Greenwood Press, 1988.

Seelye, John. "The Clay Foot of the Climber: Richard M. Nixon in Perspective." *Literary Romanticism in America*. Ed. William L. Andrews. Baton Rouge: Louisiana State University Press, 1981.

Simon, Anthony, and David Owen, eds. *Multiculturalism and Political Theory*. Cambridge: Cambridge University Press, 2007.

Selected Bibliography

Solberg, Winton U. *The Constitutional Convention and the Formation of the Union*. Urbana: University of Illinois Press, 1990.

Sorabji, Richard. *Self: Ancient and Modern Insights About Individuality, Life, and Death*. Chicago: University of Chicago Press, 2006.

Stewart, David O. *The Summer of 1787: The Men Who Invented the Constitution*. New York: Simon & Schuster, 2007.

Stowe, Harriet Beecher. *Harriet Beecher Stowe: Three Novels*. New York: Library of America, 1983.

Taylor, Yuval, ed. *Growing Up in Slavery: Stories Told by Young Slaves as Told by Themselves*. Chicago: Lawrence Hill, 2005.

Thoreau, Henry David. *Walden and Civil Disobedience*. Ed. Owen Thomas. New York: W.W. Norton, 1966.

Trees, Andrew S. *The Founding Fathers and the Politics of Character*. Princeton: Princeton University Press, 2004.

Von Rad, Gerhard. *The Message of the Prophets*. New York: Harper & Row, 1967.

Watson, David Kemper. *The Constitution of the United States: Its History Application and Construction*. Chicago: Callaghan, 1910.

Weems, Mason Locke. *A History of the Life and Death, Virtues and Exploits of General George Washington*. Philadelphia: J.B. Lippincott, 1918.

Whitman, Walt. "Pioneers! O Pioneers!" *The Harvard Classics*, vol. 42. Ed. Charles W. Eliot. New York: P. F. Collier & Sons, 1976.

Wills, Garry. *Lincoln at Gettysburg: The Words That Remade America*. New York: Simon & Schuster, 1992.

Wilmore, Gaylaud S. *Black Religion and Black Radicalism*. New York: Doubleday, 1972.

Wolffe, Richard. *Renegade: The Making of a President*. New York: Three Rivers Press, 2010.

_____. *Revival: The Struggle for Survival Inside the Obama White House*. New York: Crown, 2010.

Wright, Richard. *Native Son*. New York: Harper & Row, 1940.

Zinn, Howard, ed. *New Deal Thought*. New York: Bobbs-Merrill, 1966.

Index

Index